BER
A GUIDE FOR THE PERPLEXED

Continuum Guides for the Perplexed

Continuum's Guides for the Perplexed are clear, concise, and accessible introductions to thinkers, writers, and subjects that students and readers can find especially challenging. Concentrating specifically on what it is that makes the subject difficult to grasp, these books explain and explore key themes and ideas, guiding the reader toward a thorough understanding of demanding material.

BERKELEY:
A GUIDE FOR THE PERPLEXED

TALIA MAE BETTCHER

continuum

Continuum International Publishing Group

The Tower Building	80 Maiden Lane
11 York Road	Suite 704
London	New York
SE1 7NX	NY 10038

www.continuumbooks.com

British Library Cataloguing-in-Publication Data
A catalogue record for this book is available from the British Library.

ISBN-10: HB: 0-8264-8990-7
PB: 0-8264-8991-5
ISBN-13: HB: 978-0-8264-8990-6
PB: 978-0-8264-8991-3

Library of Congress Cataloging-in-Publication Data
Bettcher, Talia Mae.
Berkeley : a guide for the perplexed/Talia Mae Bettcher.
p. cm.
Includes index.
ISBN 978-0-8264-8990-6
978-0-8264-8991-3
1. Berkeley, George, 1685-1753. I. Title.
B1348.B477 2008
192—dc22

2008016678

Typeset by Newgen Imaging Systems Pvt Ltd, Chennai, India
Printed and bound in Great Britain by MPG Books Ltd, Bodmin, Cornwall

To Susan Beth Forrest,
the love of my life
For showing me that the meaning of it all is
to live well, to love well, and to write well
(not necessarily in that order)

CONTENTS

ACKNOWLEDGMENTS

I express gratitude to my colleagues Jenny Faust, Henry Mendell, and David Pitt for kindly reviewing earlier drafts of the monograph. Randall Parker and Susan Forrest went well beyond any reasonable expectations of assistance. Their comments and suggestions helped improve this book immeasurably. Thank you. (Thank you, thank you). The core insights which shaped this monograph were first grown when I worked on my dissertation with John Carriero, my dissertation supervisor. My approach to Berkeley is informed by the invaluable lessons that I learned from him.

ABBREVIATIONS

All references to Berkeley unless specified are from A. A. Luce and T. E. Jessop (eds.) *The Works of George Berkeley, Bishop of Cloyne,* 9 volumes (Thomas Nelson and Sons: Edinburgh, 1948–57).

3D   *Three Dialogues between Hylas and Philonous.* Cited by dialogue and page.

ALC   *Alciphron; or, the Minute Philosopher.* Cited by dialogue and section.

DM   *De Motu.* Cited by section.

NTV   *An Essay Towards A New Theory of Vision.* Cited by section.

PHK   *A Treatise Concerning the Principles of Human Knowledge.* Cited by section.

PC   *Philosophical Commentaries.* Cited by entry.

TVV   *Theory of Vision. . . Vindicated and Explained.* Cited by section.

Citations of other writings of Berkeley refer to *Works* volume and page.

Other abbreviations:

CSM   Descartes, René. *The Philosophical Writings of Descartes,* 2 volumes, John Cottingham, Robert Stroothoff, and Dugald Murdoch (trans.), (Cambridge: Cambridge University Press, 1984). Cited by volume and page.

E   Locke, John. *An Essay concerning Human Understanding,* Peter H. Nidditch (ed.), (Oxford: Clarendon Press, 1975). Cited by book, chapter, section, and page.

Enquiry Hume, David. *An Enquiry concerning Human Understanding,* 3rd ed., L. A. Selby-Bigge and P. H. Nidditch (ed.), (Oxford: Oxford University Press, 1975). Cited by page.

Treatise Hume, David. *A Treatise of Human Nature*, 2nd ed., L. A. Selby-Bigge (ed.) with revisions and notes by P. H. Nidditch, (Oxford: Clarendon Press, 1978). Cited by page.

PREFACE

George Berkeley (1685–1753) is one of the most well-known philosophers in the Western philosophical tradition; he wrote during the early modern period, one of its most intellectually fertile ever. He is traditionally considered the middle figure of "The Three British Empiricists" (flanked by John Locke and David Hume), usually contrasted with "The Three Continental Rationalists" (Descartes, Spinoza, and Leibniz).

Given his impact on both Hume and Kant, as well as the overall importance of this period of time to the rest of the philosophy that followed, the influence of Berkeley must be minimally reckoned as considerable. He is most well-recognized for his dictum *esse* is *percipi* (to be is to be perceived) and his immaterialist doctrine (the rejection of matter). Although he did not use the term, Berkeley is generally regarded as the father of modern "idealism" (roughly, the view that the world—or at least the world as known to us—is in some sense mind-dependent), which was defended in different forms by Kant, Hegel, and Schopenhauer.

SCOPE OF THE TEXT

Because of their particular importance, this guide will focus on Berkeley's *Treatise concerning the Principles of Human Knowledge* (1710) and *Three Dialogues between Hylas and Philonous* (1713). While this does not do justice to the scope of Berkeley's rather rich corpus, any responsible introduction really does need to take this kind of focus. It is in these two chief works that Berkeley develops his most well-known and influential metaphysical and epistemological doctrines—doctrines which have simply achieved a philosophical significance that his other views have not. That said, this guide will not ignore some of the issues discussed in other works. In particular, it will discuss Berkeley's *Essay Towards a New Theory of Vision*, as well as Berkeley's argument for God's existence in his 1732 Christian apologetic, *Alciphron; or, the Minute Philosopher*. It will do so, however, for the purpose of further illuminating Berkeley's central philosophical masterworks.

Some commentators have held that Berkeley's *Principles* constitutes his strongest, most definitive statement of his philosophy, while others represent the *Dialogues* as a more developed, mature elaboration of the view. Berkeley himself, however, merely explained the latter was intended to "treat more clearly and fully of certain principles" presented in the *Principles*; and "to place them in a new light" (*3D* Preface, 167–68). Instead of focusing on one or the other of Berkeley's major works or else ignoring the differences between them, one goal of this guide is to compare and contrast the argumentative strategies deployed in both works. My hope is that this approach will provide readers with a nuanced account of Berkeley's philosophy, which does not erase the differences between his two works or else emphasize one of his works to the exclusion of the other.

THEME OF THE TEXT: PHILOSOPHICAL PERPLEXITY

If Berkeley is one of the most important philosophers, he is also one of the most perplexing. His philosophy can seem wildly counterintuitive, even outrageous: Does Berkeley think the external world doesn't *actually* exist at all, that there *aren't* material things whatsoever, that there are *only* mere ideas which we perceive in our own minds? Does Berkeley (as the Irish poet Yeats wrote) prove all things a dream?[1]

One wonders how Berkeley could have endorsed such a radical philosophical picture of the world, and how he could have expected anybody to take it seriously. Even Berkeley's contemporaries were wary of his opinions. Gottfried Leibniz, for example, suspected Berkeley seemed a man who wanted to be known only for his paradoxes—a kind of Zeno, if you will, who rather than defending a coherent philosophical account of the world, rested content in defending absurdities that couldn't possibly be true.[2] It is certainly easy to understand why his contemporary, Dr. Samuel Johnson famously attempted to refute Berkeley by simply kicking a stone, in response to Boswell's claim that Berkeley's arguments could not be refuted.[3]

To this day, Berkeley continues to be viewed as a philosopher entirely at odds with common sense. In picking up an introductory philosophy text, one could easily flip to a chapter entitled "Common Sense Undone" and find an excerpt from Berkeley's *Principles of Human Knowledge*.[4] In keeping with the theme of this monograph series, then, I'd like to make the issues of paradox and perplexity central to our own investigation into Berkeley's philosophy. Is Berkeley somebody who departs wildly from common sense? Can he be reconciled more comfortably with an everyday view of the world? The theme is important to Berkeley who, especially in his major philosophical work, *Three Dialogues between Hylas and Philonous* (1713) develops the surprising view that his own position is much *closer* to common sense than those of his opponents.

GOAL OF THE TEXT

This guide is intended as an introduction to the philosophy of Berkeley; it does not presuppose prior knowledge of Berkeley, not does it presuppose familiarity with modern philosophy more generally. It does, however, presuppose *some* background in philosophy (or at least some background in reading philosophy).

My aim is to present Berkeley's philosophy in the best light possible. Too often, Berkeley is represented as one who endorses "crazy" views by providing (far from irrefutable) poor arguments in favor of them. In reading Berkeley over a long period of time, grappling with his views and his arguments, my respect for him as a philosopher has waxed with each successive reading. Berkeley is a very elegant, compact writer; he accomplishes much through very few words. And the issues he addresses are exceptionally *deep*; most of them remain salient 300 years later. Yet it is easy to lose sight of this, and it is very tempting to use Berkeley as a kind of philosophical punching bag or voodoo doll, especially in an introductory text. I have resisted that temptation. As a consequence, I have not shied away from depth and complexity in my presentation of Berkeley.

One of the reasons Berkeley is so easily misunderstood is that he offers a barrage of arguments which when examined on their own seem inadequate. However, Berkeley's reasoning is complex: Various arguments connected together intricately constitute a broader argumentative strategy that itself needs to be understood within the broader context of Berkeley's project and core assumptions. I have therefore attempted to embed Berkeleian arguments within their larger argumentative trajectories. This presents a challenge in presenting the material (and also in reading it): One must be prepared to follow a complex (and longish) philosophical strategy all the way through. I hope to have presented the strategies as clearly as possible, as well as pointing to the ways in which Berkeley's strategies in the *Principles* and the *Dialogues* both diverge and converge.

Because I have tried my best to stay very close to Berkeley himself, I would recommend that in reading this book, the reader try to follow along with the original text as well. Berkeley's writing is lively, engaging, and clear. And this guide can be no substitute for Berkeley's own masterworks. For each chapter, I will indicate the sections of text that I am discussing. The reader would do well to read those sections after reading the chapter. By then returning to the chapter afterwards, the reader should be in a good position to understand the key moves Berkeley is making in that section. Thus, my hope is that this guide not only facilitates an understanding of Berkeley's position but, more importantly, helps the reader navigate through Berkeley's own philosophical writings.

The composition of an introductory text presents its own unique challenges: There are many diverse and sophisticated interpretations of Berkeley in the secondary literature. And any introductory presentation of Berkeley therefore requires some (over) simplification. This guide is no exception; I have tried to keep discussions of competing interpretations to a minimum. That said, it would be dishonest to pretend there isn't this complexity and to suppose there is one universal interpretation of Berkeley accepted by all Berkeley scholars. So I have judiciously attempted to discuss *some* salient readings of Berkeley without burdening the book with them.

In aiming to present Berkeley views as both as accessible and compelling, I have also inevitably found myself advancing my own interpretation of him. This yields an obvious tension. While one wants to present Berkeley in the way one feels is most correct (and which represents Berkeley in the best light possible), one must also represent Berkeley in a way that respects traditional accounts of him. While I have attempted to "do justice" to the common readings of Berkeley that a student of Berkeley should be expected to know, I nonetheless unfold my own reading of Berkeley. This attitude has been shaped largely by my goal of presenting Berkeley in the strongest (and most accurate) light possible. If Berkeley can't be accessibly presented as a deep and compelling philosopher, why present him at all?

STRUCTURE OF THE TEXT

In Chapter One, I provide a biographical account of Berkeley's life as well as a brief sketch of his core philosophical views. Then, in Chapter Two, I situate Berkeley's views within his philosophical project and I situate the project within the context of prevailing issues of Berkeley's day. In Chapter Three, I explain what I take to be the underlying philosophical assumptions which shape Berkeley's philosophy. I show why (and how) Berkeley has been too frequently dismissed while pointing to some of the deeper issues at work in his position.

In Chapter Four, Five, and Six I discuss Berkeley's main arguments for his immaterialist doctrine. In Chapter Four and Five, I outline Berkeley's argumentative strategy in the *Dialogues,* while in Chapter Six I discuss the strategy in the *Principles.* In Chapter Seven and Eight, I present Berkeley's arguments for the existence of God (fundamental to Berkeley's account of the world). In Chapter Seven, I emphasize Berkeley's arguments as presented in the *Principles.* However, I also include his argument from *Alciphron* which is dependent upon his theory of vision (which I also discuss in this chapter). In Chapter Eight, I present Berkeley's argument for God's existence as found in the *Dialogues* and I develop Berkeley's account of the world in greater detail. In Chapter Nine, I examine Berkeley's views about natural science and mathematics as well as the question to what degree Berkeley agrees or disagrees with common sense. In the Conclusion, I provide a general assessment of his philosophical account by looking forward to the philosophy of David Hume.

PART ONE: PRELIMINARIES

CHAPTER ONE

THE MAN AND HIS PHILOSOPHY

In the first part of this introductory chapter, I sketch out a biographical account of Berkeley's life. In the second part I provide a brief overview of Berkeley's philosophical account of the world and its relation to philosophical perplexity and common sense.

SECTION ONE: BERKELEY'S LIFE[1]

The Early Period: Young Berkeley

George Berkeley was born to the fairly well-to-do William and Eliza Berkeley in the county of Kilkenny, Ireland on March 12, 1685. His grandfather had come to Ireland from England after the Restoration, having received the collectorship of Belfast and his father also held a collectorship. Berkeley was the eldest of six sons—Rowland, Ralph, William, Robert, and Thomas. While we know little of the first two, we know William was a soldier and Robert was a churchman and a chief support of Berkeley during his declining years. We also know that Thomas, the youngest, had been condemned to death for bigamy in 1726.

Berkeley lived at Dysart Castle, near Thomastown until he entered the boarding school, Kilkenny College in 1696 (at the age of 11). He entered Trinity College, Dublin in 1700 (at the age of 16). Locke's *Essay* was already part of the course, thanks to the influence of Irish philosopher, William Molyneux (1656–98). Berkeley was elected Scholar of the House in 1702 and received his BA degree in 1704 (at the age of 20).

Early accounts of Berkeley's life circulated questionable details about his student days, helping to promote the negative image of

Berkeley. In particular, he was represented as a recluse and the butt of student jokes—"the greatest dunce in the whole university."[2] In a famous joke, he is said to have walked into a post, whence someone responded, "Never mind, Doctor, there's no matter in it."[3] Additionally, some alleged fondness for reading "airy romances" was considered as one peculiar source of his immaterialism. Generally such caricatures have been discredited. Certainly, it seems clear that Berkeley was hardly a recluse given his involvement in at least two student societies during these years.

After receiving his BA in 1704, Berkeley remained at Trinity College in order to wait for an opening so that he could become a University Fellow (this involved teaching and administration in the college). After a highly competitive examination, Berkeley was elected Junior Fellow in 1707 and received his MA a month later. That year he anonymously published his first work *Arithmetica and Miscellanea Mathematica* (a minor contribution much of which Berkeley had written three years earlier).

Fellows were obligated to take Holy Orders; and in 1709 Berkeley was ordained a deacon and in 1710 ordained a priest. On both occasions he was ordained by Dr. Ashe, Bishop of Clogher and the former Provost of Trinity. Apparently there was some controversy concerning Berkeley's 1710 ordination: William King, Archbishop of Dublin, was angered that Berkeley had been ordained without his permission, and Berkeley issued an official apology in 1710. There is other evidence that the relationship between Berkeley and King may have been far from agreeable.[4]

Between 1707 and 1710 there is tremendous work on Berkeley's part, culminating in his 1710 masterpiece, *A Treatise Concerning the Principles of Human Knowledge*. In 1871, A. C. Fraser first published Berkeley's private notebooks. And while Berkeley's notebooks have been the source of considerable scholarly dispute, this much seems relatively clear: the notebooks were written around 1707–08 and they reflect Berkeley's developing philosophical views. Additionally, there exists an earlier version of Berkeley's *Introduction to the Principles* (concerning his antiabstractionism) which was probably written in 1708. There are important discrepancies between this and the one which was published with the *Principles* in 1710, again indicating Berkeley's philosophical development.[5] In 1709, Berkeley's revolutionary *Essay Towards a New Theory of Vision* was published. An important contribution to the science of vision, the overall Berkeleian approach came to play a dominant role until the mid-1950s.[6]

In 1710, Berkeley published the *Principles*. While this philosophical work has ultimately secured an important place in the philosophical canon, it was hardly well received initially. Indeed, it seems to have been generally rejected and ridiculed without a fair reading (or any reading at all). Influential philosopher Samuel Clarke, placing him in the same camp as Malebranche, accused him of an abstruse metaphysics that was of no use to practical affairs. This was anathema to Berkeley, who commented to his friend Percival that, "Fine spun metaphysics are what I on all occasions declare against, and if anyone shall shew me anything of that sort in my 'Treatise' I will willingly correct it."[7] When further pressed by Percival to offer his objections to Berkeley's position, Dr. Clarke refused to respond at all. Undaunted by this reception, however, Berkeley began working on *Three Dialogues between Hylas and Philonous* in order to put his theory "in a different light."

In 1712, Berkeley published three earlier sermons assembled together as *Passive Obedience*—his most detailed discussion of moral and political philosophy. His reasons for publishing involved his desire to respond to accusations that he was a Jacobite, which emerged as a consequence of his sermons.[8] In this work, Berkeley argues, *pace* Locke, that it is always wrong for subjects to actively rebel against their sovereign. While subjects may be bound to refuse an immoral law requiring positive action (and so receive the punishments determined by the sovereign) in cases when the sovereign requires subjects to act contrary to morality, outright rebellion is never acceptable. Berkeley's view that rebellion against the state is against moral law is easily applied to the Glorious Revolution itself by which William III and Mary II ascended to the throne—so it is easy to see why such accusations might have been made. Yet, it could also be taken as him urging restraint on the part of the Jacobites with respect to the current reign, and Berkeley explicitly endorses an anti-Jacobite position in *Advice to the Tories* (1715). So it is a matter of some ambiguity what Berkeley's actual political position was and whether it was a position that changed over time. It is worth noting that in a letter to his friend, Percival, Berkeley denies there is any legitimate distinction to be drawn between a king *de jure* and a king *de facto*.[9] If so, while the Glorious Revolution may have been against the moral law, once established, submission to the sovereign would have still been required.[10]

Berkeley left Ireland in 1713 for London in part to publish his *Dialogues* there (which he did in May of that year), in part to meet "men of merit." There, Berkeley quickly became friends with many of the leading London intellectuals of the day: Joseph Addison, John Arbuthnot, Alexander Pope, Richard Steele, and Jonathan Swift. In 1714, Berkeley contributed several essays to Steele's new periodical *The Guardian*. Scholarly controversy still continues over authorship of at least some of these essays, all of which were published anonymously. Recent evidence also shows that Berkeley was the editor of Steele's *Ladies Library* (1715), an educational book for women which was published anonymously "by a Lady."[11]

Around this time, Berkeley embarked on two Continental tours. During the first one which lasted ten months between 1713–14, Berkeley had the occasion to visit Paris, the Alps, Turin, Genoa, Sicily, Pisa, and Florence. While in Paris, Berkeley may have had the opportunity to meet Malebranche. Whether this is the case or not, a fanciful story emerged that they *did* in fact meet and that during heated dispute, Malebranche became so worked up that he died a few days later (Berkeley is cited as the *occasional* cause). The story can't be true, however, since Malebranche died a few years later (rather than a few days later) in 1715.

Before Berkeley began his second tour, the issue of Jacobism returned to haunt him. In 1715 he published *Advice to the Tories Who Have Taken the Oaths* urging Tories to acquiesce to the ascension of George I (of the House of Hanover) after the death of Queen Anne. This has been taken as evidence that Berkeley was not—at least not at this time—a Jacobite, since many of the leaders of the Tories had Jacobite sensibilities. The pamphlet preceded the failed Jacobite Rebellion of 1715. But in 1716 Berkeley had sought the church preferment of St. Paul's in Dublin. Initially confident of his chances, he was ultimately denied in favor of Duke Tyrrell who had written a letter denouncing Berkeley. In addition to criticizing Berkeley's long absence from Trinity College, he cited *Passive Obedience* as evidence of Berkeley's Jacobism.

Berkeley began his second Continental tour in 1716. Dr. Ashe, Bishop of Clogher granted Berkeley a tutorship to accompany his son George Ashe on his travels. The tour lasted considerably longer than the first one, ending in 1720. They traveled through France to

Turin, Rome, Naples, Florence, and Sicily. And Berkeley kept journals (some of which remain) of his travels in Italy. Of note, it is apparently sometime during his travels in Italy that Berkeley lost his draft of the second part of the *Principles* which was to concern his views about the mind. Upon returning to France in 1720, Berkeley submitted *De Motu* to the Royal Academy of Sciences at Paris, which had offered a prize for essays on motion. In this contribution to natural science Berkeley argued against the real existence of dynamic forces (*pace* Leibniz). While Berkeley did not win the contest, he published *De Motu* in 1721.

The Middle Period: Dean Berkeley

Berkeley returned to Trinity College where he had already been appointed Senior Fellow in 1717 during his absence. In 1721, Berkeley published *An Essay Towards Preventing the Ruine of Great Britain* in reaction to what has been called the bursting of the South Sea Bubble. After incurring significant national debt, the South Sea Company was instituted to take over much of the debt and reduce it through trade. The Company managed to manipulate an increase in the price of its stock, leading to a proliferation of other companies, some of them illegal. When the "bubble" burst the stock of the South Sea Company plunged. Many, including Ministers of the Crown, were brought to trial in this scandal which led to poverty and disorder. In this *Essay,* Berkeley points to the more general decline in moral and religious values; he argues that the only source of wealth is work and that luxury ought to be curbed by laws.

In late 1721, Berkeley earned the degrees of B.D. and D.D., and he was also appointed Divinity Lecturer. During this time, he again began to seek a preferment. He initially applied for the Deanery of Dromore, with the support of the Duke of Grafton, which would have allowed him to retain his Fellowship at Trinity. However, the bishop of the diocese had another man in mind, leading to a conflict. Ultimately, Berkeley applied for the Deanery of Derry in late 1722 when a vacancy came open. In 1724, he was installed as the Dean and resigned his Senior Fellowship at Trinity after 24 years.

Disappointed with the moral state of Old Europe, in part dismayed by the South Sea Bubble, Berkeley began to conceive a plan for missionary work in the New World. His plan was to build a college called St. Paul's to educate students to become clergymen. His aim was to reach both the colonial folk as well as the natives who were to become missionaries to their people. Berkeley selected the questionable location of Bermuda partially due to its equal proximity to the major colonies.

Berkeley began working on this plan in earnest in 1724, publishing *Proposal for the Better Supplying of Churches in our Foreign Plantations.* He also wrote the poem *America or the Muse's Refuge, A Prophecy* (1726), which includes the following famous (and now eerie) stanza:

Westward the Course of Empire takes its Way;
The four first Acts already past,
A fifth shall close the Drama with the Day;
Time's noblest Offspring is the last.[12]

Between 1724 and 1728 he worked to garner support for his project. After obtaining a charter and a promise of £20,000 from the British Parliament, Berkeley set sail for America in late 1728. He lived in Rhode Island (near Newport) in the house he built, called Whitehall, which still stands to this day. In 1731, however, he realized that the grant he was promised would never be paid to him. Just before sailing to America, Berkeley married Anne Forster. During their stay in America, Anne had two children: Henry and Lucia. Lucia died just before the Berkeley's return to London.

While his "Bermuda Scheme" generated considerable enthusiasm and support (by the likes of Jonathan Swift, for example), it was also significantly flawed. While equidistant to the major colonies, it was very far away from the mainland (600 miles) so native Americans would have to be convinced to make the long trip to St. Paul's. While these considerations no doubt helped sink the project, the political maneuverings which occurred behind the scenes were also considerably more complex.

While Berkeley's Bermuda project ended in failure, his visit to America had its own successes. Berkeley had traveled to Rhode Island in order to wait for the grant payment, and he lived there for almost three years. During that time he composed *Alciphron: or, the Minute Philosopher* which he published in 1732. Aside from *Alciphron* itself, Berkeley promoted philosophy in America. His American friend and correspondent Samuel Johnson (not to be confused with the English Samuel Johnson) generated a correspondence with Berkeley of considerable philosophical and scholarly merit (1729–30). Indeed, Johnson went on to write his own *Elementa Philosophica* (1752) which he dedicated to Berkeley. He became the President of what would become Columbia University (King's College) and was the instructor of the great American theologian Jonathan Edwards (1703–58). Moreover, Berkeley promoted both Harvard and Yale by donating to them a considerable collection of books. And the city of Berkeley, California is named after the Irish philosopher.

Instead of returning to Derry, Berkeley lived in London for two and a half years, where his son, George, was born in 1733. Given the Bermuda failure, it was imperative for Berkeley to await royal approval in order to determine his next steps (so it would not have been appropriate for Berkeley to return to Derry). In 1732, he anonymously published his highly regarded *Alciphron* which reached a second publication the same year and was publicly commended by the Queen. A powerful Christian apologetic, this work addressed philosophical and theological issues such as the freedom of the will, human knowledge of God, and the Divine Mysteries. In 1733 Berkeley published *The Theory of Vision . . . Vindicated and Explained* in response to a published letter which criticized his *Essay Towards a New Theory of Vision* (which was republished together with *Alciphron*). Berkeley's response (published as a tract) was only rediscovered in 1860.

During this same year, Andrew Baxter published his *An Enquiry into the Nature of the Human Soul*, which included a chapter that offered the first sustained critique of Berkeley's immaterialism (a critique to which Berkeley did not reply). What is most notable is a change in climate: During this time there seems to have been some increase in serious engagement with Berkeley's philosophy and even a new found respect for it. By 1739, Hume had recognized Berkeley as a *great* philosopher in his *Treatise of Human Nature*. [13]

In 1734, Berkeley's wait for royal approval was over: he was granted the Bishopric of Cloyne. That year, he traveled to Dublin were he was consecrated Bishop. During this time, Berkeley published a second edition of the *Principles* and a third edition of the *Dialogues*. Both editions contain important revisions including Berkeley's use of the term "notion" in a more technical way, and the addition of two exchanges between Hylas and Philonous concerning whether the rejection of material substance ought to lead to rejection of spiritual substance. Berkeley also published the *Analyst or a Discourse Addressed to an Infidel Mathematician*, which provoked considerable controversy among the mathematicians. In this work, Berkeley powerfully criticized the calculus of both Newton and Leibniz, thereby making a notable contribution to 18th century. As the controversy unfolded, he published *A Defense of Free-Thinking in Mathematics* and *Reasons for not Answering Mr. Walton* in 1735.

The Latter Period: Bishop Berkeley

Berkeley lived in Cloyne and served as its Bishop for 18 years. There he fathered four more children (John, William, Julia, and Sarah). Between 1735 and 1737, Berkeley published *The Querist* in three parts (a work concerning politics and economics comprised entirely of questions), earning his place among Irish nationalists. In his contribution to the theory of money, Berkeley urged, among other things, the creation of a National Bank. In late 1737, Berkeley visited Dublin for a meeting of Parliament to speak against an antitheistic society called The Blasters (a group associated with the Hellfire Club). While in Dublin, Berkeley also wrote and published *A Discourse Addressed to Magistrates and Men in Authority* (1738) against this group.

In 1744, Berkeley published his (at the time) widely celebrated *Siris: A Chain of Philosophical Inquiries Concerning the Virtues of Tar-water and Diverse Subjects Connected Together and Arising One from Another* (which went through six editions in six months). The erudite and mysterious work blended Berkeley's views about tar-water (and the actual process for producing it) with reflection on physics, metaphysics, and medicine. Tar-water is produced from an infusion of tar into cold water which is supposed to extract from tar what were considered its medicinal virtues (such as the capacity to cure fevers and other ailments). Berkeley based his views on experimentation. Tar-water became wildly popular yielding increasing reports of its apparent value; and Berkeley speculated that it might be a panacea. While Berkeley's celebration of tar-water has been the object of considerable mirth, as A. A. Luce has pointed out it was reasonable for Bishop Berkeley to be concerned with the health of the poor in Cloyne. And it continued to be listed in the British Pharmacopoeia well into the 20th century, from which we can conclude that Berkeley was hardly alone in his beliefs.

In 1745, the final Jacobite rebellion brought unrest in Ireland, and Berkeley responded by raising troops and purchasing equipment for them, as well as writing letters (including letters to the Roman Catholics of his diocese) against the rebellion. In 1749, Berkeley published *A Word to the Wise*, asking all Roman Catholic clergy of Ireland to put aside differences and work toward the good of the country, and in 1750 *Maxims Concerning Patriotism* was published. In 1751, Berkeley lost his son William who died at the age of sixteen; this struck at the Bishop quite deeply.

In 1752, Berkeley traveled to London where he lived for five months before dying there. He apparently moved to London to supervise the education of his son, George. There, he published the third edition of *Alciphron*. Berkeley removed the sections of Dialogue VII, *Alciphron* in which he argues against abstraction. Some have imagined this to indicate an "about face" on one of his central doctrines: The issue is obviously controversial. And he also published *Miscellany* which includes some of his old work along with *Farther Thoughts on Tar-Water*. In 1753, Berkeley died, while his wife, Anne, read to him from Paul's first letter to the Corinthians. He was buried in the chapel of Christ Church.

SECTION TWO: BERKELEY'S PHILOSOPHY

Philosophical Perplexity

While some have viewed Berkeley as an extremely counterintuitive philosopher with no good arguments to support his claims,[14] others have considered Berkeley a *great* philosopher—not least of which was David Hume.[15] And although the crude picture of Hume as *merely* the empiricist successor of Berkeley has been largely discredited, it remains true Hume was influenced by Berkeley in very profound ways. Indeed, it is worth noting Hume endorsed the opposite (but equally legendary) view that Berkeley's arguments are actually *irrefutable* (although entirely incapable of producing any conviction)—a view also mentioned by James Boswell and Thomas Reid.[16] Notably both extreme representations—Berkeley as fool and Berkeley as genius—centralize this profound opposition to common sense.

What one perhaps wants is a less dramatic and somewhat more moderate assessment of Berkeley's philosophy. Certainly, it is easy to misunderstand a philosopher, and I am afraid Berkeley is one very good example. Yet while I do think Berkeley has been a victim of serious caricature and misrepresentation, I don't think Berkeley can be plausibly understood as offering a philosophically cautious and unsurprising account of the world. Moreover, I think the outrageousness of Berkeley is part of what is so captivating about him. Philosophy tends to be at its most gripping when it shocks and unsettles. And radical views from exceptionally intelligent philosophers are often indicative of the emergence of deep and troubling philosophical questions—perhaps due to profound shifts in how the world is conceptualized. Such was the early modern period which was characterized by the impact of the rise of modern science upon the older (largely Aristotelian) account of reality.

Berkeley himself, especially in his major philosophical work, *Three Dialogues between Hylas and Philonous* (1713), develops the view that his own position is much *closer* to common sense than those of his opponents. On the face of it, of course, this seems only to be adding insult to injury (or heaping the ludicrous upon the unbelievable). Yet there have been important interpreters of Berkeley who have found a way to see a more palatable Berkeley, so the question is not so easily dismissed.

That being said, Berkeley's views about common sense are complex. While the Berkeley of the *Dialogues* really does seem especially interested in restoring philosophers to common sense, the Berkeley of the *Principles* also proudly endorses the view that one ought to "think with the learned and speak with the vulgar" (*PHK* I §51). One example of "speaking with the vulgar" offered by Berkeley, is that we continue to say the sun rises and sets, despite the fact that it is not the sun but the earth that is moving. This proud endorsement, however, raises the real possibility that on several philosophical issues, Berkeley's commitment to common sense is merely verbal. The worry is that while Berkeley's own considered ontological views may differ in serious ways from the views of the common folk, that nonetheless the *speech* of the common folk is to be preserved, but only for propriety's sake.

Unsurprisingly, a recurring motif in the literature has been a split Berkeley, a kind of Janus Berkeley. On the one hand, we seem to have Berkeley the man of the people, friend of the masses, and defender of common sense, while on the other hand we seem to have Berkeley the metaphysician, philosopher, and chief source of outrage and perplexity.

One good way to frame this tension is to recognize that for Berkeley there is an important contrast between the views of those he calls the "vulgar" (or the common folk—the "illiterate bulk of mankind" as he sometimes calls them) and those he calls the "philosophers" (the learned, the men of speculation). This distinction, equally important to Hume, plays a significant role in the orientation of Berkeley's own view. He explicitly aims to show where both the vulgar and the philosophers fail; to reconcile the parts that he accepts and to, in some sense, go beyond both. This obviously raises an interesting question about the very positioning of Berkeley's intellectual efforts: To what extent would he seek to describe them as part of the enterprise of philosophy at all? To what extent is he advocating a return to the views of the vulgar? Berkeley's positioning of his work presents itself as a kind of third option that is neither quite of the vulgar nor quite of the philosophers. In this way, Berkeley's work poses interesting metaphilosophical questions about the nature of philosophy itself, and its relationship to common sense and the views of the ordinary person.

BERKELEY'S METAPHYSICAL ACCOUNT OF THE WORLD: AN OVERVIEW

Immaterialism

Berkeley's immaterialism is a negative thesis which denies that matter exists (more strongly it denies that the notion of matter is intelligible). Berkeley doesn't simply mean one thing by the term "matter." Rather, he recognizes that it can be used a host of different ways and he aims to undermine materialism in *any* way of understanding it. Indeed, Berkeley imagines that the term is used in shifting ways in order to preserve the materialist thesis in the face of arguments to the contrary.

Yet Berkeley also argues against the views of the vulgar and the philosophers specifically. He identifies a core form of materialism— that the everyday items which comprise the world (e.g., tables, trees, cows) are the causes of our sense experiences. According to the vulgar view, the everyday items that we immediately perceive are mind-independent causal powers. The philosophers, by contrast, understand matter as an unperceived substance in which the sensible qualities we perceive exist (or "inhere"). I therefore distinguish between vulgar and philosophical materialism.

Analogously there is a contrast between both vulgar and philosophical accounts of perception. While the vulgar suppose that we immediately perceive the everyday items themselves, the latter suppose that we immediately perceive only our private ideas which resemble, and therefore allow us to "mediately" perceive, the properties of the material substance. We can call the former "naïve" (or "vulgar") realism and the latter "philosophical" (or representational) realism. According to Berkeley, while the vulgar do not appreciate that their objects of immediate perception are mind-dependent ideas, the philosophers falsely suppose that ideas are not real things, but merely representations thereof. Berkeley's explicit intention is to reconcile the two views by maintaining we immediately perceive the real things themselves, which are nonetheless mind dependent.

Spirits and Ideas

According to Berkeley there are only two kinds of thing: spirits and ideas. Spirits are simple, active beings which produce and perceive ideas; ideas are passive beings which are produced and perceived by spirits. The everyday items which populate the world (tables, trees, etc.) turn out to be nothing but collections of ideas and as such, they are dependent upon spirits for their existence.

In defending this view, Berkeley is effectively maintaining that spirits are the only substances (i.e., fundamental beings) which exist. Matter is rejected and everyday items depend upon spirits for their existence. Thus, in addition to Berkeley's immaterialism (his denial of matter), it will also be worth speaking of his spiritualism (his affirmation that spirits are the only substances).

According to Berkeley, one is immediately aware of one's ideas along with one's own self. However, this seems to leave one in an entirely private or egocentric world. Consequently, Berkeley initiates a second, more advanced stage of his idealism, which moves beyond what is given to our immediate awareness. Berkeley accomplishes this by trying to demonstrate the existence of God. He also maintains that we can infer the existence of other human spirits as well, although here the conclusion is less certain. One's awareness of one's own self can provide some understanding of what these other spirits must be like.

Using God as the foundation, Berkeley then aims to maintain the existence of an external, public world in the face of this pressure toward subjectivism. The resulting picture is one in which human spirits and God are connected together through communicative exchange, while the everyday items of nature are causally inert signs which facilitate this communication. God himself is immediately causally responsible for the things we sense-perceive, which are related together as signs to things signified. As such, they are part of a communicative system whereby God directs our conduct on a daily basis. Part of the picture involves the view that God perceives every-day items independently of our own sense-perception of them and that, as a consequence, these items are somehow still public.

As I conclude this chapter, let me briefly return to the shocking character of Berkeley's account: Why would Berkeley maintain the everyday items are nothing but collections of ideas? How does one drive a *motorcycle*, if it's only a collection of ideas? Ideas don't seem nearly *sturdy* enough! It is perhaps not so surprising that Samuel Johnson famously kicked the stone in order to refute Berkeley. Alas, he was not successful, since according to Berkeley, Johnson first saw a visible idea (of a rock) and when he moved his leg in a kicking motion, experienced the tangible ideas resistance and pain in his foot. Berkeley's theory nicely explains Johnson's attempted refutation. It also explains why Johnson (rightfully) supposed that upon seeing the visual idea and then kicking, he would experience the feelings of resistance and pain in his foot. The visible and tangible ideas are both immediately caused by God. However, in learning their regular-ity, we can predict that upon seeing certain visual ideas and acting accordingly, we will thereby experience certain tangible ideas. We are simply responding to the Divine Language, which we have long ago mastered.

CHAPTER TWO

BERKELEY'S PROJECT

Reading: *The Principles*: Title-Page, Preface, Introduction §1–5, §156

The Dialogues: Title-Page, Preface

Understanding Berkeley's philosophical project is essential to understanding his philosophical views. Why would somebody go to such great lengths to show that tables and trees cannot ever exist unperceived? Without recognizing some kind of *point* to this stunning thesis, Berkeley's key ideas can only seem both perverse and unmotivated. In this chapter, I situate Berkeley's overall philosophical account within the context of his philosophical agenda, and I situate his philosophical agenda within the context of the salient issues of his day.

SECTION ONE: BERKELEY'S PROJECT: AN OVERVIEW

The best-received view is that Berkeley's agenda is primarily a religious one. Yet while this is correct, it is incomplete. Berkeley's religious views are peculiar. He has an idiosyncratic agenda to press which is deeply bound up with his distinction between "the philosophers" and "the vulgar." Berkeley makes it clear in the *Dialogues* that his goal is to retrieve learned men from a kind of useless philosophical speculation and to return them to the real world of everyday affairs. In particular, he aims to have "speculation referred to practice" (*3D* Preface). For Berkeley "reference to practice" concerns everyday virtue, morality, and piety. More specifically, he is interested to dispose men of speculation "to reverence and embrace the salutary truths of the Gospel, which to know and to practise is the highest perfection of human nature" (*PHK* §156).

Berkeley expects real consequences in restoring men of speculation to practice. In particular, he believes this would have "a gradual influence in repairing the too much defaced sense of virtue in the world." He blames "the prejudices of philosophers" as hitherto prevailing "against the common sense and natural notions of mankind" (*3D* Preface 168). In this way, Berkeley aims for his work to have a real impact upon the world; the chief function of his philosophy is the improvement of human life by way of religion.

This general framework is important in beginning to tackle the tough question concerning the relationship between Berkeley's own philosophy and "common sense." Berkeley's criticism of the philosophers who stray from common sense is largely connected to his desire to bring these men "down to earth" by reconnecting speculation to practice. The learned, for Berkeley, are supposed to be restored to common sense largely by becoming reengaged with the world around them, rather than merely amusing themselves with speculation that has no connection with the everyday world. This is important because it helps explain, at least in part, why common sense plays such a central role in Berkeley's philosophy: It is central to his project of referring the philosophers to practice. And Berkeley's explicit disagreements with the vulgar can be understood in terms of Berkeley's sense that pernicious beliefs and behavior abound even among the common folk. Berkeley's philosophy, therefore, is positioned as a kind of third point in relation to the learned and the vulgar. Its intended function is to reengage the learned, bring them on his side, so that any immoral and irreligious conduct of the "illiterate bulk of mankind" can be corrected, and the world restored to virtue.

Berkeley's concern with the learned is that practicing speculation in a way that is divorced from the practicalities of the everyday, while "amusing" is selfish and irresponsible. Yet if such speculation involves determining genuine *truths*, despite the fact that they are useless to the betterment of mankind, then there remains the sticking point that such pursuits may still be valuable for their own sake. Consequently, one of Berkeley's major strategies in addressing the learned is to convince them that it involves mere verbal dispute and gamesmanship. In this respect, Berkeley may be characterized as a kind of antiphilosopher, one who is interested in tearing down the edifice of speculation to expose a naked emperor. However, Berkeley's views extend well beyond traditional philosophy. He also aims to cut out pointless speculation from the natural sciences and from mathematics, and refer these sciences to practice and the betterment of human kind as well.

Yet while this negative philosophical approach may aim to show that standard speculation for its own sake has no genuine content, Berkeley also needs to motivate such men of speculation to return to everyday practice—that is, to the practice of Christian virtue. In order to secure this end, Berkeley believes that he needs to establish the existence of God and the natural immortality of the soul as "the readiest preparation, as well as the strongest motive, to the study and practice of virtue" (*3D* Preface 168). His positive philosophical account, therefore, has also a decidedly functional role to play.

SECTION TWO: THE NEGATIVE PROJECT—BERKELEY AS ANTIPHILOSOPHER

Philosophical Perplexity

Questions concerning philosophical perplexity were taken quite seriously by philosophers such as Locke, Berkeley, Hume, and Kant. Locke claimed his *Essay* was originally inspired by a philosophical conversation among friends that reached no resolution. Indeed, he proposed a new way of approaching metaphysics specifically. Instead of trying to tackle philosophical problems, Locke thought—before sailing out on "the vast Ocean of Being" (*E*. 1.1.7, 47)—one ought to proceed with a careful examination of the human understanding. In this way, Locke hoped to determine what ideas we have and how we come by them. The payoff was to recognize that there were certain ideas that we did not have, possibly could not have, and so show certain metaphysical questions exceeded the grasp of human understanding. It is little surprise Locke's conclusions seem somewhat depressing. For Locke, in many respects our understanding of the world comes up short and the source of such ignorance lies in the limitations of human understanding. He writes:

> I suppose it may be of use, to prevail with the busy Mind of Man, to be more cautious in meddling with things exceeding its Comprehension; to stop, when it is at the utmost Extent of its Tether;

and to sit down in a quiet Ignorance of those Things, which upon Examination, are found to be beyond the reach of our Capacities. (*E*. 1.1.4, 44–45)

Yet there is a very real sense in which Locke is offering a kind of *solution* to philosophical perplexity in addition to this diagnosis. His basic strategy is to take standard philosophical problems of his day and effectively sweep them under the carpet by pointing to limitations in the human understanding. Berkeley, by contrast, is adamantly opposed to this account of perplexity. He explicitly flags it in his Introduction to the *Principles* and complains that it reflects poorly on our Maker that we should have such a desire to know these things, only to have that desire thwarted. He writes: "We should believe that God has dealt more bountifully with the sons of men, than to give them a strong desire for that knowledge, which he had placed quite out of their reach" (*PHK* Intro §3).

For Berkeley, the source of philosophical perplexity is, by contrast, *philosophy itself*. He writes: "Upon the whole, I am inclined to think that the far greater part, if not all, of those difficulties which have hitherto amused philosophers, and blocked up the way to knowledge, are entirely owing to our selves. That we have first raised a dust, and then complain, we cannot see" (*PHK* Intro §3).

What are some of the metaphysical sources of perplexity that concern both Locke and Berkeley? In order to understand the difficulties which were emerging, especially for early modern philosophers, we need to have a better understanding of the philosophical materialism Berkeley believes lies at the root of such problems. 'Substance,' for Berkeley and his fellow philosophers, is a technical notion. Roughly, one may treat it as equivalent to 'basic thing.' For example, the Aristotelians viewed human beings, cows, and oak trees as (corporeal) substances. Substances are supposed to be ontologically and causally basic. They are ontologically basic insofar as "accidents" depend upon them for their existence. And they are causally basic insofar as changes in the world are accounted for by appeal to the essence (nature) of the substances themselves. A change in "accident" is something that ultimately needs to be referred to the substance's essence.

Thus substances were typically contrasted with what philosophers called "accidents"—items that existed in substances and depended upon them for their existence. In such a view, "accidents" are allowed to have a kind of existence, although in a less robust sense or way than substances themselves. For example, sight, although less of a thing than Socrates, is nonetheless more of a reality than blindness, which is a privation of reality. Although the issues are complicated here, "accidents" may be viewed as property-like items, property instances, or in some way connected to subject-property structure, items that are individuated per the individual substances in which they exist (thus we distinguish one person's sight from another's). In this view, accidents are taken to exist in ("inhere in") the substance that possesses them.

Of course, different philosophers conceptualized material substance in different ways. According to the Aristotelians, corporeal substances are composite unities of actualizing form and potential prime matter. By contrast, for Descartes matter is nothing but three-dimensional extension, capable of size, shape, and motion. And for Locke, matter is nothing but solid corpuscles which exist in space. Regardless of the differences, however, all agree that matter is a substance in which various properties or accidents (such as extension, size, and shape) exist.

Yet the very notion of material substance seems to have been leading to some perplexity concerning mind, body, and their interrelations in light of the rise of the new science and the rejection of Aristotelian hylomorphism (the theory of form/matter). In this Aristotelian theory there is a contrast between what we can call superficial and deep change. The former merely involves the gain and loss of accidents by a given substance, which underlies this change (as a human might change size or weight). By contrast, deep change involves the generation and perishing of the substances themselves. For example, an acorn can turn into an entirely different kind of thing (an oak tree); a caterpillar can turn into a butterfly. How is this possible? Doesn't something need to survive the change?

In the Aristotelian view this involves a change in the "substantial form" itself. In this case, the thing that survives the change is nothing actual, it is only a potential to gain and lose substantial form. Together this potential (the prime matter) and the actualizing form constitute a composite substance. In this theory, the reason a substance is the kind of thing it is, is explained by appeal to the substantial form of the thing.

With the rise of the New Science, however, this view is rejected. As a consequence, all change is regarded as mere superficial change, and material things are not explained by appeal to a substantial form. Instead, they are explained by appeal to actual matter, which can gain and lose various properties (such as size, shape, location, and motion). In such a view, change in the material universe is explained mechanistically in terms of the interactions between particles of matter, rather than by any appeal to a substantial form or to an essence.

As a consequence of this shift, several difficulties move to the foreground. The theory of form and matter provides a framework for understanding the nature of the soul (the form of the human being) and the body (the matter). Once this framework is rejected, the challenge emerges as to how to explain the nature of mind and its relation to body. Famously, Descartes argues that the mind is nothing but the thinking thing we are aware of in conscious thought itself while matter is nothing but three-dimensional extension.[1] The difficulty now, however, is to explain the causal interaction between the mind (an unextended thinking thing) and the body (an unthinking extended thing). If they are so wildly different how can one exert a causal influence on the other? How can the mind make the body move, and how can impacts upon the body cause ideas in the mind?

According to Locke the question of how mind and body interact is "answered" by simply showing us that we do not have adequate ideas of the real essences of body and mind, and consequently are in no position to answer that question (*E*. 2.23.15, 305). The Lockean "solution" to perplexity, therefore, is to understand the reach of our capacities, and then to refuse to meddle in that which is beyond us.

There are other problems. Unlike Descartes, who holds that matter is nothing but sheer three-dimensional extension, Locke holds that solid particles exist in a vacuum. But how do these particles cohere? According to Locke, we do not have the capacity to understand this basic fact about matter. Nor do we, according to Locke, understand how motion can be transferred from one particle to the other. And then there's space itself. What is it? Is it a substance? An "accident?"

More generally, one starts to see how the changing world view puts pressure on the very notion of substance. We have come a long way from the picture in which cows and acorns are basic. Are material particles basic? It seems that matter itself is infinitely divisible in this account: One can keep breaking matter down into smaller and smaller parts. (This was anathema to Berkeley who felt the view led to all sorts of paradoxes.) Perhaps it is little wonder that Berkeley felt that all of these issues arose from a fundamental error, namely the very philosophical commitment to material substance in the first place.

Forms of Skepticism

The traditional view about Berkeley's response to skepticism is that he offers an answer to the question whether we can know there exists an external (material) world. Descartes, for example, had famously doubted of everything.[2] Yet he found that he could not doubt his own existence and that he was a thinking thing.[3] From this he tried to show God's existence, and from this prove the existence of the external (material) world.[4] Equally famous, his attempt has generally been found wanting for reasons, not least of which is the concern that his attempt to prove God's existence involves presupposing what needs to be established (namely, that clear and distinct ideas are reliable guides to truth). Thus, we have the notorious "Cartesian Circle." Inevitably, Berkeley is seen as "answering" this concern by effectively getting rid of the (material) external world altogether. (Problem solved!)

Yet while this concern about skepticism with regard to the external world is admittedly relevant to Berkeley, it ought to be placed within a larger context of concerns that Berkeley has about skepticism. After admitting that a skeptic is "one who doubts of everything" Hylas and Philonous (the interlocutors of *Three Dialogues*) agree to *expand* the notion to also include (1) the denial of the real existence of sensible qualities and (2) (Lockean) ignorance of everyday items (*3D* I 173).

The Denial of the Existence of Sensible Things
Hylas and Philonous agree that a skeptic is one who denies the reality of sensible things. This denial that sensible things are *real* appears to be deeply bound up with the view of modern science that secondary qualities such as colors and sounds do not really exist in the object (or more correctly, that there is nothing inherent in the object which resembles the sensation of color or sound). This commitment to the view that the world is populated with matter characterized only by the primary qualities appears to open up a gap between the world as it appears to us and the world as it really is. In this view, we experience

certain sensations in the mind (mere appearances) where neither they nor even resemblances actually inhere in the material objects outside of us.

In order to appreciate this concern, consider the following analogy. When one wears sunglasses, the world appears darker than it really is. Thus there is a gap between how the world appears through sunglasses, and how it appears without sunglasses. Suppose that these glasses are green. Not only does everything appear darker, it also appears greener. Yet this appearance is a misrepresentation of how things actually are. The sky is not green, etc. The view of the new scientists is that there is nothing at all in the world resembling how sensible qualities (such as color, sound, taste, etc.) appear to us. Instead of there being no green in the sky (but blue instead), in this view there is no color there at all!

This point is important, since it evidences a serious encroachment of the new science upon "the common sense of the vulgar" as well its impact upon the older Aristotelian views, which to a large extent, provided a theoretical basis for the vulgar views. In the vulgar view, we simply see the world as it is. The blue that one experiences (i.e., the blue that "looks like something") is taken to reside in the sky, and the sweetness that one experiences (i.e., the sweetness that "tastes like something") is taken to be part of the sugar. Moreover, such (secondary) qualities are taken to have an existence independent of any mind's perception of it. Schematically, we can formulate the vulgar model of how the orange of a cat is seen as follows:

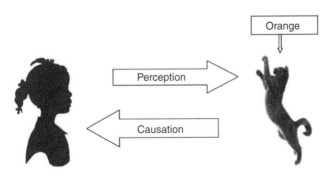

Common Sense (the Vulgar)

In the Aristotelian view, this sentiment is characterized in a more sophisticated way as the view the world "mirrors" its appearance to us. While the vulgar may not have any theory of perception, it seems that in a more sophisticated view one will need to posit a vehicle or means by which one perceives such external qualities. In this view (representational realism), to perceive such external qualities involves receiving a mental vehicle, which in some way resembles the quality itself. While this view may be a little bit unclear at this point, consider the analogy of binoculars. In order to see something a far way off such as the performers at a concert, it may be that one needs to use binoculars as the vehicle or means by which one sees. If all goes well, there ought to be a resemblance between how things appear to one through the binoculars and how they are in reality. In effect, there ought to be a resemblance between the performers on stage and how they appear in the binoculars.

In the Aristotelian view, which is a version of representational realism, the sensible accident which inheres in a substance (as orange inheres in a cat) is causally propagated to the body. As a consequence the soul is modified in a particular way; it receives the sensible species where the sensible species (although numerically distinct from the accident) is nonetheless "formally identical" (and so qualitatively resembling) the sensible accident. Schematically, we can formulate representational realism as follows:

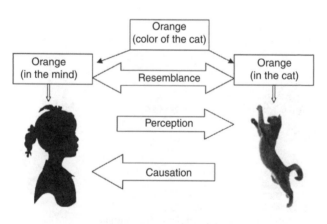

Representational Realism

With the emergence of the New Science, this view about the qualities which would now become "secondary" was rejected. In the new world view, only "primary" qualities (such as extension, shape, motion, solidity, and the like) really exist in external things. Our experience of the secondary qualities (color, sound, odor, taste) is not "mirrored" in the actual world. Instead, the primary qualities are supposed to afford an explanation of causal impact upon the body, which in turn provides a causal explanation of the sensations we experience. To be sure, not all friends of this mechanic view wished to hold a Galileo-type error theory (and deny the reality of colors and sounds), as we shall see. But regardless of whether one maintains an extreme Galilean position or not, the fact remains that a gap is now opened up between the world as it actually appears to us and the real world composed of tiny corpuscles.

Berkeley's general unhappiness with this position is brought out forcefully by Philonous' long diatribe in the beginning of the Second Dialogue about how beautiful everything is: "Look! Are not the fields covered with a delightful verdure? . . . What treatment then do those philosophers deserve, who would deprive these noble and delightful scenes of all reality?"(*3D* II 210). Berkeley sees this form of skepticism (the denial of the reality of sensible things) as flying wildly in the face of common sense. As we shall see, Berkeley works hard (in his own peculiar way) to retrieve the reality of secondary qualities.

This requires some comment. By now, 300 years after Berkeley wrote the *Principles,* the impact of natural science has led to a change in "common sense." It is certainly true that most people take for granted some version of the very view Berkeley railed against: We speak of "sound-waves" and "electromagnetic waves." We think what we call colors, sounds, and the like—if they are out there at all—are really just physical properties of some sort. At least this is how we *speak.* Such facts raise interesting questions about the status of Berkeley's philosophy which had signaled its commitment to "common sense"—a common sense which may have altered.

Berkeley points to worries about this emerging scientific picture which we shall confront in the fourth chapter. The worries he raises 300 years ago are precisely those which *challenge* somewhat the view we may now currently accept, often without much thought or reflection. For this, among other reasons, I think Berkeley can force us to think more deeply about what has now become "common sense" to us.

At present, I want to observe that while we may tacitly accept some possibly unreflective view about sound-waves and the like, we also appear to move through the world in ways that seem to presuppose the view of the vulgar. When we are interested in painting the living room, we are not interested in waves but in how the colors *look*. We go to the store and select various color swatches to help us make a good choice. In such cases, we are clearly talking about the blue we immediately experience, the blue that (to borrow a phrase) "there is something that it is like" to see. Obviously these phenomenal qualities are deeply connected to our sense-experiences—and when we project them onto the world and talk about *them* as if they were *out there*, we are in some ways overlooking the point that really, if there is anything *out there* at all, there is nothing but electromagnetic-waves. There is nothing out there that is *like* what we immediately experience. Consequently, I think that while, on the one hand, we speak "commonsensically" about waves, on the other hand, we also often talk and act as if the phenomenal properties we immediately experience resided out in the world in the physical things themselves. That is: We are *still* vulgar realists, despite the fact that we have *also* accepted the view of the new science.

Lockean Ignorance

Berkeley (unlike Locke) is not simply concerned with philosophical perplexity, but also with a kind of philosophical *skepticism*. Berkeley writes:

> Prejudices and errors of sense do from all parts discover themselves to our view; and endeavouring to correct these by reason we are insensibly drawn into uncouth paradoxes, difficulties, and inconsistencies, which multiply and grow upon us as we advance in speculation; till at length, having wander'd through many intricate mazes, we find ourselves just where we were, or, which is worse, sit down in a forlorn scepticism. (*PHK* Intro §1)

Here, Berkeley has Locke in mind, transforming Locke's invitation to "sit down in a quiet ignorance" into the tragedy that we "sit down in a forlorn scepticism."

Locke himself does not profess skepticism. Nonetheless, it seems clear that Berkeley regards Locke's professed *ignorance* as a form of skepticism. Presumably, the concern is that for Locke, there is much we are ignorant of when it comes to everyday items such as gold, cherries, and men, for example. For while we have knowledge of the various powers or capabilities possessed by such items (its "accidents"), we do not have an adequate idea of the real essence of such items, and so do not understand how they can possess the powers they do. In expanding his concern from philosophical perplexity, to this type of skepticism (i.e., Lockean Ignorance of everyday items), Berkeley takes aim at the very *account of perplexity* originally offered by Locke.

In this way, Berkeley's own account is intended to supersede Locke's treatment of philosophical perplexity, by tackling both the perplexity itself and the Lockean explanation/solution (i.e., "ignorance") through drawing on an account grounded in the misuse of language—one which was introduced and then underemployed by Locke himself.

This helps illuminate the role of Berkeley's "antiphilosophical" stance in restoring men of speculation to "common sense" through showing the sources of perplexity and/or Lockean skepticism are based on nothing but empty or misused words. More deeply, however, we can begin to appreciate why, for Berkeley to profess this type of skepticism is to depart in a radical way from the common folk. For *they* move through life utterly undisturbed by this philosophical ignorance. To *them*—the understanding of what a cherry is, for example, the simple knowledge of how a cherry looks, feels, tastes, and smells. Importantly, Berkeley takes pains to point out that this philosophical ignorance, in fact, has no consequences in terms of the day-to-day negotiations of the everyday world. (This is something with which Locke himself would have agreed; he believes that the human understanding while not fitted to grasping the true nature of things, is nonetheless effectively geared toward securing the daily conveniences of life). However, for Berkeley, it seems more than a little bit odd that we should be so in the dark about the real nature of things, and yet somehow know enough to get through our day. Philonous presses Hylas:

> But is it not strange the whole world should be thus imposed on, and so foolish to believe their senses? And yet I know not how it is, but men eat, and drink, and sleep, and perform all the offices of life as comfortably and conveniently, as if they really know the things they are conversant about. (*3D* III 228)

This embarrassing question is surely intended to underscore the fact that this philosophical ignorance actually has no bearing on how people live their day-to-day lives and is therefore an example of speculation that has been divorced from practice. Such a concern is further driven home by Berkeley, who has Philonous make the further point that skeptics such as Hylas themselves are unaffected by such ignorance in their daily lives—presumably ignoring it altogether (*3D* III 228). Not only does this ignorance have no bearing on how the vulgar blunder through life, it likewise has no bearing on how the philosopher negotiates the world. It is therefore a kind of abstruse, unimportant, wholly speculative sort of ignorance.

As it turns out, this state of affairs may indeed have bad consequences in the real world. Berkeley wishes us to appreciate how ridiculous this professed (practically irrelevant, theoretically detached) ignorance must seem to the illiterate bulk of mankind. Indeed, he explicitly points to the inherent perversity in the thought that those who spend their time in the pursuit of *wisdom*, should end up in a place of *ignorance* on issues that seem so obviously known to the people who amble unreflectively through their day. Surely it would seem to Berkeley that such a state of affairs may have very bad consequences in making the learned seem *ridiculous* to the vulgar—thereby undermining any *authority* or *respect* that they might otherwise have possessed and ultimately relied on in working toward the betterment of mankind (*PHK* I §88).

The Retrenchment of the Sciences

What I call the *Retrenchment of the Sciences* is the view that most of the theoretical content of mathematics and physics, which does not have any connection to practice (and the betterment of human beings), has no content at all. This claim occupies a central place in Berkeley's *Principles,* and it is firmly situated within Berkeley's project of returning the learned from useful speculation to the practicalities of everyday life. Berkeley identifies skepticism (i.e., Lockean Ignorance of real essences) as the central problem for natural science. His solution is to deny that there are any unknown essences, and to more strongly deny that natural science involves the study of underlying causes at all. Rather it is the study of regularities in the phenomena of nature. Indeed, Berkeley defends an instrumentalist view of science which sees scientific theories, concepts, etc. as mere conceptual tools for classifying phenomena and making predications.

This allows Berkeley to critique the natural scientist who is "overpreoccupied" with formulating exact universal rules. Instead, natural science ought to focus on the betterment of mankind through a proper exaltation of God (*PHK* I §109).

Likewise Berkeley aims to clip the pretensions of arithmetic and geometry, two branches of mathematics. With regard to the former, Berkeley maintains that subtle speculation in arithmetic has been unduly elevated, largely because the symbols of arithmetic have been taken to signify something important (such as abstract platonic objects) which can illuminate the natural world. For Berkeley, however, inquiry into arithmetic in a way that abstracts for its application to ordinary practice is a vacuous trifling with words (*PHK* I §119).

With regard to geometry, Berkeley is concerned with perplexities and paradoxes he thinks arise particularly from the assumption that a finite extension is infinitely divisible, and worse that each part in this division may be divided into an infinity of parts, and so on, an infinite number of times. Berkeley's answer to this is to show that since the only objects of geometry are ideas, and ideas cannot be infinitely divided, such a process is a great nonsense. In answer to the charge that the rejection of infinite divisibility of finite extension will destroy geometry as a science, Berkeley says that "what is useful in geometry and promotes the benefit of human life, does still remain firm and unshaken on our principles. . . . Some of the more intricate and subtle parts of *speculative mathematics* may be pared off without any prejudice to the truth" (*PHK* I §131).

SECTION THREE: THE POSITIVE PROJECT—BERKELEY AS INSPIRATIONAL PHILOSOPHER

Despite his antitheoretical tendencies, Berkeley can hardly be said to abandon philosophy. He begins the *Principles* by defining philosophy as "nothing else but the study of wisdom and truth" (*PHK* Intro §1). In Berkeley's view, philosophy appears limited to a study of the divine (i.e., God and the soul) and the duty of humankind (i.e., morality and righteousness). A large part of the enterprise of philosophy is *motivational* in nature: Motivating the study and practice of right conduct, "enflaming tempers with the love of great actions," enobling and dignifying the human being.

Like his negative project, Berkeley's positive project is best understood against the backdrop of the Lockean agenda. In addition to showing that much metaphysical knowledge is simply beyond us, Locke aims to show that, instead, *"Morality is the proper Science, and Business of Mankind"* (*E.* 4.12.11, 646). Indeed, Locke claims that a true science of morality is possible since we do have ideas of the real essences of those things relevant to ethical truths.

While Berkeley himself aims to turn philosophers away from speculation (and in particular perplexity and skepticism), he does not claim that any one science is the proper business of mankind. Instead, of turning men to a new science, he aims to turn them directly to virtuous action. This is to say: Berkeley's positive turn is action-oriented in a way that Locke's is not.

In order to motivate philosophers to return to virtue and piety, Berkeley does not believe that his elimination of speculation disconnected from practice will suffice. Minimally, he thinks, he needs to proffer *an incentive* to appropriate Christian conduct. By demonstrating the existence of God and by establishing the natural immortality of the soul, Berkeley thinks, philosophers will be motivated to goodness through a concern in securing their eternal fate. The idea here is that ultimately good action can be secured through self-interested motive.

This view may seem especially strange to us, post-Kant. According to Kant, an act can never be morally good unless it is done for the correct moral reason.[5] This means that we cannot do something moral simply because it satisfies some desires. And yet Berkeley seems to flagrantly reduce ethical conduct to action for self-interested motive. In fairness to Berkeley, a couple of points can be made. First, his position was not that wild for his time. It seems to have been generally assumed (by both Descartes and Locke, for example) that the existence of God and the natural immortality of the soul are necessary to motivate virtuous conduct.

Second, Berkeley's position about morality is more complicated than it might seem. Moral actions (for Berkeley) are those that promote human welfare *in general*. Thus, acting for solely self-interested motives is not in anyway ethical. Rather, according to Berkeley, obeying God's Laws (which promote human welfare as their end) is what constitutes ethical conduct.

Finally, Berkeley provides an explicit argument against the view that virtuous conduct as its own reward is sufficient to motivate righteous behavior. For while he is prepared to allow that virtuous behavior is itself a pleasure, he does not think this subtlety will suffice to motivate the bulk of mankind. Certainly the pleasures which attend fame and fortune can overwhelm the refined pleasure of virtuous action. As a consequence, the existence of a future state where rewards and punishments are dispensed by a Divine Being is integral, for Berkeley, to righteous conduct.

At any rate, informed by his positive project, Berkeley's proofs of God's existence are supposed to be motivational. Rather than merely establishing the existence of God, Berkeley aims to show the truth in the scriptural passage of Acts 17:28 that God is "in whom we live, and move, and have our being." For Berkeley, this means that God is "present and conscious to our innermost thoughts" (*PHK* I §155).

Rather than viewing God as remote from human affairs, he is very close to us. This, for Berkeley, ought to inspire a "holy fear" necessary to good conduct. God is not shown by Berkeley as a mere Creator of man, but as a Divine Governor, who effectively communicates to us on a regular basis—instructing us as how to behave. In this way, Berkeley can address the mechanistic notion of a Creator who does not Govern or Sustain (*ALC* IV §14). It also enables him to address what he sees as "irreligion." Here he speaks of a "sort of *atheism*" (*PHK* I §155) to which those who live in Christian countries have "through a supine and dreadful negligence sunk." "Since it is downright impossible, that a soul pierced and enlightened with a thorough sense of the omnipresence, holiness, and justice of that *Almighty Spirit,* should persist in a remorseless violation of his laws" (*PHK* I §155). Berkeley means to address not an atheism of belief (or lack thereof), but an atheism of action—behavior which manifests a lack of a genuine sense of the presence of God and the natural immortality of the soul.

Atheism, Deism, Free-thinking

Berkeley's positive, motivational project must be understood within the theological context within which he was philosophizing. He explicitly writes of combating both atheism and irreligion, which he sees as playing a significant role in enabling nonvirtuous conduct. And certainly the specters of both Thomas Hobbes and Baruch Spinoza hover in the background. Yet while both men were branded atheists, both professed belief in God. So the issues here are decidedly tricky.

First, it is important to bear in mind that the climate of "religious tolerance" in Berkeley's time was rather different from the climate in either the United States or in Europe today. In England, for example, The Blasphemy Act of 1697 forbad denying Christianity as the one true religion, the Athanasian doctrine of the Trinity, and the Divine authorship of the Scriptures. This is hardly a climate in which atheists could speak their minds freely; indeed during Hobbes' time, one could be burned for heresy. Little surprise that if Hobbes was an atheist, he never said as much. Nonetheless, his beliefs were taken as sufficient to brand him an atheist. For example, his strong materialism involved denying the existence of any other substance except body—so both the human soul and God himself would have to be material. Berkeley explicitly avers that this materialism is nothing but an "atheism a little disguised" (*TVV* §6).

Part of the difficulty is that many deviations from orthodoxy were branded "atheistic" in nature, regardless of whether they had such implications. For example, Descartes himself was unfairly accused of atheism since his identification of matter with sheer extension (i.e., space) seemed to lead to the view that matter itself was coeternal with God. (This seems to reflect badly on God, who is supposed to be causally responsible for everything as well as contradicting scriptures which indicate God created the material world). However, another part of the difficulty is given explicit expressions of atheism were illegal, atheistic views had to be expressed esoterically. Thus we have the plausible interpretation of Hobbes and others as *crypto-atheists*.[6]

At any rate, it quickly becomes evident why Berkeley saw his attack on materialism as undermining the chief support or cornerstone of atheism. Not only does matter lead to difficulties such as the problem conceiving creation of matter *ex nihilo* on the one hand, and the problem of the coeternality of matter on the other (*PHK* I §92), it renders the soul material, and appears to undercut a world in which a wise God oversees the world with providence, subjecting the world instead to the strict determinism which apparently dispenses with genuine human freedom (*PHK* I §93).

Yet the issues are also more complex. Berkeley writes during the heyday of the famous controversies surrounding deism particularly in the late 17th and early 18th centuries in England.[7] Sometimes mischaracterized as the representation of God as the noninterfering Creator who sets the world into motion and then does nothing else, the term "deism" applies to views which raised serious questions about the relation between scriptural revelation and human reason, assigning revelation either a backseat role or absolutely no role at all. This is not to say, of course, the new mechanistic picture of the world did not invite conceptions of God as a Divine Creator as watchmaker who did not have to sustain and govern the world at every instant. It did. However, to leave it at that is to miss the core of the deist controversies.

With deism, we see the emphasis on natural religion (based upon beliefs discoverable by reason, such as the existence of God, the immortality of the soul, and the existence of a future state promising reward), to the exclusion of the sacred truths based solely on revelation. At its more extreme, deism involved strong criticism of the clergy taken to admix mysteries into religion for purposes of securing power.

Berkeley himself became increasingly concerned over those called "free-thinkers." He was particularly concerned by the views of Anthony Collins, whom he believed (with decent reason) to be a covert atheist.[8] "Free-thinker" was a pejorative expression used by the clergy and then reclaimed by Collins in his *A Discourse on Free-thinking* (1713). The term "free-thinking" itself indicates refusal to submit one's free use of reason to the demands of any authority, and was at first used by Berkeley as a kind of aspersion. (Later, he preferred the expression "minute philosopher" in light of the positive meaning that Collins placed on "free-thinker.")

We see the first signs of critique in the *Three Dialogues* and then his several *Guardian* essays culminating in his systematic assault in *Alciphron; or, the Minute Philosopher*. In the Preface to *Three Dialogues*, for example, he speaks of "that loose, rambling way, not altogether improperly termed *free-thinking*, by certain libertines in thought, who can no more endure the restraints of *logic*, than those of *religion*, or *government.*"

SECTION FOUR: THE *PRINCIPLES* AND THE *DIALOGUES*

I have presented Berkeley's project as if it were not manifested differently in Berkeley's two major works, which is not the whole truth. A deeper, nuanced comprehension of Berkeley's overall project can be obtained by reflecting upon the differences. In brief, the *Principles* captures the spirit of Berkeley's project far more sharply: It aims to motivate the learned to turn away from useless speculation and to reengage with the practical affairs of life in order to restore virtue to the world; it is a stark call to action. By contrast, the *Dialogues* is far less abrasive: It aims to bring comfort to the learned by showing that the Berkeleian position agrees with common sense and avoids skepticism, and provides answers to atheistic assaults on Christianity. Berkeley writes in the Preface to the *Dialogues*:

> And although it may, perhaps, seem an uneasy reflexion to some, that when they have taken a circuit through so many refined and unvulgar notions, they should at last come to think like other men: yet methinks, this return to simple dictates of nature, after having wandered through the wild mazes of philosophy, is not unpleasant. It is like coming home from a long voyage: a man reflects with pleasure on the many difficulties and perplexities he has passed through, sets his heart at ease, and enjoys himself with more satisfaction for the future. (*3D* Preface 168)

On the title page to the *Principles,* Berkeley indicates both a major and a minor goal: The major is to inquire into the chief causes of error and difficulty in the sciences; the minor is to inquire into the grounds of skepticism, atheism, and irreligion. By contrast, on the title page of the *Dialogues,* the major goal is to demonstrate the reality and perfection of human knowledge, the incorporeal nature of the soul, and the immediate providence of a Deity (in opposition to Skeptics and Atheists). The minor goal is to open a method for rendering the sciences more useful and compendious.

It is little surprise, then that much more space is devoted to the Retrenchment of the Sciences in the *Principles* (§100–134) than in the *Dialogues.* By contrast, much more space is devoted to combating skepticism and atheism in the *Dialogues* than in the *Principles.* In the *Principles* Berkeley indicates he is only interested in the *grounds* of skepticism and atheism. These are dispensed with quickly (§85–95). That said, Berkeley explicitly addresses irreligion in the *Principles*, while he does not do so in the *Dialogues.* For Berkeley this means emphasizing the nearness of God ("in whom we live, move, and have our being") as well as the natural immortality of the soul in order to provide a deep incentive to behave well. The tactic of instilling the fear of God is much more obvious in the *Principles* (*PHK* I §155) than in the *Dialogues.* And this is consistent with the *Principles'* call to turn away from irreligion.

While the *Dialogues* is addressed against both the skeptics and the atheists, however, the attack on skepticism is far more obvious than any attack on atheism. The entire *Dialogues* is structured as a contest between Philonous ("Lover of Mind") and Hylas (his name derived from the Greek word for matter) to see who is closer to common sense and farthest from skepticism. The dramatic movement of the *Dialogues* involves Philonous (Berkeley's spokesman) gradually forcing Hylas deeper into skepticism. By contrast, Berkeley seems to combat atheism in the *Dialogues* only through his innovative argument for the existence of God and his all-too-brief demonstration of the incorporeality of the soul (*3D* III 231). However, it is worth noting that much of the Third Dialogue actually concerns God and our knowledge thereof. It may be that Berkeley is interested in (at least partially) answering attacks that threaten to undermine traditional religious beliefs about God that make room for religious mystery.

The structure of the two works can be broken down as follows. In the *Principles,* Berkeley provides an isolated introduction devoted to his philosophy of language and his attack on abstract ideas. The rest of the Principles can be divided into three parts: Sections 1–33 contain his preliminary account and defense of his philosophical position; sections 34–84 contains possible objections and replies to his position; sections 85–156 outline the consequences of Berkeley's philosophy. These consequences involve the defeat of skepticism (§86–91) and atheism (§92–96), the retrenchment of the sciences (§101–134), an account of our knowledge of the soul and a demonstration of its natural immortality (§135–144), and finally an account of the existence of God as a Divine Governor and an exhortation to Christian conduct (§145–156).

The *Three Dialogues* likewise has three main stages. The First Dialogue contains the first half of Berkeley's arguments for his position. One of the main consequences, however, is that Hylas has been forced to become a skeptic insofar as he denies the reality of sensible things. And although this consequence is not drawn out until the Third Dialogue, he is also compelled to profess Lockean Ignorance of the essence of everyday items. Moreover, the very notion of material substance is shown to be incoherent.

The Second Dialogue further advances Berkeley's position. It contains an argument for the existence of God as the Divine Perceiver of all things, and also defends the view of God as the immediate cause of natural events. One of the main consequences, however, is that Hylas now loses any basis for even inferring the existence of material substance. The Third Dialogue contains Hylas' objections to Berkeley's position and Philonous' replies. One of the first results, however, is that Hylas' skepticism is further extended. He is ignorant of everyday items, has no basis to conclude their existence, and indeed must deny their existence (since the very notion is incoherent).

CHAPTER THREE

FUNDAMENTAL ASSUMPTIONS

Reading: *PHK* §22–23; *3D* I 200–1

In the previous chapter, I placed Berkeley's account of the world within the context of his overall philosophical project to gain insight into why Berkeley might have been tempted to press for such a view. Yet, this does not detract from the admitted oddity of his view. Nor does it provide any arguments in favor of it. Alas, Berkeley has also been traditionally viewed as offering a host of arguments in favor of his position, all of which seem to involve some type of obvious error or fallacy. Far from "unanswerable" he has seemed all too refutable despite the barrage of philosophical arguments. This leaves Berkeley as a kind of entertaining (and useful) philosophical target for those wishing to hone their own critical skills. In this chapter, I want to start by showing why this is so.

I will examine one of Berkeley's most famous arguments ("The Master Argument") and point to some of the difficulties with it.[1] My overall point, however, is not to argue that Berkeley is only useful for target practice. My point, rather, is that a less superficial reading of Berkeley is required. My fear is such readings of Berkeley are superficial at best, and prevent us from wrapping our minds around some of the most deep and provocative philosophical issues that Berkeley is addressing. In the second part, therefore, I provide the core ideas behind this interpretation and the key assumptions which ground Berkeley's metaphysics. In the third part, I explain how this interpretation can illuminate Berkeley's Master Argument.

SECTION ONE: THE MASTER ARGUMENT

Berkeley famously offers what has come to be known as his "Master Argument" in both the *Principles* and the First Dialogue. In both versions of the argument, Berkeley audaciously claims this argument *alone* is sufficient to establish basic idealism (the view that everyday items of the world cannot exist without a perceiving mind). Indeed, he boldly asserts that he will bet all of his chips on this one hand: If it is so much as possible to conceive the existence of an everyday item existing unperceived, then he will grant it is so. Berkeley is radically claiming that it is *impossible* to so much as *conceive* of an everyday item (such as a tree) existing unperceived. In other words, the mind-independence of everyday items is *inconceivable*.

The mechanics of the Master Argument involves considering a specific attempt to answer the challenge to conceive of an everyday item existing unperceived and then showing this attempt fails to count as genuinely conceiving an unperceived everyday item. The Master Argument therefore depends upon two claims: (1) The considered attempt to conceive of an everyday item existing unperceived fails, and (2) this considered attempt is the *only* possible way to conceive of an everyday item existing unperceived.

Berkeley examines a specific attempt to conceive an everyday item existing unperceived. It involves imagining a tree in a forest or a book in a closet (or keys in your pocket, gum on your shoe) with nobody around to perceive them. In the *Principles*, Berkeley says this involves (1) forming ideas of the tree, (2) failing to form ideas of somebody perceiving the tree. What he means is that one does not imagine visible ideas of a human (or rather, human body) "looking" at the tree. Why is this attempt a failure for Berkeley?

It seems the problem is that one has nonetheless formed an *idea*: "When we do our utmost to conceive the existence of external bodies, we are all the while contemplating our own ideas" (*PHK* I §23). The challenge, for Berkeley, is to conceive of the tree *without* contemplating our own ideas and this, Berkeley argues, cannot be done. In the *Dialogues*, Berkeley makes his view somewhat clearer by having Philonous give the following argument:

1. One cannot see a thing which is unseen.
2. So, too, one cannot conceive something which is unconceived.

The reasoning is this: Necessarily, if a thing is seen, it not unseen. So it is impossible to see an unseen thing. Analogously: It is necessarily the case that if a thing is conceived, it is not unconceived. So it is impossible to conceive an unconceived thing. But then, if to conceive something is for it "to be in the mind" (i.e., for it to be perceived), then it is necessarily the case that whenever one conceives something it is "in the mind" (i.e., perceived). So it is impossible to conceive of an unperceived thing.

The general reaction to this argument has been one of incredulity—even contempt. One difficulty with the argument is this: Berkeley tries to move from the claim that one cannot conceive of a thing unconceived to the claim that one cannot conceive of a thing unperceived. However, this assumes the conceiving is a form of perceiving, but it isn't clear why this is so. Perhaps forming imaginary ideas (of a tree by itself) might be loosely construed as a form of perceiving, but it isn't clear why simply thinking about such a tree (without any imagined ideas) by itself counts as a form of perceiving (while it may count as a form of conceiving).

That said, even if we grant this objection, the modified conclusion is still a strong one: One cannot so much as conceive of a thing existing unconceived (or unthought of). But surely this is easy to do. So the overwhelmingly recognized difficulty with this argument is this: Even if it follows that whenever one conceives of a thing, that thing is thereby "thought of" or "in the mind," it does not follow that one has failed to conceive of that thing *as* "without the mind" (or unperceived). While it may, in fact, be "in the mind" that does not mean that it cannot still be *conceived* as "without the mind." One way to understand the problem is this: If one conceives of one's own death, it is nonetheless true one exists. But it doesn't follow from the fact that necessarily one is in existence whenever one conceives of oneself as dead, that one cannot *conceive* of oneself as dead. On the contrary, this seems entirely possible. Moreover, if this argument is actually allowed to go through, then it seems it will rule out *too much* for Berkeley. It is also impossible for me to conceive of a thing which is, as a matter of fact, unconceived by me. Should it not then follow that I cannot conceive of a thing *as* existing unconceived by me? If so, Berkeley is stuck with a radically solipsistic universe—at complete odds with his theocentric idealism.

The point is well characterized by commentator Kenneth Winkler.[2] On the face of it, there is a difference between the content of one's thought and the fact that one is entertaining the thought: One can "isolate" the content itself from the thinking itself. Berkeley needs to show why the fact that one is thinking about a thing "bleeds into the content" so that one cannot think of the thing without thinking of that thing *as thought of.* If Berkeley does manage to explain this, however, it is then unclear how he is to exclude the fact that *he himself* is thinking of the thing from "soaking into the content" as well.

Aside from being almost universally recognized as a bad argument, the Master Argument has raised the puzzle why Berkeley himself thought the argument was so wonderful. It serves as a good example of the awesome gap between Berkeley's arguments for his much ridiculed idealism, and our regular intuitions and argumentative insights. Is there anything that can help us bridge this gap? Should we even *want* to bridge this gap? Yes, we should. As we shall see, it's always darkest before the dawn. And there is more going on in the Master Argument than meets the eye.

One of the things that may be at work is Berkeley's view that one only ever immediately perceives one's own ideas. If we further assume that ideas themselves are only ever in the mind *as* perceived (i.e., if ideas include their being perceived as part of their own content), then Berkeley's train of thought becomes somewhat clearer. One cannot ever conceive of ideas *as* unperceived, and it is hard to see how these ideas could represent mind-independent things to us. That is, if our ideas always include their being perceived right in their content, how can they possibly represent something else *as* unperceived.[3]

While this interpretation sheds some light on Berkeley's Master Argument, it focuses attention on Berkeley's apparent assumption that we only ever immediately perceive *ideas*. It has traditionally been assumed that the view we only ever immediately perceive ideas is one which Berkeley inherits from Locke and which, more generally, is characteristic of modern philosophy as a whole. The view that perception is facilitated by inner ideas has sometimes been called "the way of ideas." But, surely on the face of it, this view is hardly obvious. Rather than seeing mere ideas, for example, don't I actually see the *real* table itself—the same table that everybody else sees? It seems rather odd (and certainly presumptuous) that all perception (including sense-perception) extends no further then our own private ideas. Consequently, if Berkeley had wanted to boast a single argument which could carry the burden of his idealism, this argument no longer seems sufficient. *Why* should we accept this assumption?

In order to try to press beyond this difficulty, I want to undertake a fairly deep discussion about the nature of consciousness, ideas, and spirits. This journey, I think, will cast Berkeley's Master Argument in a new light and it will provide a provocative and persuasive account of what is of such concern to Berkeley.

It requires that we take seriously the following, somewhat more subtle question: What *is it* for an idea to appear in the mind *as* perceived? A related way to put the concern is this: According to the Master Argument, we apparently don't recognize that the content of what we conceive *includes* its being perceived. But what is this additional feature that we don't recognize? It isn't just that we haven't appreciated some fact (namely that we are engaged in perceiving) but, rather, we haven't noticed that *what* we are thinking about is thought about *as* perceived. This suggests that there is a kind of phenomenological feature of our experience which is being missed. *What* is this feature? It's an important question, and it leads us to the heart of the Master Argument.

SECTION TWO: BERKELEY'S CORE ASSUMPTIONS

The Reflexivity of Thought

In the prevailing view of the early moderns, thinking is essentially reflexive. By this I mean that being conscious that one is thinking is constitutive of thinking itself. Whenever one thinks, one is conscious that one thinks. Let's call the view that to think is to be conscious that one thinks "the reflexivity of thought" (RoT) and the consciousness involved "essential consciousness."

It is important to distinguish between essential consciousness and the reflection whereby one directs attention to one's own mental states—making them the content of one's cognition. This latter reflection involves expressly attending to one's mental activities. For example, one might attend to one's migraine—how long it has lasted, how intense it is, its particular quality. This express reflection need only occur sometimes, while essential consciousness is constitutive of cognition itself. Moreover, while express reflection occurs only when mental activity is itself the content of cognition, essential consciousness occurs regardless of the content of cognition. Even if one is thinking about one's new book, for example, one is nonetheless conscious one is having this thought. Since consciousness that one is thinking about one's new book itself *constitutes* thinking about one's new book, one can be said to immediately perceive one's thoughts. By contrast, it seems express reflection involves a second-order act of mental examination. For example, in *thinking* about one's headache ("God that hurts! I wish it would stop!"), in addition to the state of pain itself there is now some new state of thinking which takes the pain as its object.

That thought is inherently reflexive is obviously a very weighty philosophical assumption. I want to briefly clarify what the claim involves, so that it is not too easily dismissed. First, even philosophers such as Descartes recognize that the mind could have various dispositions to act in certain ways which are "unconscious." RoT does not concern mental habits, dispositions, or capacities. Rather, it concerns *occurent* thoughts, which might be described as phenomenological in nature (i.e., there is something that it is like to have them). The weighty claim of RoT is that in all occurent, phenomenological thoughts, one is *conscious* that one is having the thought.

Second, we need to continue to bear in mind the distinction between essential consciousness and express reflection. By wrongly conflating essential consciousness with express reflection, it becomes easy to dismiss the former out of hand. Consider that when one is utterly absorbed in a film, one may be "lost to oneself." In such a case, one would not be reflecting upon one's own mental states and activities—to do so would involve failing to pay attention to the movie itself! The claim being made is not that one is always thinking about one's mental activities. Rather, the more meager claim is that one is in all cases *aware of them.* For example, even though one is not thinking about the fact that one sees the movie, this does not mean that one is not *aware* that one is seeing a movie. More generally, the claim involves the idea that intentional action involves being (at least tacitly) aware of what one is doing. Even as one drives a car without thinking about it, one can be aware of what one is doing. (If one weren't—certainly the risk of accidents would be greatly increased). Similarly, it does not seem unreasonable to suppose that whenever one thinks, one "knows what one is doing." While the status of RoT is a large topic that we have only briefly broached and I certainly do not take myself to have fully defended the thesis, I do think that I have pointed to the *prima facie* plausibility of this view.

Subjective-Objects[4]

What is one conscious *of* when one is essentially conscious that one is thinking? I call the items that constitute an answer to that question "the elements" of consciousness. So what are the *elements* of essential consciousness? One answer is that one is conscious of one's various *thoughts*. In the view accepted by Berkeley's predecessors (such as Descartes and Locke), one is more specifically conscious of one's mental states or activities. In experiencing a pain, one is conscious of the very state of pain itself. Similarly, when one doubts the existence of a tree, one is conscious of one's act of doubting (i.e., one's doubt). The answer provided by Descartes and Locke is that *mental states* are elements of consciousness.

In this view, there are *two* ways in which thoughts are dependent on the mind. First, they are dependent insofar as they are states of mind which cannot exist without a substance in which to exist. The state of pain cannot exist without a subject of pain; doubting cannot exist without a doubter. Second, they are thoughts which cannot exist without being elements of consciousness due to RoT. Another way to put this last point is that the very existence of a thought consists in being consciously perceived by a mind: There cannot be "unconscious" pain (pain that one does not feel); there cannot be an occurrent thought that exists beyond the conscious awareness of a mind.

In my reading, Berkeley rejects this traditional model of essential consciousness by refusing to recognize these variable elements as mere mental acts (states or episodes) of thinking, which depend upon minds in the first way. They are elements of consciousness which depend upon minds in only the second way: their existence consists in being perceived by a mind. However they are not states, acts, or episodes of mind. What are they?

If you close your eyes and experiment, you can produce the image of a unicorn, an imaginarily "audible" thought such as "I feel sleepy," the faint imaginary "recording" of your favorite song, an odor, or a taste. It isn't obvious that such objects of consciousness are mental states or activities. Instead, *they* may simply seem to be entities in their own right which one can produce. Nonetheless, these objects are decidedly "creatures of consciousness" in that *they* cannot exist *except* as variable elements of consciousness. Another way to put the point is that their existence *consists* in being perceived. When you imagine a unicorn, you are essentially conscious that you are imagining a unicorn. What is it to be conscious in this way? In the model I think Berkeley endorses, you are conscious of the imaginary unicorn itself.

Without a doubt, the question of whether the variable elements of consciousness are mental states or subjective-objects is a philosophically delicate question. For us, it is certainly not without its historical precedent: Berkeley endorses what some philosophers have (somewhat misleadingly) called "an act-object" conception of consciousness:[5] One is conscious of "thing-like" items that we have been calling "subjective-objects" (i.e., sense-data). Such items are distinct from mental states. Rather "mental states" are in fact nothing but relations between the mind and its subjective-objects. For example, the analysis of "I am in pain" does not involve a mental subject and the intrinsic state of being in pain; it involves a mental subject and a subjective-object (the pain) which are connected by the relation of experience ("I experience the pain").

One initial reason for wanting to speak of these subjective-objects is that they appear to bear certain properties one cannot reasonably attribute to a mental state. For example, if it is correct to say the subjective-object I produce in imagining a unicorn is pink and has a horn, it is plainly absurd to say my state of imagining a unicorn is pink and has a horn. Again, if one closes one's eyes and presses on them one can experience various images (subjective-objects which it would seem have different colors and shapes). Certainly one's mental state does not have color or shape. With somewhat more delicacy, it would appear that while the pain one experiences is burning, throbbing, and so forth, it is incorrect to say that one's state of being in pain is itself burning, throbbing, and the like.

For the most part, the "act-object" conception of consciousness is now commonly rejected by philosophers for many reasons. One major one, however, is this: On the face of it there doesn't seem to be anything on ontological par with them in the physical world. Hence, if one wanted to maintain a materialist account of the mental, it is hard to see what physical thing a subjective-object could possibly be. Indeed, this appears to be immediately ruled out of the question given the curious properties of subjective-objects (such as color, shape, etc.) that one may not wish to attribute to neurological states.

As a consequence, the *adverbial* account has been suggested.[6] In this view these apparent subjective-objects are really nothing over and above the intrinsic mental state the mind is in. Instead, they are simply *ways* of thinking. For example, when I imagine a patch of red, I do not strictly speaking produce an image (a subjective-object) which I "perceive"—rather I imagine "redly." That is, imagining red is not to produce an object at all, it is simply a *way* of imagining.

While the relative merits of the act-object and the adverbial account involve philosophical complexity beyond our present scope, let me simply observe that the "act-object" conception squares well with our common way of speaking (at least sometimes). We say, "I have a migraine," "I have a sick feeling in my stomach," and so forth. Likewise, the notion of "subjective-object" appears to reflect what is phenomenologically the case (at least sometimes). I imagine a unicorn, think a thought, experience shapes when I press my eyes, etc. By contrast, the adverbial account mandates a departure from the common way of speaking (as in "I experience orangely and squarely") and indeed, sometimes borders on the unintelligible. It is certainly a view that Berkeley himself would have greeted with suspicion (not that this might be of considerable concern at this point). And, clearly, objecting to subjective-objects merely by appealing to a commitment to *materialism* is not something *Berkeley* would have countenanced: it begs the question against him in a fairly dramatic way. Obviously, this objection could just as easily be an objection to *materialism* itself as it is to subjective-objects.

The Self as Datum

Consider again the question: What is one conscious *of* when one is essentially conscious that one is thinking? One is not only conscious of one's thoughts, but also that these thoughts belong to *oneself* (or that it is *oneself* who is thinking). What is to be aware of oneself in this way? Is the self a kind of datum over and above one's thoughts? This is a terribly slippery issue in philosophy, perhaps made famous by Hume's claim that he only ever perceives perceptions when he turns reflection upon himself.[7] For while both Descartes and Locke seem to think that one is aware of oneself over and above one's thoughts, Hume thinks the self is nothing more than the very perceptions themselves.

It seems clear enough that Berkeley agrees with Descartes and Locke. To schematize this, I will speak of both the variable element (thought) and the constant element (the self or "I") of essential consciousness.

The difference between the older conception of consciousness (held by Descartes and Locke) and the one held by Berkeley is that for the former variable elements of consciousness are mental states or activities, while for Berkeley they are instead "subjective-objects." Both conceptions agree, however, that the self is a constant element of consciousness.

Now certainly, the view that the self is a kind of additional datum in essential consciousness that one is thinking is a very weighty philosophical assumption—certainly one that can be contested. However, I do not think it is an entirely implausible view, either. To see this, I want to contrast three kinds of "Humeanism" (strong, medium, and weak).

In the strong view, not only is there no datum of a self, but it is actually false that one is conscious that *one* is thinking. Instead, one is conscious only that there is thinking occurring (or that there exists some thought). In such a view, it is, strictly speaking, incorrect to say "I am thinking." Instead, one is only entitled to say (as apparently Lichtenberg would have it) that "It is thinking" (as in "It is snowing"). Obviously this is a very extreme view that, without further motivation, seems entirely shocking and without merit. Hence, I put it to the side.

In the medium view, while there is no datum of a self, it is still true that one is conscious that *one* is thinking. Rather, essential consciousness simply does not include that self as element. Consider: In seeing that one's neighbor (John's) house lights are on, one is aware that *John's* house lights are on. Yet it seems a mistake to suppose one is, in any sense aware of John *himself*. Similarly, it might be argued, while one is aware that one is thinking, one is not in any sense aware of *oneself*. One is aware only of house lights and of thoughts.[8] While the issues here are very tricky—and beyond what we can fully discuss now—note at least one difference in the two cases. While (in seeing the lights) one might be aware that John's house lights are on, one is not thereby aware that John now exists. For all one knows, John might have unfortunately died 2 days ago. By contrast, insofar as one is aware that one is thinking, one is thereby aware that one (now) exists. One simply cannot think *unless* one exists (as Descartes famously argued). And *this*, I take it, is precisely the datum that Descartes, Locke, and Berkeley have in mind when they speak of an awareness of the "I" or the self: To be aware of the "I" is to be aware that one exists and that one is a thing (i.e., that one is something instead of nothing). To be sure, this is far thinner than the sense-perceptual awareness of say, John the neighbor. By itself, this awareness gives no specific information other than the sheer existence of this thing and its being *oneself.* However, it is still *something* and therefore more than what one is aware of in the case of John's house lights.

Finally, in the weakest "Humean" view (and the one I think Hume himself holds), a datum of the self is actually admitted (i.e., it is admitted that one is aware of one's own existence). However, this awareness is then reduced to an awareness of one's perceptions or thoughts. In other words, in this view, to be aware of one's self is simply to be aware of the various perceptions or thoughts. In effect: The self simply *is* the collection of perceptions. The difficulty with this view, however, is that thoughts seem like discrete existences (especially if they are viewed as subjective-objects). And it is very hard to see how an awareness of so many discrete things could constitute an awareness of one's own existence. Indeed, this may have been the very difficulty which caused Hume to despair over his own account and pronounce the issue beyond his capacities.[9] Moreover, it simply seems intuitively odd to identify oneself with all of the subjective-objects one perceives. Instead, one seems to be something distinct from them. This, I take it, is precisely *Berkeley's* view, which is then not so entirely implausible. And so, as we shall now see, the confusing darkness is now behind us, as we can begin to more deeply understand Berkeley's insight.

The Substantiality Thesis

With these three notions in mind, we can conceptualize how consciousness itself can constitute a relation of support between ideas and spirit. Recall my claim that for Berkeley variable elements of consciousness cannot exist *except* as objects of consciousness: One cannot have a pain and not be aware of it. More generally, there cannot *be* a pain of which nobody is aware. Again, one cannot have a thought and not be aware of it. More generally, there cannot *be* a thought which exists beyond consciousness awareness. For the existence of thoughts *consists in being perceived.*

What is it for a spirit to be conscious of an idea? How do we understand this relation? According to RoT, to think is to be conscious that one thinks. And according to Berkeley's account, to be conscious one thinks is to be conscious of two kinds of thing: oneself and one's subjective-objects. Thus, to think is to be conscious of oneself and one's subjective-objects. Fundamental to thought itself then, in Berkeley's view, is a connection between oneself and one's objects. One could never be conscious of oneself without being conscious of one's subjective-objects, one could never be conscious of one's subjective-objects without being conscious of oneself. Whenever one thinks, one is conscious of both. And the claim that pain cannot exist unfelt or that a thought cannot exist beyond consciousness can be understood as the claim that pain (or a thought) cannot exist without a spirit which is conscious of both itself and the pain (or thought). This is to say: Pain (or thought) cannot exist except as elements of consciousness, and pain (or thought) cannot be elements of consciousness without a spirit to perceive them (i.e., to be conscious of itself and the object). From now on, I will speak of the "Substantiality Thesis" according to which spirits support ideas by perceiving them. And I propose that we understand this as the claim that subjective-objects cannot exist without a self insofar as thinking is nothing but consciousness of self and subjective-objects.

If the relation of support between spirit and idea is consciousness itself, however, some peculiar views about one's knowledge of spirit arise that are worth digressing to discuss. For it seems that in an important sense, spirits cannot be the objects of thought. Consciousness of self involves consciousness of oneself as a perceiver of subjective-objects. Since the self is the perceiver of subjective-objects and not a subjective-object itself, it could never be an object of immediate perception—not even if we turned the perception back around on the "I." And neither could one use a subjective-object to represent the self (by means of resemblance) and thereby perceive it mediately. According to Berkeley, spirits and ideas are far too different for the latter to represent the former. Because of this, Berkeley says, "to expect that by any multiplication or enlargement of our faculties, we may be enabled to know a spirit as we do a triangle, seems as absurd as if we should hope to *see a sound*" (*PHK* I §142).

Of course, it is still possible to be conscious of oneself. And according to Berkeley, we use this awareness of ourselves to understand other spirits as well: We ourselves can function as a kind of image or representation of other spirits (including God). In this way, the term "spirit" can be provided with content through the awareness of one's own existence, which accompanies all variable elements of consciousness. We can also use human language to *discourse about* oneself or spirits in general (thereby making oneself or spirits more generally, the "content" of thought in this sense). What one cannot do, however, is to think about *oneself* (i.e., make oneself the content of thought) prior to the use of language. If there is a kind of express reflection allowed at all—it is reflection by means of *discourse*.

This helps us answer a very long-standing concern about the apparent incompatibility between Berkeley's philosophical immaterialism and his view that spirits are substances which support ideas. It is worth digressing briefly to discuss it. The traditional worry has been that *if* Berkeley rejects material substance, *then* he is bound to reject spiritual substance as well. Consequently, minds should turn out to be nothing but collections of ideas. This concern is aggravated by the fact that Berkeley emphatically *denies* that a spirit can be perceived and that there can be an idea of it (*PHK* I §27). But if matter is rejected because we do not have an idea of it, then shouldn't spirit be rejected as well? In the 1734 editions of the *Principles* and the *Dialogues*, Berkeley introduces a slightly more technical use of the term "notion," alleging that while we have no idea of spirit, we nonetheless have a notion of it. Yet this has mostly struck commentators as *ad hoc*. Why not likewise introduce a notion for material substance?

A preliminary response is that Berkeley's reasons for rejecting material substance do not even concern the fact that it cannot be perceived (as we shall see in the following chapters). In the third edition of the *Dialogues* (1734) Hylas presses these types of parity of reasoning concerns against Philonous. And one important point of clarification made is that Philonous rejects material substance because the very definition (notion) of it is inconsistent. By contrast, the definition of spirit (as a thing that perceives and will) is *not* inconsistent.

Yet a deeper response can also be offered. Berkeley's conception of spiritual substance departs from the traditional one: He does not view ideas as mental states at all. Instead, they are virtual things on their own—"subjective-objects". While traditional substance involves a relation of dependence between property (or state) and subject, the dependence relation between a subjective-object and spirit is that a subjective-object cannot exist unless it is perceived by one.

Berkeley himself explicitly denies sensible things exist in the mind "by way of mode, property, or attribute" (*PHK* I §49, *3D* III 237)—instead they exist there only "by way of idea" or "as a thing perceived in that which perceives it" (*3D* III 236). If this interpretation is correct, then Berkeley is denying that variable elements of consciousness are mental states, acts, or properties of the mind which are "supported" as the traditional way that substances where thought to support their modes or accidents. Instead, the variable elements are subjective-objects which are "supported" in that they are objects of consciousness which cannot exist *except* as objects of consciousness.

Berkeley's denial that spirits can't be perceived shouldn't be understood as the claim that there is no awareness of them at all. In claiming that there is a "notion" of spirit, Berkeley is not helping himself to something after the fact. Instead, Berkeley is following Descartes and Locke in claiming that one has a consciousness of one's own existence, that it is a constituent of essential consciousness. For Berkeley, however, the self is never a variable element of consciousness. One can, as it were, never think *about* oneself as one can think about colors and sounds. One is only ever aware of oneself as that which is thinking about something else (such as colors and sounds).

SECTION THREE: THE MASTER ARGUMENT REVISITED

With all of this work behind us, we are now in a position to return to the Master Argument. Recall the challenge: Conceive of a tree existing unperceived. The apparent reason Berkeley discounts imagining a tree where nobody is around to see it, is because since one imagines the tree, it follows the tree exists in one's mind (i.e., is perceived). As we observed, however, this is insufficient. It is not enough to show that the imaginary tree exists in one's mind; it must be shown that the tree is represented *as* being perceived in one's mind. And it isn't obvious how Berkeley can do that.

One solution is to suppose that Berkeley assumes that we only ever immediately perceive our own ideas. If it is true that *ideas* only exist in the mind *as* perceived, then it follows one could never represent a thing unperceived by an idea. However two questions then arise: One, *why* does Berkeley assume we only ever immediately perceive our own ideas in the first place? Two, what *is it* for an idea to exist in the mind *as* perceived? That is, what is the phenomenological feature one wrongly ignores in claiming that imagining a tree with nobody around suffices to have conceived it existing unconceived?

Question One

While we are not yet in a position to answer the first question, we now have a better formulation of it: Why does Berkeley assume that we only ever immediately perceive subjective-objects? In other words, why does Berkeley view all perception as a form of essential consciousness? Part of the issue is that Berkeley more specifically believes that sense-perception *itself* is a form of essential consciousness. And so now we have this question: Why are sensible qualities such as colors and sounds viewed by Berkeley as *subjective-objects* which cannot exist unperceived?

This view, for us, has some historical precedent. In the first half of the 20th century, the view that we sense-perceive only these types of items (called "sense-data") had considerable proponents. Indeed, this is precisely the view that was branded the "act-object" conception of mental states mentioned above. Since then, the view has certainly fallen into disrepute (although it is still defended by some). But my point, once again, is that while this doctrine seems far less plausible than some of the delicate claims I defended about consciousness above, it is nonetheless a philosophical view that has at one point garnered wide acceptance. From now on I will call this the Ideality Thesis. It is the position that in sense-perception we (immediately) sense-perceive our own ideas. In my interpretation it is the claim that we (immediately) sense-perceive subjective-objects, or that sense-perception is a form of essential consciousness. It will be our business, in the following chapter, to examine Berkeley's detailed arguments in favor of it.

At present, I simply point to the radical tendencies of Berkeley's position. For Berkeley's view generalizes well beyond sense-perception to perception of any sort. In the view I take Berkeley to hold, *all* thought contents are nothing but subjective-objects. That is, everything we can possibly think about is a mind-dependent subjective-object. This view (which I shall call "cognitive closure") is certainly radical.[10] For while our imaginary ideas *are* subjective-objects, it doesn't mean they can't resemble external things (like horses and so forth). However, if our imaginary ideas derive from (and resemble) our objects of sense-perception, and our objects of sense-perception are themselves nothing but subjective-objects, then it follows that imagined ideas can only ever resemble subjective-objects.

There are a couple of ways to escape this (trap of) "cognitive closure." One possibility is to suppose that one may, through a process of abstraction, ignore the mind-dependence of subjective-objects and think only of their other features. For example, even if the sensible quality blue is nothing but a subjective-object, perhaps one may focus only on the color aspect of the subjective-object, rather than its mind-dependence. If so, mind-independent color (or at least color that is not mind-dependent) could be the object of cognition. Another possibility is that our subjective-objects actually resemble other items which are not subjective-objects and which are not mind-dependent. In a representational realist account of sense-perception, one could then "mediately" sense-perceive mind-independent objects. As we shall see in Chapter Five, Berkeley spends the early stages of the *Principles* arguing for "cognitive closure." His argument depends largely on his rejection of abstract ideas.

Question Two

While we have not yet answered the first question (Why does Berkeley think all objects of perception are nothing but subjective-objects?), we do have an answer for the second question (What *is it* for an idea to exist in the mind *as* perceived?). A subjective-object is mind-dependent because it cannot exist except insofar as a self-conscious spirit perceives it. This allows us to identify the overlooked feature as the awareness of *oneself*. In brief, what characterizes a subjective-object *as* perceived is precisely the further datum of the self.

Berkeley says as much: "But the mind taking no notice of itself, is deluded to think it can and doth conceive bodies existing unthought of or without the mind; though at the same time they are apprehended by or exist in itself" (*PHK* I §23). Berkeley's view seems to be this: It is insufficient to merely ignore the self. Rather, one must eliminate the self altogether (something which seems truly impossible to do) in thinking of the tree unperceived. One is never simply aware of a subjective-object alone—one is also aware of oneself. And this is precisely the way a subjective-object appears *as* in the mind.

One worry about this interpretation is that in rehearsing the Master Argument, Berkeley claims that the mind is *not noticed*. If it is *not noticed*, it is hard to see how it can be the constant element of essential consciousness. Yet given that Berkeley is *explicit* that one is conscious of one's own existence, one must find a way to reconcile this consciousness with his treatment of the Master Argument. A good solution is to appeal to the distinction I mentioned earlier between essential consciousness and express reflection. While one might be conscious of one's own existence, this does not mean that one is expressly *thinking about it*. Rather, according to the widely accepted view of the moderns, one is conscious of one's existence *regardless* of what one is thinking about. Indeed, in Berkeley's view, the self can never be expressively reflected upon—if by this one means *perceived*. It can, however, be made the object of discourse. One can *talk* about it and in this way notice and pay attention to it.

Since the self is not the object of cognition, it is easy to see why one's own existence might be easy to discursively ignore. As one watches a film, one's objects of cognition are from the film itself (not oneself as the perceiver). So if one discursively thinks about anything at all, it will tend to be about the film. To "notice oneself" is to expressively reflect on oneself (i.e., to discursively think about oneself). Berkeley's point in the Master Argument is the following: In order to conceive of a sensible thing as existing unperceived, one must be conscious only of the sensible thing and not one's self. This, however, is impossible since to conceive any object is to be conscious of both oneself and one's object of cognition. To be sure, one might discursively attend only to the object of cognition. But this is not to eliminate oneself as an element of consciousness. One has simply not noticed (not discursively thought about) oneself.

Note that Berkeley also has a way to answer the concern that, given his reasoning, it should likewise follow that one cannot conceive of an object existing independently of *oneself*. For one can use one's own self as a way of representing other minds as well. In such a use, one's self-awareness functions as a kind of image for other minds. This means that while one cannot conceive of an object except as perceived, because one cannot eliminate the self, it does not follow one cannot conceive of any object except as perceived by *oneself*.

With this in mind, let us return to the original problem with the Master Argument. Recall Winkler's concern that one should be able to "isolate" the content itself from the thinking itself: Berkeley needs to show why the fact that one is thinking about a thing "bleeds into the content." On the face of it, it appears that the self is precisely *not* part of the content: One is aware of oneself thinking *about* a sub-jective-object. Yet, in the view I have proposed, Berkeley's view is that subjective-objects only appear "as perceived" insofar as they are accompanied by a self. So we now have a way to tell when something exists in the mind *and* it exists there "as perceived."

This suggests that we can actually drop the highly controversial assumption that we immediately perceive only subjective-objects. We can leave the question *open*. The question now is whether in imagin-ing a tree one has successfully eliminated the perceiving self. If not, it would appear the tree has been represented "as perceived" after all. The complaint that the self has not intruded into the content has no merit, since things are never represented *as* perceived in the content. Rather, the content is *only* ever represented as perceived insofar as there is a self-evident self perceiving it. Berkeley's Master Argument would now appear to hinge on the following assumption: An object is represented *as* perceived by the mind just in case there is an accom-panying self. And if accepted for true, the argument then stands or falls on whether one is always conscious of oneself when one con-ceives of something else. While this is still a highly contestable assumption, it is clearly more subtle and less flagrantly controversial than the thesis that one only ever immediately perceives subjective-objects.

Indeed this latter assumption seems to be established on the basis of the Master Argument since it seems to lead to a commitment to "cognitive closure." If objects are represented *as* perceived insofar as there is an ineliminable self, then no object can be represented except *as* perceived. That is, no object can be perceived except *as* a subjec-tive-object. Nor can one abstract certain aspects (such as color or sound) from their being perceived. For in abstractly thinking about color, one will nonetheless by aware of oneself as well. Since this is precisely what is involved in a thing being represented to the mind *as* perceived, it would appear that any attempted abstraction is of no use in escaping cognitive-closure. Thus, Berkeley's Master Argument has the potential to secure cognitive-closure without even defending the view that abstract thinking is impossible and without defending the view that the ideas we immediately perceive cannot resemble mind-dependent objects. It is little wonder that he was willing to wager so much on it.

PART TWO: BASIC IDEALISM

IDEALISM IN THE *DIALOGUES*

Reading: *3D* I

In the last chapter, we encountered the controversial thesis that one only ever perceives ideas. This can be broken down into the Ideality Thesis that one only immediately sense-perceives ideas, coupled with "cognitive closure"—the view that the ideas one immediately sense-perceives cannot "mediately" represent anything other than ideas and that one cannot abstract the existence of an idea from its being perceived. The Ideality Thesis, coupled with the view that everyday items (such as trees and boats) are nothing but collections of the things that one immediately sense-perceives (what I shall call the Collections Thesis) can yield another argument in favor of the view that everyday items are mind-dependent. As we discussed in the previous chapter, Berkeley accepts the Substantiality Thesis that ideas are mind-dependent insofar as they cannot exist unperceived by a self (that is, ideas and selves are fundamentally bound together in thought). All together, then, we have the following Basic Argument in favor of Berkeley's (basic) idealism:

1. Ideas depend upon spirits for their existence (The Substantiality Thesis).
2. The things we immediately sense-perceive (such as colors, sounds, etc.) are ideas (The Ideality Thesis).
3. Everyday items are nothing but collections of the things we immediately sense-perceive (The Collections Thesis).
4. So, everyday items depend upon spirits for their existence (Basic Idealism).

For the rest of this chapter (and much of the following one as well), I want to examine Berkeley's argument for the Ideality Thesis in the *Three Dialogues*. In the following chapter, I will also examine Berkeley's argument in favor of the Collections Thesis. Together, this will give us an account of Berkeley's defense of the Basic Argument.

PRELIMINARIES

It is seldom sufficiently appreciated that the entire *Three Dialogues* constitutes a unified argumentative strategy. One of the principal aims of the *Dialogues* is to show that Berkeley's position is closer to common sense and farther from skepticism than the views of his opponents. It is, however, the First Dialogue that really sets Hylas up to be forced into this skepticism. In particular, Hylas makes some major philosophical commitments there that lead to this skepticism. The arguments in the First Dialogue can therefore be viewed as a reduction of these major assumptions to an absurd skepticism.

The two assumptions that Hylas makes are interrelated. First, he assumes that everyday items are material substances in which sensible qualities inhere (*3D* I 176). The essences of these everyday items (material substances) are also supposed to be the causes from which these qualities "flow." Hylas thereby endorses *philosophical materialism*. Second, he distinguishes between the perception of sensible qualities and their existence; he affirms that real existence requires *absolute* independence from perception (*3D* I 175). In affirming what I shall call the Independence Condition (a thing is real only if it can exist unperceived), he thereby endorses the *representational realist* view that sensible qualities have two modes of existence: (1) existence in the mind (as represented in the mental state) and (2) real existence as an accident which inheres in a material substance.

The *Dialogues* argument, then, is effectively a *reductio* of philosophical materialism and representational realism. It is also an argument in favor of the Collections Thesis and the Ideality Thesis, which can be viewed as Berkeley's own positive replacement of the rejected theses respectively. Instead of viewing everyday items as material substances in which sensible qualities inhere, Berkeley views them as nothing but collections of sensible qualities. Instead of drawing a distinction between sensible things as they are perceived and sensible things as they exist in reality, Berkeley accepts the Ideality Thesis that sensible things are subjective-objects, elements of essential consciousness which cannot exist unperceived. So, in reducing philosophical materialism and representational realism to skeptical absurdity, Berkeley is also attempting to argue for two key premises in his Basic Argument. His *reductio* argument proceeds as follows.

In the First Dialogue, Philonous and Hylas agree to the "rules of the game" that they will follow for the rest of the *Dialogues*. They define their terms, and Hylas comes clean on his two major assumptions. For most of the First Dialogue, Philonous then deploys arguments to show that sensible qualities are mind-dependent. As a consequence, Hylas is forced to deny that the sensible qualities are the real qualities inhering in the everyday items (i.e., the material substances). He thereby becomes a skeptic who denies the reality of sensible things.

In the last section of the First Dialogue, Hylas then makes several attempts to evade the main argument that has been used against him. Here, Philonous argues that according to Hylas' principles, everyday items cannot be sense-perceived at all. Because of this he will (in the Third Dialogue) be led to profess a Lockean Ignorance of the real essence of everyday items. Additionally, at this stage Philonous destroys one reason for *inferring* the existence of material substance (in the Second Dialogue, he will destroy another). Given the identification of material substance with everyday items, it will turn out that we don't even have any *reasons* for believing in their existence, yielding an ever more extreme form of skepticism.

However, in the First Dialogue, in showing that that *all* sensible qualities, including extension, are mind-dependent, Philonous also aims to show the very notion of material substance is inconsistent. This is the alleged inconsistency: (1) A material substance does not perceive anything; (2) Extension exists in material substance. The inconsistency obtains because extension (a sensible quality) can only exist in a perceiving thing. Consequently, this will lead to the most egregious form of skepticism of all, namely the outright denial of the existence of everyday items (which have been unfortunately identified with something that cannot possibly exist). In this way, the materialist will be shown to deny the reality of things. The only solution, argues Berkeley, is to abandon the two assumptions which lead to this difficulty.

THE GAME BEGINS

Everyday Items and Sensible Things

Philonous and Hylas begin by expanding the definition of "skeptic" to include one who (1) denies the reality of sensible things; (2) professes to know nothing of everyday items. By the end of the *Dialogues* Hylas will be shown to meet the definition of skeptic in both of these ways. Philonous then defines "sensible thing" as that which is "*immediately* perceived" by the senses. Philonous contrasts the notion of "immediate perception" with "mediate perception." For example, while one immediately perceives the sound of clomping, this sound may *suggest* the visible idea of a horse-drawn coach, allowing one to mediately perceive the coach.

Suggestion, is a technical notion which as we shall see, does considerable work in Berkeley's philosophy. Upon experiencing x and y consistently together on multiple occasions, one can come to suggest the other. This is possible, for Berkeley, as a consequence of the development of a psychological habit. For example, upon experiencing the word "dog" spoken while a dog is present, one can come to associate the two, so that when somebody says "dog," an idea of a dog is suggested. One can think of this habit as a tendency or inclination to imagine a dog when the word "dog" is uttered in the appropriate context. Again, upon experiencing a constant correlation between the visible idea of glowing red, and the tangible idea of heat, one may find oneself thinking about heat upon seeing the visible idea of glowing red. As a consequence, one can be said to *mediately* see the heat (by means of the visible idea).

Philonous (and Berkeley) takes the expression "sensible thing" to apply to colors, light, shape, sounds, odors, tangible qualities—items he also sometimes refers to as "sensible qualities." He *also* sometimes uses the expression to apply to collections of these distinct items, grouped together under one name (i.e., "everyday items" such as cherries). While some commentators take Berkeley to use the expression "sensible thing" mostly with respect to everyday items, it actually seems to me the opposite is the case—the expression being applied most properly to the basic items such as colors and sounds (only subsequently grouped together under common terms). At any rate, I will use the expression "sensible thing" to apply mainly to primitive sensible things such as colors and sounds, while using the expression "everyday item" to refer to more compound items such as cherries and trees. One of the reasons I hesitate to call everyday items "sensible things" is because it is a tricky question whether Berkeley thinks everyday items such as tables and trees are immediately or only mediately perceived. I shall return to this issue a few chapters from now.

Immediacy

At the beginning of the First Dialogue, Philonous spends some time with Hylas clarifying the notion of immediacy. He says that perception is immediate if it does not involve the "intervention" of anything else which serves as the "means" by which one perceives (*3D* I 174). What exactly does he have in mind? The question is important, and so I want to spend some time now exploring it.

I have claimed that Berkeley is interested in rejecting representational realism in the *Dialogues*. However, there are different versions of this view. The version of representational realism that Berkeley is generally taken to reject can be called "indirect." In this view, one sense-perceives only mental items which themselves represent the external things in the world. One can understand this form of representationalism by way of analogy: At an arena concert, there might be a large screen which enables members of the audience to see the performers who are scarcely visible to the naked eye. In this case, one doesn't perceive the performers themselves. Rather, one perceives the screen (or rather, the images on the screen) as the indirect means by which one perceives the performers. In such a view, the representational realist (like Berkeley) commits to the Ideality Thesis that we immediately sense-perceive only mental items. The difference is that the representationalist also thinks that in immediately sense-perceiving mind-dependent objects (ideas) one can "mediately" sense-perceive mind-independent things by means of this.

There is another form of representationalism, however, which can been called "direct." In this view, while one sense-perceives external objects by means of representation, the immediate objects of sense-perception are not mere ideas, but rather the mind-independent things themselves. Again an analogy might help. Suppose that at the concert there is no screen. Instead, one uses binoculars to see the performers. In this case, one perceives the performers *through* the binoculars. The set is the *instrument* by which one perceives the performers. And it can emerge as a question to what degree the performers (as they appear in the binoculars) *resemble* the performers as they actually are on stage. Despite the fact that this question of resemblance emerges, however, it is still true that one perceives the performers *themselves*. One does not perceive *something else* (such as a screen) in order to perceive the performers. And so, in this version of representational realism, there is no commitment to the Ideality Thesis at all.

It is generally recognized in the literature that Berkeley attributes to the philosophers he attacks, the "indirect realist" account of sense-perception. Alas, it is actually far from obvious that all philosophers of Berkeley's day held to the indirect realism Berkeley appears to attribute to them. The issue whether philosophers such as Descartes or even Locke were instead *direct* realists is now very controversial in early modern scholarship.[2] And it seems probable that the Aristotelian view was one of direct realism.[3] If so, Berkeley appears to get some of his predecessors wrong. In my view, however, Berkeley does *not* get his predecessor wrong. His view is more subtle than has been supposed. In order to see this, I want to distinguish two different kinds of immediacy—strong and weak.

Strong Immediate Perception: To perceive x immediately$_S$ is to perceive x without the use of a vehicle of perception at all.

To press our analogy, this sort of immediacy$_S$ would involve perceiving the performers with no intervening instrument at all (i.e., by the naked eye). In distancing ourselves from this analogy, however, caution is required. Certainly one's eyes are a kind of instrument by which one sees. Thus, even seeing *with one's eyes* would appear to not count as immediate in this account. Yet this is not the issue for our purposes, since Berkeley would agree that (in some sense) we currently require eyes in order to see. The issue is that in sense-perceiving an external object it seems that the perceiver himself/herself must be altered in some way—she must be put into some specific mental state. If an external object doesn't make a difference in the mind itself, it is hard to see how the mind could register anything external. Thus, one could say that even in such a case one sense-perceives an external object *by means of* some intrinsic mental state or change, where being in such a state or being changed in the appropriate way is tantamount to sense-perceiving the external object itself. In this case, it is now at least a conceptual possibility that the perceiver be put into this mental state despite the fact that it does not accord with the external reality. For example, under a chemically induced state, it might seem that one sees performers on stage, when there aren't any performers there at all. Thus, there is now the potential of a gap between how things appear in the mind and how they are in reality.

As we have already seen, however, it was recognized by philosophers of Berkeley's day that the mind requires no further act of perception or mental state at all in order to perceive *its own internal thoughts* through essential consciousness. For example, one has an immediate$_S$ awareness of one's headache. It is transparent to the mind and requires no further mental state in order for one to be aware of it. Thus, according to this very strong notion of immediacy$_S$, one can only ever immediately perceive one's own thoughts (and one's existence). In this sense, all the philosophers *did* agree that we only ever immediately$_S$ perceive ideas (i.e., our thoughts). Indeed, taken this way the claim scarcely seems that controversial: Only our thoughts can be objects of immediate$_S$ awareness (i.e., variable elements of consciousness). Berkeley is *right* to attribute this view to them.

Berkeley, however, is claiming something far more radical: Sense-perception *itself* is a form of essential consciousness. The objects we sense-perceive are just as immediate$_S$ as our thoughts and pains, and as a consequence they (as subjective-objects) cannot exist unperceived. This is *not* something that all philosophers held. For there is a weaker sense of "immediacy" according to which external objects *can* be immediately perceived:

Weak Immediate Perception: To perceive x immediately$_w$ is to perceive x without perceiving some y as a means of perceiving x.

In this sense of "immediacy," one can immediately$_w$ sense perceive some object even by means of a vehicle, just so long as immediately$_S$ perceiving that vehicle first is not itself the *means* by which one then sense-perceives that external object. The difference can be nicely explicated by help of our analogy. In the case of perceiving the performers at the concert by means of the larger screen, one perceives the screen itself in order to thereby (indirectly) perceive the performers. By contrast, in the case of perceiving them by means of binoculars, one does not perceive *the binoculars themselves* in order to then perceive the performers. Rather, one sees the performers *through* the binoculars. In this case, one immediately$_w$ perceives the performers (whereas in the case of perceiving the screen, one does not).

Departing from the analogy, we can say that when one immediately$_S$ perceives one's own internal mental items in order to perceive some external object, one does not immediately$_W$ perceive those objects. By contrast, if the mind is put into a mental state, and that mental state enables the mind to perceive the external object without it being the case that one immediately$_S$ perceives that mental state itself *as the means* by which one perceives the object, then one has immediately$_W$ perceived the external object.

Direct representationalism (unlike indirect) does *not* involve a commitment to immediate$_S$ sense-perception. While mental states can be immediately$_S$ perceived, colors and sounds are *not* mere mental states. Rather mental states bear representational content and being in such a state is the way in which one immediately$_W$ perceives nonmental things (such as colors and sounds). In other words, immediate sense-perception is not a form of essential consciousness. In order to sense perceive an external object one must be put into a state which represents the object. While being in that state involves being essentially conscious that one is in that state, one's consciousness of that state is not *itself* a form of sense-perception.

With this in mind, I want to suggest that while Berkeley explicitly claims that according to the philosophers, one only immediately perceives ideas, he does *not* actually attribute this stronger, more controversial Ideality Thesis to them. To see this, I want to note that at the very conclusion of the *Dialogues*, Philonous claims the following:

> My endeavours tend only to unite and place in a clearer light that truth, which was before shared between the vulgar and the philosophers: the former being of opinion that *those things they immediately perceive are the real things*; and the latter, that *the things immediately perceived, are ideas which exist only in the mind*. Which two notions put together, do in effect constitute the substance of what I advance. (*3D* III 262)

According to the vulgar, we actually *immediately$_S$* sense-perceive the real things. They do not suppose that the mind itself needs some sort of mental vehicle or instrument by which it perceives external objects. In siding with the vulgar, Berkeley wants to maintain that we immediately$_S$ sense-perceive the real things. However, despite the fact that Philonous aims to reduce to skeptical absurdity Hylas' philosophical stance, he also wants to retain a philosophical insight: We can only immediately$_S$ perceive our ideas. In other words, he agrees with the philosophers that only essential consciousness is a form of immediate$_S$ perception, and he agrees with the vulgar that sense-perception is immediate$_S$. Since essential consciousness only takes mind-dependent objects (as the philosophers say) and since sense-perception is immediate$_S$ (as the vulgar say), it follows that the objects of sense-perception are mind-dependent. Thus, the vulgar err in not recognizing the mind-dependence of the things immediately$_S$ perceived, while the philosophers err in viewing them as nothing but mental states rather than the real objects of sense-perception. Thus, insofar as this Ideality Thesis that sense-perception is a form of essential consciousness is the intended *reconciliation* of the philosophers and the vulgar, it is *not* a view which Berkeley takes any of the philosophers to hold on their own. It is a view, rather, that he must defend *against* them. In my reading, much of the First Dialogue is actually an argument *against* the possibility of immediate$_W$ sense-perception.

The Meaning of "Idea"

In order to understand Berkeley's argument more clearly, I want to consider several different ways in which the word "idea" was used by the early moderns. In one sense, "idea" was used as a straightforward synonym for "object of knowledge" or "object of perception." When used this way, there is no reason to suppose they are mind-independent. Just because a tree is an idea (i.e., an object of knowledge) does not mean it cannot exist unperceived. Another way to put the point is to say that the term "idea" applies to anything that happens to be perceived (or known). It is a mere *extrinsic* application of the term, which says more about the perceiver himself/herself than it does of the actual things perceived. Using our analogy, we can say that the performer which is perceived through the binoculars is the "idea" (i.e., the object of perception).

Second, "idea" can be used to refer to the mental state (the vehicle) *by which* one perceives external objects. Here it usually applies to the mental state which secures immediate$_W$ perception of an external object (in the case of direct realism). In this way, an idea (the mental state) is dependent upon the mind which has it. In terms of our analogy, the set of binoculars itself would be the idea in this sense.

Finally, "idea" might be used to refer to the object *as* perceived (*as* it appears to the mind). With respect to our analogy, this sense of "idea" refers to the performers *as they appear in the binoculars.* While this last use seems closely related to the first use of the term, the idea in this case is mind-dependent (although merely trivially so). In this third sense, one is referring to the thing perceived *as* it appears. Another way to put the point across is to say that in this sense, an idea is the representational content of a mental state.

Suppose, for example, one sees a tower which appears round while being in reality square. The tower (insofar as it is represented to the mind as round) is the content of one's act of sense-perception and it can be distinguished from the actual tower (i.e., the tower that is in reality square). In this use, there can be a more serious kind of mind-dependence in case there ceases to be any resemblance between what is in reality and what appears in the mind (as when the world appears green through sunglasses).

For example, in the case of visually hallucinating a castle, what one "perceives" does not exist in reality at all (it exists only in the mind). In speaking of an idea, one is referring to the representational content of the thing perceived insofar as it appears to us. Here, however, the "object of perception" does not exist in reality. It only exists in the mind insofar as "it" is the representational or imagistic content of the vehicle of cognition by which one imagines. In such a case, it is perhaps somewhat strained to say there is an object of knowledge (or perception) at all. While there is representational content (in one's mind), it doesn't correspond to anything in reality. In such cases, I will speak of "restricted content" of the mental state. Obviously, there is a much stronger kind of mind-dependence when the content is "restricted." Not only is it true the object as it appears cannot exist unperceived, it is also true that the object *only* really exists as it appears to us.

Berkeley's agenda in the First Dialogue is to raise considerations used by modern philosophers to show that the world as it appears to us is very different from how it is in reality. In particular, Berkeley will argue that sensible qualities (such as colors, sounds, odors, and tastes) exist only in the mind and in this sense are mind-dependent. Effectively, he will press the view that sensible qualities are nothing but restricted representational content, and hence mind-dependent in the same way that a unicorn is mind-dependent insofar as it exists in the mind and nowhere else.

In endorsing the Independence Condition, Hylas is alleging that anything which cannot exist unperceived is unreal. To reconsider our analogy: If objects should appear in the binoculars alone (and not independently of how they appear there), then one would deny that those objects are *real*. In accepting this view, Hylas accepts that the mind perceives external objects by means of some mental vehicle and he thereby believes that the objects of essential consciousness are nothing but mere mental vehicles or states which purport to represent the external world. So in light of Philonous' argument against resemblance, Hylas will be forced to deny that sensible things are real. They are, as Berkeley says, "a false, imaginary glare."

It is important to recognize, however, that while the modern arguments designed to defeat any resemblance between how things appear to us and how they are in reality will seriously cripple the view that sensible things are immediately$_w$ perceived, there was more than one way to accommodate the modern primary/secondary distinction. Some thinkers attempted to work out a view that was less extreme than the Galilean "error theory" that sensible qualities such as colors and sounds don't exist in the external object at all but exist only in the mind. Just because there is a lack of resemblance, doesn't necessarily mean that sensible things are *nothing* but restricted content. Consider this analogy: Just because one sees the tower as round despite the fact that it is square (and there is consequently a difference between the tower as it appears and the tower as it really is) does not mean that the tower is nothing *but* restricted content. As we shall see, the overall argumentative strategy in the First Dialogue includes attempts to show why these moves fail to stay in agreement with the vulgar as well. Ultimately, then, these attempts at escape will fail, and Hylas will be forced to claim that sensible things are nothing but restricted content.

A False Imaginary Glare?

Before launching his argument for the existence of God in the Second Dialogue, Philonous spends considerable time pointing to how beautiful the world seems to be. Consider the speech which begins "Look! Are not the fields covered with a delightful verdure?" and ends:

How should those principles be entertained, that lead us to think all the visible beauty of the creation a false imaginary glare? To be plain, can you expect this scepticism of yours will not be thought extravagantly absurd by all men of sense? (*3D* II 211)

It is one of the longest speeches in the *Three Dialogues* and clearly points to Berkeley's unhappiness with the view of the New Scientists that, with respect, to secondary qualities, the world is not in reality how it appears to us. More specifically, Hylas has been argued into accepting an error theory of secondary qualities according to which fire is not really hot, sugar is not really sweet, and so forth. While Hylas takes consolation in his expectation that Philonous, who likewise has accepted the mind-dependence of sensible qualities, will also deny the reality of sensible things. However, Philonous makes it clear he has rejected the Independence Condition, and is therefore *not* bound to view sensible qualities as unreal.

It is an important question what is involved in Berkeley's rejection of the Independence Condition. Is it merely a nominal change (i.e., does Berkeley merely decide to count what others might view as a "false, imaginary glare" as something *real*)? Or are there more substantive changes involved in the rejection of this principle? I want to claim the latter. In particular, rather than turning things into mere ideas, Berkeley aims to turn ideas into things (*3D* III 244). This is to say, in recognizing sense-perception as a form of essential consciousness, he rejects the view that the variable elements of consciousness are nothing but mental states which fail to adequately represent the world. Instead, they are the objects of sense-perception itself. This is to say, sensible things are subjective-objects.

Let's revisit the position of the direct realist. If we assume that Berkeley defeats the direct realist view, then according to the background picture, one has various sensory states with representational content that themselves do not resemble anything in the external world. It is a situation as that in which a Cartesian Evil Deceiver causes one to have various different states that only seem to track reality—or a state in which one dreams of a world that does not exist. For the representational content of the dream-state is not mirrored at all in the "real world." And as in the dream-state, one does not strictly *perceive anything at all.* It merely seems as such; there seems to be nothing but a "false, imaginary glare." In such a view the content of immediate$_w$ "perception" is restricted to the merely representational. In other words, the mind-dependence is that of "restricted content."

Suppose now that Berkeley merely decides to *call* the restricted content of such representational states "real." Then the view that Berkeley has somehow preserved reality is deeply disappointing. One is merely in some mental state which has some representation content not to be found anywhere beyond that state. And even if Berkeley can show that there are various different finite minds in analogous states, along with a God who is in some divine (nonsensory) state of perception with similar content, it now seems that all spirits are in some state of mind, seeming to perceive something that does not answer to the representational content. To be sure, one may call this situation the "perception of the real thing." However it seems as if the very original which the representational content is supposed to represent, has fallen away. The fact that we have introduced God is not consoling. How can what God "perceives" count as an archetype, if God himself is merely in a state with representational content. In order for what we perceive to *really* exist, we expect the representational content to represent something more than more representational content!

Fortunately, Berkeley has a deeper point to make. In accepting the vulgar view that one immediately$_s$ sense-perceives the real things themselves, Berkeley is recognizing sense-perception as a form of essential consciousness. Consequently, he departs from the philosophers in viewing the variable elements of essential consciousness as mere mental states. Instead, they are subjective-objects.

Notably one of the earliest arguments that Berkeley provides in the First Dialogue accomplishes much more than undermining the resemblance involved in immediate$_w$ sense-perception. Instead, it also purports to show that sensible things (colors and sounds) are in fact nothing but variable elements of essential consciousness. To be sure, by itself, this leaves open the possibility that they are nothing but mental states which do not have anything in the real world answering to them. However, in arguing that the assumptions of the philosophers result in the unacceptable forms of skepticism, Berkeley rejects the Independence Condition. The rejection of this, and his affirmation of the vulgar view that one immediately$_s$ sense-perceives the real things, leads to the view that sense-perception itself is a form of essential consciousness.

This interpretation squares with Berkeley's reconciliation of the philosophers and the vulgar. For, according to the vulgar, we immediately$_s$ sense-perceive the things themselves; according to the philosophers, we immediately$_S$ perceive only the variable elements of consciousness. By rejecting the view that the variable elements of consciousness are nothing but mental states (i.e., "unreal" or "a false, imaginary glare") and maintaining that, as subjective-objects, some are the very objects of sense-perception itself, Berkeley can allow for the vulgar view that we immediately$_S$ sense-perceive the real things, while retaining that philosophical insight that we immediately$_S$ perceive nothing but ideas (i.e., variable elements of consciousness). Thus, Berkeley's rejection of the Independence Condition is more than nominal. It involves the rejection of the view that variable elements of consciousness are nothing but mental states—mere vehicles of sense-perception. Instead, they are subjective-objects—the very objects of sense-perception.

For the remainder of this chapter, I want to examine this initial argument deployed by Philonous in *Three Dialogues*. I show how this argument prepares the way for this overall shift by purporting to establish that sensible things are variable elements of consciousness.

THE PAIN/PLEASURE ARGUMENT (TPA)

One of the main arguments which Philonous uses to establish the mind-dependence of sensible qualities derives from Galileo[4]—and it is used by others such as Locke. For example, Locke argues that while a fire may cause the sensation of warmth from a distance, it may cause pain upon a nearer approach. But if we grant pain is not really in the fire, then why should we think warmth is really in the fire either (*E*. 2.8.16, 137)? Berkeley has Philonous explicitly use this type of argument. He points out that the sensation caused by a pin prick is on par with the sensation caused by a hot coal. Since nobody thinks the pain from the prick is in the pin (or, indeed, anything resembling that pain), why should one think that any sensations caused by the coal (or anything like them) exist in it (*3D* I 179)?

Clearly this argument threatens the representationalist view by undermining the possibility of anything *resembling* the sensation of heat existing within the coal. If there is nothing resembling pain which is mind-independent and which exists in the coal, why should we suppose otherwise in the case of heat? This seems to seriously damage the possibility of immediately$_W$ sense-perceiving the heat. And it likewise damages the possibility of the actual heat existing in the coal.

Berkeley, however, radicalizes this argument, by maintaining that the sensation of intense heat simply *is* an instance of pain, while a sensation of warmth simply *is* an instance of pleasure. Indeed, he seeks to maintain that many sensations (of tastes and smells) are likewise pleasures and pains: Philonous maintains that bitterness is a kind of pain (or displeasure) while sweetness is a pleasure. And while he does not use this argument with respect to colors and sounds, it seems he thinks that they, too, are instances of pleasures and pains. Philonous refers to sounds as "sweet" and "grave" (*3D* I 182), and speaks of beholding the natural beauties of earth "as a pleasure" (*3D* II 210). In general, Berkeley suggests that the secondary qualities have something "vividly pleasing or disagreeable" about them in a way that primary qualities do not.

The core of the argument is this: If heat, cold, bitter, and sweet are nothing but pleasures and pains, then they are obviously mind-dependent (since pleasures and pains are mind-dependent); and since pleasures and pains can exist only in something that perceives, they cannot exist in matter. This argument also shows that if nothing resembling the pain exists in the external thing, so nothing resembling heat (which just *is* pain) exists in an external thing. The possibility of immediate$_w$ sense-perception is thereby undermined.

Hylas tries to defeat this argument in three ways (and I defer the third way until the following chapter). First, he claims that even though intense heat is a pain, it is not true that warmth is a pleasure. Rather, he maintains, there is a lack of either pain or pleasure (an "indolence"). By denying warmth is a pleasure or pain, Hylas hopes to maintain its mind-independence (and therefore its reality). However, Philonous will ultimately respond to this by pointing out that if intense heat is mind-dependent, then it is hard to see why warmth should not be likewise mind-dependent. One way to see this point is this: If it is true the immediate perception of intense heat is nothing but essential consciousness itself, then why should immediate perception be anything other than essential consciousness itself in the case of warmth? Even if warmth is neither a pleasure nor a pain, it is still an element of essential consciousness and hence mind-dependent.

The second (more interesting) strategy that Hylas adopts is to deny the highly controversial premise (3) of the argument: He now insists that the intense heat and pain are actually distinct (the pain is caused by the heat in his altered view). In order to further defend this crucial premise, Philonous offers another argument:

1. In placing one's hand by the fire, one feels a simple, uniform idea
2. The heat is immediately perceived
3. The pain is immediately perceived
4. So, the intense heat immediately perceived is not distinct from the pain.

The first premise is supposed to be based upon experience: One tries the experiment and notices one feels only one, simple idea. The second and third premises are designed to rule out the possibility that any *mediate* perception is involved. Consider, for example, that in seeing a red, glowing poker, one can in some sense be said to see the heat (i.e., one sees the *hot* poker). In Berkeley's view, this means one has, through experience, associated the visible idea with the tangible experience of heat. In immediately perceiving the visible idea, the tangible idea of heat is *suggested* to the imagination, and consequently one can be said to mediately perceive the heat. This argument rules out the possibility that in immediately perceiving the pain (for example), the heat is merely suggested. Moreover, it affirms there is only one, simple idea that is immediately perceived. If so, it would seem that the conclusion follows.

However, this argument is largely dissatisfying, since the first premise remains open to dispute. It is an empirical claim, and it is not altogether obvious it is true. One might argue that when one places one's hand on a hot stove, one first feels the contact, then the heat, and then the pain. If so, it seems that one feels two distinct sensations (of heat and of pain).

While Berkeley does not consider this objection, he might respond as follows: It takes a second or two for one's hand to heat up sufficiently for the heat to become painful. So, one might at first experience a heat that is less intense than the subsequent, burning, painful heat one feels a second or two later. Thus, there would be two distinct ideas, one of a strong but not painful heat, the other of a stronger, painful heat.

That said, such a response isn't enough for Berkeley's purposes. Since he needs premise (3) of TPA, he needs to rule out the first interpretation of the data. Simply proposing a counterinterpretation doesn't do that. Berkeley does, however, offer an argument to show sensible pain is nothing distinct from sensations of heat, cold, and the like in an intense degree:

1. A vehement sensation (of heat, cold, etc.) cannot be conceived without pain or pleasure.
2. It is impossible to form an idea of sensible pain abstracted from particular sensations of heat, cold, and the like.
3. So, sensible pains are nothing distinct from those sensations in an intense degree.

The first premise is delicate. In the imagined objection, one first feels the heat and then the pain. If the heat one first feels is sufficiently vehement, then not only can such a sensation be conceived, it can be literally experienced. The delicate question, I think, is whether upon experiencing a vehement heat that is accompanied by pain, the heat is *more* vehement than the first sensation of heat (without pain). If it is, then there is a more intense degree of heat one has experienced at first, and there are therefore two distinct ideas of heat. If so, the example can't show that the second experience of heat and the pain are distinct ideas.

Now the overall thrust of Berkeley's argument is that very extreme heats are pains. If it should turn out there are some strong heats that are not pains, but nonetheless very extreme heats are indeed pains, then Berkeley's argument still goes through. Recall Hylas' denial that warmth is a pleasure. So long as *some* immediately perceived heats are pains or pleasures, it follows immediately perceived heats are mind-dependent. The challenge issued in this premise is to conceive of a very vehement heat to which pain could be added or subtracted while remaining in the same degree of intensity. Yet it does seem the addition of pain to heat always corresponds to an augmentation in the intensity of the heat.

While this does place the imagined objection into serious jeopardy, it does not yet establish the identity between a vehement sensation and pain (or pleasure). It only shows, at best, the most intense heats cannot be conceived without pain. Yet even if it is true in such cases pain necessarily accompanies the heat, it does not follow that the heat itself simply is a pain.

The second premise of Berkeley's argument claims that one cannot abstract an idea of sensible pain from sensible ideas such as heat, cold, and the like. This obviously depends upon Berkeley's controversial views about abstraction (and we haven't examined those yet). How-ever, what he appears to have in mind is that every sensible pain has a sensible quality: Pains don't just hurt plain and simple, they hurt in a particular way. The pain is burning, freezing, piercing, throbbing, and so forth. And the challenge in abstracting sensible pain from its sensible conditions is to mentally pull apart the pain from such con-ditions. Berkeley's view, however, is that this is impossible. For the burning, freezing, and so forth is not incident to the pain itself, but is rather constitutive of the pain. It is the very burning that hurts.

To be sure, one still might object to this premise, by arguing that with an increase in intensity the pain ultimately overwhelms the heat.[5] If so, one then feels pain without the heat (and so it seems once again that there are two distinct sensations that are not even necessarily connected). I think that Berkeley's answer to such a concern would involve the view while a heat can become so intense that only the painfulness is relevant (and consequently, one may think only about the fact that the pain *hurts*), this does not detract from the fact that every sensible pain has a sensible quality: They are always experi-enced as either burning, freezing, piercing, throbbing, and so forth. It is only that when the pain is very intense, such qualities are largely irrelevant.

CONCLUDING REFLECTIONS

What is especially notable about this argument is that it does not *merely* show that sensible qualities are "restricted content"; it shows that perceiving (intense) heat *is the same* as perceiving pain. In other words, it shows that (intense) heat is a variable element of conscious-ness, and therefore that all sensible heat is a variable element of consciousness.

According to the philosophers Berkeley is attacking, variable ele-ments of consciousness are nothing but mental states. Consequently, once intense heat is identified with pain, it seems intense heat must itself be nothing but a mental state. However, instead, of viewing heat-pain as a sensory state that is itself only an object of a parasitic essential consciousness, one might view heat-pain as the content of sensory-perception, where sensory-perception is nothing but a form of essential consciousness itself.

Essential consciousness is peculiar kind of perception whereby the objects thereof (e.g., thoughts, pains, imaginary sounds, and smells) cannot exist *except* as objects of consciousness. Essential consciousness can be described as "sticky" in that the *only* objects it takes are ones that *can't* exist *except* as objects of consciousness. This is to say: Sticky perception is a genuine relation of support which connects subjective-objects (ideas) with the constant element (spirit).

In this way, the very use of the word "idea" is altered. While Berkeley retains the second use of "idea," he does so only in seeing variable elements of essential consciousness as mind-dependent. However, he does not view these elements as mere mental states. Instead, they are subjective-objects. And since, for Berkeley, the *only* kind of immediate perception is essential consciousness itself, he can now also use "idea" in the first sense (as a mere synonym for "object of perception") and have it also yield mind-dependence since all immediate perception is "sticky."

Of course, in order to yield this result, Berkeley must reduce philosophical materialism and representational realism to skeptical absurdity. And he certainly has not accomplished that yet. Indeed, there remains a crucial objection to TPA that we have not yet considered: While it may be true that intense heat, bitterness, and so forth are mind-dependent insofar as they are appearances in the mind, it isn't clear why one can't still speak of heat, bitterness, and the like insofar as they exist in themselves (unperceived). After all, water can have a certain fixed temperature which can be measured scientifically. Surely this is not to be conflated with the mere pain that we experience. In order to answer these concerns, then, there is much more work to be done.

CHAPTER FIVE

IMMATERIALISM IN THE *DIALOGUES*

Reading: *3D* I

In the previous chapter, we began our examination of Berkeley's Basic Argument:

1. Ideas depend upon spirits for their existence (The Substantiality Thesis).
2. Sensible things (such as colors, sounds, etc.) are ideas (The Ideality Thesis).
3. Everyday items are nothing but collections of sensible things we immediately sense-perceive (The Collections Thesis).
4. So, everyday items depend upon spirits for their existence (Basic Idealism).

We considered Berkeley's grounds for the Substantiality Thesis in Chapter Two. In Chapter Three, we considered Berkeley's argument for the Ideality Thesis. In this chapter, I want to examine Berkeley's defense of the Collections Thesis, which is connected to his corresponding reduction of philosophical materialism to skeptical absurdity. This objection will be discussed in depth in the following chapter.

SENSIBLE QUALITIES "IN THEMSELVES"

While Berkeley's Pain Argument may show that sensible qualities such as intense heat, bitterness, and the like, insofar as they are experienced by us are mind-dependent, it does not follow that heat and bitterness insofar as they exist in the actual material things (such as fire or sugar) are likewise mind-dependent. A fire, a red-hot poker, a bucket of water—all of these have a particular temperature independent of individual perceptual experiences. Indeed, there is something belonging to the poker say (such as an increase in the motion of particles) which can be said to constitute the heat of the poker. Just because the sensations one experiences upon touching the poker are mind-dependent, it does not follow that this physical property of the poker itself is mind-dependent.

Berkeley is quite aware of this distinction, and he has Hylas draw it early in the First Dialogue. Philonous' initial response to it is both revealing and disappointing: He reminds Hylas that they are discussing only the reality of *sensible* things: Heat (as it is in itself) is not immediately perceived by the senses, only heat (as it is for us) is immediately perceived. Consequently, only the latter is a *sensible* thing, and so is germane to the conversation. Even if the poker does have such mind-independent qualities that we denominate "heat," this has nothing to say about the mind-dependence of *sensible* qualities. And if sensible qualities immediately perceived are mind-dependent, then due to his commitment to the Independence Condition, Hylas will be still forced to deny these sensible qualities are real.

While this response is disappointing, since it advocates we simply ignore the heat as it is in itself, it is also revealing when understood within the context of the modern distinction between primary and secondary qualities. In defending the mind-dependence of sensible-qualities against the philosophers, Berkeley must undermine any attempt to show that sensible things are immediately$_w$ perceived. His strong denial that heat (as it is in itself) is immediately perceived is nontrivial insofar as it flags his rejection of Hylas' attempt to rehabilitate this possibility. Clearly, a possible lack of resemblance between the pain/heat (as it is in us) and the heat (as it is in reality) makes it hard to see how having the sensation of a heat can be the vehicle by which the heat in the fire is immediately$_w$ perceived.

However, as I mentioned earlier, there are different ways of making sense of the modern view about secondary qualities. And Berkeley has more to say on this topic. One way to make sense of secondary qualities, as we have seen, is the "error theory." In this view, secondary qualities are not real, and they are wrongly attributed to material things. Consequently, we err in thinking that sugar is sweet, the sky is blue, water is hot, and the cat is orange. Such a view, for Berkeley, is plainly contrary to common sense.

In making a distinction between "qualities as they are in us" and "qualities as they are in themselves" one might try to find a way to continue to maintain that sugar is sweet, the fire is hot, the cat is orange, and so forth. This would also allow one to believe in qualities, which although not sensible, are mind-independent and exist in the external substance. Berkeley develops this strategy in greater detail, by having Philonous and Hylas discuss the secondary qualities of sound and color. As we shall see, Berkeley thinks this move leads to a position that is just as counterintuitive as the "error theory."

Although, it seems for Berkeley sounds and colors are like pleasure and pains (or at least may be described in ways that suggest positive or negative valences), Berkeley does not attempt TPA in these cases. Instead, he appeals to the natural science of his day in order to force Hylas into a similar position. This time, however, Hylas attempts to make more sense of his distinction between qualities as they exist in us, and qualities as they are in themselves.

Hylas begins by granting that sound cannot exist in a sonorous body (such as a bell). He appeals to experiments which show a bell, when struck in a vacuum, can make no sound. He concludes from this that the air, rather than the bell, is the substance in which sound exists. While Philonous objects to that inference, Hylas then goes on to identify sound (as it is in itself) with the "vibrative or undulatory motion" in the air which impacts the body and causes us to experience

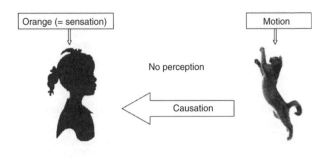

Error Theory

sound-sensations (i.e., sound as it exists in us) (*3D* I 182). He then distinguishes between two senses of the word "sound"—the philosophical and the common. In the philosophical sense, sound is the vibrative motion of the air (i.e., sound-waves); in the common acceptation, sound is nothing but the sensations we experience in our mind as a consequence of the impact of sound-waves upon our auditory system. Thus, instead of offering an "error theory," Hylas now offers an "equivocation theory" according to which sound is mind-independent and real (in the philosophical sense of the word "sound"), but merely apparent and mind-dependent (in the common sense of the word).[1]

Hylas is forced into offering this equivocation theory in the case of colors as well. Here, however, he begins by maintaining that the real colors exist in the external objects themselves. In order to undermine this view, Philonous begins by pressing concerns about the relativity of sense-perception. The first concern involves the denial there is any nonarbitrary standard by which to determine "the true" color. The second concern involves undermining the view that colors are inherent (nonrelational) properties of substance.

Philonous begins by noting that the sky which appears purple and red at a distance, may look otherwise up close. Hylas' task is to distinguish the apparent and the real colors of something—he is supposed to determine the standard or "true" color. Philonous is not merely pointing out that, for example, an object's color may appear differently to somebody with an illness of the eye (such as jaundice) or that sugar may not taste sweet to somebody who is ill. Such a move, by itself, leaves intact the notion there is a nonarbitrary standard

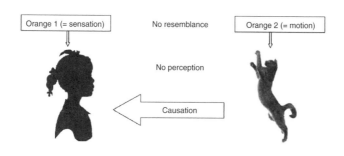

Equivocation Theory

(natural, healthy) way of perceiving the color. Rather, Philonous is aiming to argue against the very hope for determining any just standard.[2]

Hylas proposes the color, which upon the closest scrutiny the object is said to have, should constitute the object's real color. Yet Philonous assaults this by suggesting there is no clear standard to assess "the closest scrutiny"—microscopes ought to provide a better understanding of the "real colors." However, this seems to be variable with the increasing power of the microscope. Moreover, he argues, smaller animals may, as a consequence of their size, perceive different colors. Which kind of animal perceives "the true" color?

Philonous also argues that external objects can change their color in case the light is changed. For example, an object looks different by candlelight than by daylight. And an object appears to have no color at all in dark. Philonous also appeals to the science of his day by pointing out that an object in the light from a prism (all heterogeneous rays separated) will change color. Such considerations are deployed to show that changes in colors are not inherent changes in the objects themselves. Rather, they seem to be mere relational or circumstantial changes.

In response, Hylas maintains that light itself is the substance in which color truly exists. According to Hylas, light is nothing but "a thin, fluid substance" and color is nothing but the motion or agitation of the substance which impacts the eyes and causes us to experience various color sensations. Again, Hylas distinguishes between the philosophical sense of "colour" (which allows that color *as* the motion of light really exists in the substance) and the common sense of "colour" (which is merely apparent and exists only in the mind). In such a view, while there is no nonarbitrary standard concerning the various apparent colors, there is one (nonrelative) motion (i.e., color) of the light. While there can be a fixed frequency of a wave, for example, there is no nonarbitrary standard for determining which of the multiple sensations involved (such as blue, green, orange, and the like) should be assigned to it. And while changes in apparent color are merely relational (depending upon features of the perceiver herself as well as her surroundings) changes in the motion of the light are clearly inherent. In accepting this distinction, Hylas once again endorses the equivocation theory of secondary qualities.

Philonous' first response to the equivocation theory is to point out that it makes an important concession in granting that only the sensible qualities (as they are in us) are immediately perceived. If the qualities such as color, sound, heat, and bitterness (as they are in themselves) are *not* immediately$_w$ perceived, then the attempt to reha-bilitate the philosophers view that sensible things are immediately$_w$ sense-perceived has failed (and the mind-dependence of sensible qualities has been established). As a consequence, a defender of the equivocation theory still counts as a skeptic since sensible things (i.e., the things immediately perceived by us) are mind-dependent, and by the Independence Condition, unreal.

Philonous' second response to the equivocation theory is to point out the ways in which it departs from common sense. First, owing to the preceding considerations, it is still the case that colors and sounds (in the customary vulgar sense) are unreal. Consequently, the vulgar are still guilty of an error—the error of supposing what they ordinar-ily mean by "colors" and "sounds" exist in the external objects and *are* real. Second, it is odd to think that colors and sounds which are real (and which exist in external bodies) are themselves invisible and inaudible respectively. So, are the invisible colors the real ones? Are the inaudible sounds the real ones? Yet the colors immediately seen and the sounds immediately heard are themselves unreal? Ultimately, then, it seems the equivocation theory collapses into the error theory: What the vulgar suppose to be the real properties of everyday items exist nowhere but in their own minds.

To be sure, one might worry that Hylas has conceded too much. Why not maintain that the sound in the air and the color in the ether are indeed immediately$_w$ perceived? If one could maintain this view, then not only would the most important argumentative thrust be defeated, but one could still maintain that the real philosophical colors and sounds are visible and audible respectively.

Alas, the deployment of perceptual relativity considerations deci-sively blocks this move. For it seems there is a multitude of visible ideas (apparent colors) which can be associated with any given par-ticular motion in the ether (the real color). Indeed, it would seem the same visible ideas (apparent colors) can be associated with differ-ent motions in the ether (real colors). And there is no nonarbitrary standard by which any one apparent color can be selected as the one which "tracks" the "real color." Given this, it is hard to see why having the sensory experience of blue should constitute immedi-ately$_w$ perceiving some specific motion of ether as opposed to any other.

Here Berkeley's point forces us to reflect upon our own contemporary use of secondary quality terms as well as our appeal to "sound-waves" and the like. While it seems to make sense to grant that science has taught us sounds are sound-waves and colors are a particular range of electromagnetic waves, it is then a question of what it means to say we hear sound-waves or see electromagnetic waves. In the view proposed, these physical phenomena cause certain sensations in us. But there is nothing in our own sensations which is mirrored in the world itself. It seems then, we immediately sense-perceive qualities that do not actually exist in the world. Consequently, it seems we do *not* really see sound-waves and electromagnetic waves themselves; indeed, it turns out that sound-waves can never be heard and electromagnetic waves can never be seen. But if sounds just are sound-waves and colors are just electromagnetic waves, then sounds can never be heard and colors can never be seen. This is absurd.

The only possibility, it seems, is that one means one thing when one applies secondary quality terms such as "sound" and "color" to what one immediately sense-perceives, and another when one applies such terms to physical properties like waves. That is, the meaning of secondary quality terms is nonunivocal. If so, however, it seems what one immediately sense-experiences is *distinct* from the physical causes thereof. So, the view that secondary qualities one immediately sense-perceives can be reduced to physical properties (such as waves) is actually *false*. It also means our own current common sense about secondary qualities may conceal an equivocation. For example, on the one hand we may grant that colors and sounds are nothing but waves. On the other, we may continue to speak of the sky as having a blue color and by that apply to it the sensible quality connected to our sensation of blue. Unbeknownst to us, however, we are not actually talking about the same thing in the two cases. Indeed, the very meaning of the word has shifted. Properly speaking, however, one ought to recognize that the sensible qualities one immediately sense-experiences don't really exist in the physical objects at all. While one might *want* to say that the sky is blue, this is (at least in one important sense) entirely false.

THE POWER THEORY

Berkeley is not done. There is another strategy for accommodating the modern view about secondary qualities besides the error theory and the equivocation theory. This view, endorsed by both Robert Boyle and John Locke, is that secondary qualities insofar as they exist in the material things are nothing but powers (dispositions) to produce specific sensations within us.[3]

In this view, to say that some everyday item is orange is to attribute to it the power to produce the sensation of orange in us. To call it sweet is to attribute to it the power to produce the sensation of sweetness in us. Such powers are supposed to arise from the primary qualities. Thus, owing to a configuration of extended, material particles there arises a texture which, in the right situation, can have a causal impact upon a human body thereby yielding sensations in the mind. Yet, in a way, this account of what it is to attribute secondary qualities to everyday items is neutral with respect to the physics. For regardless of how it is that any particular everyday item acquires the power to produce the sensation of orange, once it has that power it can be called "orange" at least insofar as it can cause the sensation of orange to exist within us.

The power theory is different from the equivocation theory in some important respects which enable it to escape Berkeley's concerns above. While in the former, the secondary quality is merely relational, it is inherent in the latter. And while in the equivocation theory there is one true "philosophical" quality which is attributed to the material thing (such as a vibrative motion), in the power theory there can be many powers (consistent with the various sensations the thing is capable of producing). For example, while the second account gives

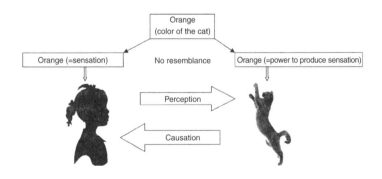

Power Theory

us only one true temperature attributed to the water, the former account can allow the water to be hot (insofar as it has the power to produce the sensation of hot) and cold (insofar as it has the power to produce the sensation of cold).

This allows the power theory to escape pressure from the perceptual relativity to give up any nonarbitrary connection between the sensations experienced by us and the actual qualities in the entities. Recall that since so many apparent qualities can be associated with any of the "true philosophical" qualities, the view that one immediately$_w$ perceives a true quality in perceiving an idea is surely undermined. The power theory avoids this difficulty, however, by allowing an entity to have as many secondary qualities/powers as secondary qualities immediately perceived. There is no problem of correlation since every sensation is correlated with the power to produce it.

Consequently, characterized as powers to produce sensations, secondary qualities in this latter view have a reference to our experiences. By contrast, characterized purely in terms of primary qualities alone (such as motion), secondary qualities lose any significant connection with the sensations. Thus, while there is a difference between "orange" (as it exists in the everyday item) and "orange" (as it is immediately perceived by us), this does not require a complete distinction between vulgar and philosophical senses.

For example, Locke contrasts the sensation of pain from the power to cause pain in us. We might call the fire "painful" insofar as it has the power to cause the pain. In this way, the attribution "painful" is not altogether unrelated to the attribution "pain" which is strictly applied to the sensation in us. Similarly, we might call a jackhammer "noisy" insofar as it has the power to produce certain sensations of sound in us, a food "tasty" insofar as it causes certain good tastes. Here, it seems at least possible to preserve the view that in receiving a sensation one thereby immediately$_w$ perceives the quality (i.e., the power to produce it). To be sure, one does not immediately$_w$ perceive a quality by means of resemblance. Rather, one immediately$_w$ perceives noisiness in receiving the sensation of an unpleasant sound.

According to Locke, in common parlance, the vulgar may go further than this and attribute the sensation itself to the everyday item as if the sensation itself or some resemblance thereof existed in it (*E.* 2.31.2, 374–5). For example, we say that the cat is "orange" although the more accurate way of speaking (in this view) is that it is "orange-looking." The benefit of this view is that, at the very worst, the only error made by the vulgar is to speak as if the sensation itself (or something resembling it) exists in the everyday item. The vulgar are nonetheless correct in attributing various properties to those entities and in supposing that those entities bear those properties. Consequently, this view manages to avoid assigning a gross error to the vulgar. In the error theory, no secondary qualities exist in the everyday items at all. In the equivocation theory, the vulgar are mistaken in supposing that what they call "orange" and so forth exist in the everyday items—only what philosophers denote by such terms really exist there. Yet in the power theory, the vulgar are correct in assigning various sensible qualities to the entities.

Does Berkeley address this position? He needs to, if he wants to undermine the view that sensible qualities are mind-independent. While the power theory attributes a degree of mind-dependence to secondary qualities it does not do so in an especially strong way. Consider that, insofar as the powers to produce sensations in us are dependent upon the existence of sensations and the perceivers that have them in order to exist, secondary qualities are to that degree mind-dependent. In other words, secondary qualities are mind-dependent insofar as they cannot exist except as possible objects of perception. There is, however, no requirement that the world "mirror" what we experience, and so no requirement that the sensible things which populate the world be actually perceived in order to exist. At least on the face of it, this is a stronger claim that Berkeley seeks to secure.

Berkeley's objections to the equivocation theory leave the power theory untouched. And if Berkeley feels these objections sufficient to address the latter, it seems he does not appreciate the salient differences between the two accounts. Fortunately, I think there is another place in the opening dialogue where Berkeley does appear to address the Lockean position. After presenting the dilemma between the error theory and the equivocation theory and then extending mind-dependence to primary qualities as well, Philonous allows Hylas to recover from any missteps. One attempt that Hylas makes involves an appeal to Locke's notorious notion of *substratum*. It is here, I suggest, that Berkeley actually addresses the Lockean power theory of secondary qualities. And as we shall see, Berkeley's attempt to address the power theory is also an important step in his defense of the Collections Thesis (and his rejection of philosophical materialism). In order to start mobilizing this additional argumentative strategy,

I want to pause briefly to consider once again the question of the vulgar.

THE POWER THEORY AND THE VULGAR

In many respects, the power theory seems to be an improvement over both the error and equivocation theories, at least with regard to the views of the vulgar. For example, the view that true sound can never be heard seems a tough pill to swallow. So, too, does the view that the sound we immediately hear does not really exist in the world at all. Locke's theory, by contrast, affords a happy way of avoiding these consequences. The sound and the color referred to by the vulgar (i.e., the sensible qualities immediately perceived) do indeed exist in the everyday items, but they are nothing but powers to produce certain sensations in us. Is there any way this power theory likewise flies against the views of the vulgar?

According to the vulgar, one sense-perceives everyday items such as tables and trees: One can see the sky, feel the fire, and taste a cherry. Yet, in the power theory, one experiences, at best, only the various powers possessed by the item; and these qualities are merely relational. Instead, in the Lockean view the existence of the thing that possesses the various powers ("ties them altogether" in one single item) is something one *infers* on the grounds that such powers need a thing to possess them and in order to explain the apparent grouping together of various different powers. Consequently, the power theory requires that we relinquish the commonsense view that we see trees, feel fires, and taste cherries.

It is notable, however, that Berkeley seems to think this problem arises in *any* theory which adopts the standard philosophical distinction between accident (or property) on the one hand, and the underlying substance on the other. He argues that we sense-perceive only sensible qualities such as colors and sounds, and since a material substance is supposed to be distinct from its sensible qualities, it should follow that we don't sense-perceive the everyday item (taken as a material substance) after all. But this, he argues, conflicts with the vulgar (and surely commonsensical view) that we *do* sense-perceive everyday items such as tables and trees.

Berkeley also makes the same point about causes. At the very beginning of the First Dialogue, in defining a sensible thing as something perceived immediately ("without intervention") by the senses,

Philonous argues that one *cannot* be said to immediately perceive the *cause* of the sensible things. This is a controversial claim. For if one immediately sense-perceives the everyday item itself, and this item is the cause of the various sensible qualities, then one thereby immediately perceives the cause.

Why does he deny that causes can be immediately perceived? He takes Hylas to suppose the cause is something *over and above* the sensible qualities immediately perceived. Since Hylas accepts philosophical materialism, he believes that sensible qualities inhere in a material substance (which is the cause of the qualities). In the traditional view, substances are the basic causes, and the various qualities (accidents) possessed by it can be explained by appeal to the substance's essence (from which the various properties "flow"). If, for Hylas, a material substance is something *distinct* from a mere collection of qualities, then it is something that is *not* immediately perceived.

Notably, Hylas also accepts the view that no inferences are ever involved in sense-perception (the senses draw no inferences). Yet if the causes of sensible things are not immediately perceived by the senses, then it would seem that some inference would have to be involved. Certainly, one could not come to mediately perceive the cause as one can mediately perceive the heat in seeing the glowing red poker. This is because, such mediacy involves association, which requires immediate perception. As a result of this, Hylas has unwittingly stepped into a trap that is going to ultimately force him to deny that everyday items can be sense-perceived at all.

The Lockean, however, *explicitly* bites the bullet on this point. And, indeed, the situation becomes far worse. Certainly in the error theory, it turns out that the essences of everyday items are hidden to us. For we sense-perceive qualities which do not even really exist in the items themselves. A serious gap is opened between the world as it appears to us (through sense-experience) and the world as it really is. The power theory scarcely saves us from such consequences. While we can come to know various relational properties (usually "powers") of a substance (such as gold), we do not know the underlying configuration of the intrinsic primary properties which give rise to such powers, nor do we know the real essence of the thing which gives rise to its various properties. We know, if anything at all, only the "nominal essence" (which is nothing but the collection of various properties). Thus, in the power theory, the real essences of everyday items become hidden to us—inaccessible to sense-experience. Instead, a material substratum is inferred as the thing in which the qualities inhere and as the cause which explains how the qualities are all tied together. Effectively then, the power theory also yields the dreaded "Lockean Ignorance" of everyday items, which so troubles Berkeley.

THE ARGUMENT AGAINST MATERIAL SUBSTRATUM

Locke's view about the philosophical concept of substance is both notorious and controversial. One of his main claims is this: While we possess a relative notion of what a substance (in general) *does*, we do not possess a positive notion of what it *is*. While we understand the relationship between a substance and its accidents, properties, or modifications (it "supports" them) and therefore have a notion of substance in this relative way (as a "supporter" of properties), we cannot characterize substance in terms of any intrinsic feature which makes a substance *a substance*. This is closely related to Locke's view that we do not know the "real essences" of particular substances. If we don't have access to the real essences of particular sorts of substances, it makes some sense for Locke to deny we have any positive idea of substance in general. It seems we do not have a good handle on any exemplars of substance, and so cannot move by abstraction to yield a more general idea.

Hylas appeals to this Lockean view in an attempt to hold out against Philonous' arguments in the First Dialogue. He begins:

> I acknowledge, Philonous, that upon a fair observation of what passes in my mind, I can discover nothing else, but that I am a thinking being, affected with variety of sensations; neither is it possible to conceive how a sensation should exist in an unperceiving substance. But then on the other hand, when I look on sensible things in a different view, considering them as so many modes and qualities, I find it necessary to suppose a material *substratum,* without which they cannot be conceived to exist. (*3D* I 197)

That this is an attempt to formulate *Locke's* view is uncontroversial. Hylas, like Locke, denies he has a positive idea of (material) substratum; he claims to have only a relative idea of its supporting accidents (or "being spread under them"). Instead of immediately perceiving the substratum, it is inferred only by reason. One notable point, however, is that contrary to a "folkloric" account, Berkeley does *not* reject the substratum on the ground that it cannot be perceived or even on the ground that there is no positive idea of it. Instead, he argues there is not even a relative notion of "supporter" since there is no way to understand the kind of support which is supposed to exist between substratum and accident.

The argumentative strategy deployed in both the *Principles* and the *Dialogues* involves pointing out that this use of "support" (and like expression such as "being spread under") cannot be understood in the common, literal, spatial sense. Effectively, then, Berkeley is claiming that this Lockean notion of support between substance and accident (and the philosophical notion of it more generally) involves a departure from common usage. Given this departure, Berkeley thinks, some explication of what it means philosophically is required. Yet no explication is forthcoming. By contrast he thinks that his own appeal to "existence in the mind" can be explained in a nonspatial (nonliteral, noncommon) way—namely as "perception by the mind" (*3D* III 250). Thus, while he can say that sensible qualities exist in the mind (insofar as they are perceived by it), he does not allow that sensible qualities can exist in (be supported by) a substratum, since the appeal to the relation of "support" or "existence in" is tantamount to an appeal to an unexplained metaphor.

What is important for our current purposes is this: Hylas' response begins once again with a distinction between two ways of viewing sensible things. On the one hand they are sensations which exist only in the mind. On the other, they are modifications or properties of a material substratum. This distinction, however, nicely follows Locke's own distinction (deployed to accommodate modern views about secondary qualities):

> It will be convenient to distinguish them [ideas], as they are *Ideas* or Perceptions in our own Minds; and as they are modifications of matter in the Bodies that cause such Perceptions in us: that so we *may not* think (as perhaps usually is done) that they are exactly the Images and *Resemblances* of something inherent in the subject. (*E.* 2.8.7, 134 my insert)

The argument against material substratum not only attacks the substratum itself, but also the second way of viewing sensible things. If the relation of support makes no sense, it likewise makes no sense to view them as modifications which warrant an inference to some substratum. It is notable, then, that Philonous concludes the argument with a reference to this alleged second way of viewing sensible things as accidents: "when you conceive the real existence of qualities, you do withal conceive something you cannot conceive" (*3D* III 199).

Caution is required here to appreciate Berkeley's move. A folkloric reading of Berkeley has it that in rejecting a material substratum, he is left with only the various qualities (accidents) which are then grouped together under one name (such as gold). My proposal that he also refuses to view sensible things as accidents at all (in rejecting the support relation) raises the question "What is left, then?" What needs to be recognized, however, is that the view that sensible things are to be viewed as *accidents* or *modifications* (which require a substratum to bear them) is a very specific conception of sensible things. In Berkeley's view the particular color that one immediately perceives also has a particular size and shape (it's a color *patch*). Here one can speak of the sensible *thing* one immediately perceives and recognize that the patch has a color, size, and shape. Yet this does not necessitate any commitment to an underlying substratum. What Berkeley rejects, in jettisoning the view that sensible things may be viewed as "so many modes and qualities" is a view that sees color, for example, as a discrete quality which cannot exist without a substance. In Berkeley's view, by contrast, there is a single-item (an extended-blue-color patch) which can stand on its own as the thing itself to which the properties of extension, shape, and color are attributed.

This is useful in clarifying the Collections Thesis. The thesis that everyday items are nothing but collections of sensible qualities (i.e., things) is supposed to be a view congenial to the vulgar. Yet the notion of "accidents" is a highly technical philosophical notion. So it would be odd to attribute the view that everyday items are nothing but collections of accidents to the vulgar. Instead, the very philosophical position which divides beings up into either accident or substance is rejected. The vulgar apparently accept that everyday items are nothing more than what they immediately$_S$ sense-perceive. And they sense-perceive nothing but patches of color and the like.

At any rate, in rejecting the view of sensible things as "so many modes and qualities," Berkeley effectively rejects the power theory and thereby shuts down the final strategy for escaping the force of TPA and the perceptual relativity considerations. As a consequence, the possibility of immediate$_w$ sense-perception is now completely eliminated. Hylas is forced into an error theory account of sensible qualities: They are nothing but restricted content—a false, imaginary glare. This is one of two steps in his defense of the Ideality Thesis.

The second step, as we have already seen in the previous chapter, is Berkeley's use of TPA to show that sensible things (such as intense heat) are variable elements of consciousness. One is now confronted with the choice of continuing to view variable elements of consciousness as mere mental states, or of viewing items such as heat/pain as subjective-objects and this essential consciousness as itself an instance of sense-perception. The representationalist distinction between sensible things as they exist in reality and as they exist in the mind yields this commitment to mental states. It also leads to the skeptical denial of the real existence of sensible things. It leaves us with an error theory (and a "false, imaginary glare"). The best solution, according to Berkeley, is to relinquish this representationalist model (and the Independence Condition). The result is an affirmation of the Ideality Thesis and a reconciliation of the vulgar and the philosophers.

THE REJECTION OF INDIRECT REALISM

It is curious that an explicit discussion of representational realism should appear at the very conclusion of the First Dialogue. If Berkeley has been arguing against it all along, why should it suddenly pop up at the end? The answer is that this final stage constitutes the culmination of his progressive assault on the position. In particular, this is the final stage (in the First Dialogue) in the reduction of representational realism and philosophical materialism to radical skepticism. Here, however, Hylas is not only forced to deny the reality of sensible things, he is also forced into a Lockean Ignorance. He will have to deny that he knows the real essences of everyday items. And what leads to this embarrassment, for Hylas, is his continued identification of everyday items with material substance. The pressure at this stage of the argument, therefore, concerns mostly Berkeley's Collections Thesis. Unsurprisingly, then, while all discussion thus far has concerned the status of the reality of sensible qualities, the argument against representational realism is specifically geared toward *everyday items*.

Another noteworthy feature is that Hylas explicitly endorses a form of indirect realism rather than direct realism. Hylas proceeds with an analogy: In sense-perceiving a picture of Julius Caesar, one thereby sense-perceives Julius Caesar mediately. In the same way, in immediately sense-perceiving sensible things, one thereby *indirectly* sense-perceives the everyday items (i.e., the mind-independent matter). Why does Hylas now propose an indirect (rather than direct) form of representational realism?

The answer is that direct representational realism has already been ruled out. Hylas has already acquiesced to the view that the content of immediate sense-perception is "restricted" and as a consequence, we only "perceive" our own ideas (we only "perceive" the representational content; we only "perceive" things as they appear to us). More strongly, owing to the failure of the power theory, he also agrees to an error theory of sensible qualities: There is nothing corresponding to our sensations of them in the material substance itself. His hope, however, is that by taking all of our sensations together, they can somehow serve as the means by which we "mediately" sense-perceive the everyday items themselves.

Philonous begins by arguing that what Hylas proposes *cannot* be a form of "mediate" sense perception at all, since it would have to involve reasoning and/or memory and the senses don't involve any such reasoning: A man who never knew of Caesar could see the picture perfectly well without thinking of Caesar. So one's thoughts are only directed to Caesar himself on the basis of reasoning (and memory). In such a case one perceives only the colors and shapes which compose the picture (i.e., one perceives only the individual sensible things). Perception of anything else (such as a picture of Julius Caesar) involves more than just sense-perception. It involves memory and/or reasoning.

Philonous contrasts this account of "mediate" perception with his own account. He admits that he allows a kind of mediate sense-perception in which one can see the heat of an iron bar (the visible idea suggests the idea of the heat) just as one can hear a color (the audible idea suggests a visible idea). However, in these cases the object mediately sense-perceived can also be immediately sense-perceived. By contrast, in the case we are imagining, the matter cannot. It therefore requires some reasoning and/or memory to yield it.

Aside from pointing to the fact that this undermines any claims about "mediate" sense-perception, Philonous goes on to claim that neither memory nor reasoning *can* deliver us the notion of the resembling matter. Hylas agrees. He says he has no reason whatsoever for inferring the existence of matter. This seems a bit odd, until we remember that the Lockean view of sensible qualities as modes and accidents which warrant an inference to a material substratum has already been rejected. It now seems that Hylas *has no basis* for inferring material substance. Consequently, he obstinately affirms that he will maintain its existence until it has been rejected as an absurd possibility.

Yet on the face of it, there is an obvious objection to Philonous' argument: Just because one's thoughts may not be directed to Julius Caesar by perceiving a picture of him, this does not mean that one does not "mediately" sense-perceive him. Can it not be said that this person *unwittingly* perceives Caesar? There are several occasions in which we sense-perceive things, and we do not know what they are. A representational realist can say no reasoning is required in "mediate" sense-perception so long as the causal transmission of representational mental state is in working order.

Philonous, however, reminds us of the extreme relativity of appearances an alleged material thing may have. Given all of these appearances are so different from each other, it seems impossible that they should all resemble some one material thing. And if one attempts to identify which of these appearances is "true," one is likewise headed for trouble given that it is hard to determine a nonarbitrary standard. This move is especially important in that it reminds us that immediate$_W$ perception has been knocked out of the running, placing considerable pressure on a direct realist account in its entirety. If it did not seem necessary to invoke reasoning before, it certainly does *now* given the plurality of possible appearances and the arbitrary nature of any one standard appearance.

At this point, Philonous has Hylas concede that material things are imperceptible in themselves ("Properly and immediately nothing can be perceived but ideas" *3D* I 206). He then argues that it is impossible for something imperceptible to resemble an idea ("Can a real thing in itself *invisible* be like a *colour*; or a real thing which is not *audible*, be like a *sound?*"). Why does Philonous claim that material things cannot be sense-perceived at all?

Philonous had *initiated* the First Dialogue, pressing very hard on the very notion of "immediate perception." In particular, he had strongly insisted that the involvement of *inference* invalidates any claim to immediacy. Yet, it is precisely such considerations which now "come home to roost." Given the considerations of perceptual relativity, an inference is indeed required. This invalidates the view that material substances can be immediately$_w$ sense-perceived. And given that sense perception does not involve reasoning, it also rules out this possibility of *indirect* sense-perception. Once it is concluded that material substance cannot be sense-perceived *at all*, however, Philonous can now appeal to the view that something inaudible, invisible, and the like cannot resemble sounds and colors.[4]

Consequently, Berkeley continues to force a gap between what we immediately sense-perceive and the everyday items themselves (which are supposed to be material substances which exist independently of being perceived and are distinct from mere ideas). In the view Hylas must now hold what we immediately sense-perceive cannot resemble the real everyday items themselves. As a consequence, they are hidden from us. Berkeley thereby shows how in addition to yielding skepticism about sensible things (by leading to a denial of their existence), philosophical materialism also leads to Lockean Ignorance of the very everyday items the vulgar suppose they know well.

THE REJECTION OF MATTER

Hylas' commitment to Lockean Ignorance goes largely unacknowledged until the beginning of the Third Dialogue. Here, however, the full extent of Hylas' skepticism is made apparent. Because Hylas does not subscribe to the Collections Thesis, but rather identifies everyday items with material substance, he is forced into a position of Lockean Ignorance: The everyday items cannot be sense-perceived, their real essences cannot be known. Because the Lockean notion of "support" is rejected, Hylas loses one basis for inferring the existence of these unknown essences in the First Dialogue. (And by the end of the Second Dialogue, he has also been forced to reject the view that material substance can be the *cause* of sensible ideas). Since Hylas has identified everyday items with material substances, he has no basis for concluding the existence of such things and must therefore also commit to a more radical Cartesian skepticism about the very existence of everyday items.

The situation, however, is far worse: Hylas has also been forced to admit that the very notion of material substance is contradictory. For after using perceptual relativity considerations to rule out the equivocation theory, Philonous uses the same considerations to argue for the very incoherence of material substance.

In the case of extension, Philonous considers that the same object will appear big or small relative to a kind of animal: a stone might appear small to a human, but very large to a mite. The upshot is supposed to be that there is no nonarbitrary standard for determining "the true" size of the object. Aside from this appeal to different animal species, Philonous also observes the same visible object appears big or small depending upon its distance from us. For example, it is unclear whether the tiny size of a car (from an airplane) or its larger size (up close) is the "true size." To be sure, one might appeal to the regular visible size of a car (as it looks from a "standard" distance). However, the issue of the microscope as delivering the "truest" representation once again emerges. A tiny speck that appears rather small (up close to the naked eye), may appear much larger in a microscope. Which is the "true" visible size of the object? Philonous argues that changes in the visible size of an object are not inherent, but merely relative. As one changes one's distance from the object, its visible size increases or diminishes. Surely a change in the perceiver's relation to an object is not an inherent change in the object itself.

Philonous harnesses these perceptual relativity considerations to provide an argument against material substance: If the same object can appear big to one eye (using a microscope) and small to another, then it is both big and small at once (which is a contradiction). This echoes one of the earlier relativity considerations he raises (in response to Hylas' reluctance to accept TPA), that water to one hand may feel cold while to the other hand hot. Is it not a contradiction to say an object is both hot and cold at the same time? Berkeley then extends similar arguments to shape, motion, and solidity. If a material substance is supposed to be the subject of sensible qualities, how can it be the subject of *inconsistent* sensible qualities? While sensible qualities such as bitter and hot can simply be stripped from a material substance, leading to an error theory account of secondary qualities, once the same considerations apply to *extension itself*, the very notion of material substance (as an unperceiving, extended thing) is placed in serious jeopardy.

Of course, the natural response to this argument is simply to distinguish between "extension as it is in us" and "extension as it is in itself." Just because an object may appear to be both big and small, this does not alter the fact that it has some fixed extension. For example, just because a person may seem small from a distance and large up close, this does not change the fact that s/he is six feet tall. And while Hylas does not use the preceding expressions, he does distinguish between "sensible" and "absolute" extension (and motion and so forth).

As with sound and color, Berkeley might point out "absolute" extension is not a sensible thing, that consequently this distinction is irrelevant to the argument, and that "sensible" extension is nonetheless mind-dependent (and hence, unreal). Yet this leaves intact the view that there is such a thing as mind-independent extension and this seems sufficient to retain the notion of material substance. Moreover, this time no appeal to common sense is available to Berkeley. While it may seem absurd to postulate philosophical colors which can never be seen and philosophical sounds which can never be heard, no such similar absurdity seems to attend extension. It seems *prima facie* intelligible to speak of nonsensible extension.

Berkeley makes a different move: He appeals to his antiabstractionism (which we shall examine in greater detail in the following chapter). The chief argument Philonous uses is to challenge Hylas to form an abstract idea of extension distinct from sensible extensions (such as big and small). Philonous concludes that no such idea of nonsensible extension can be formed. In addition to this argument, Berkeley provides a second antiabstraction argument which obviates any need to appeal perceptual relativity considerations with respect to the primary qualities. Here, Berkeley argues that primary qualities cannot be abstracted from secondary ones: They are "blended together." Yet if the perceptual relativity considerations above show that the secondary qualities are mind-dependent, then it would appear to follow that the primary qualities are mind-dependent as well.

If this argument goes through, since Hylas has identified everyday items with material substance, he must deny the very existence of everyday items. Philosophical materialism, like representationalism is thereby reduced to absurdity. "And so," says Philonous as he concludes his reduction of Hylas' position, "you are plunged into the deepest and most deplorable *scepticism* that ever man was" (*3D* III 229).

The solution, for Berkeley, is to reject the identification of everyday items with material substances. Instead, if one follows the vulgar and accepts that everyday items are perceived by the senses, then it should follow that they are nothing but collections of sensible qualities—the things we immediately perceive with the senses. In this way, the Collection Thesis, like the Ideality Thesis, is defended.

CHAPTER SIX

SPIRITUALISM IN THE *PRINCIPLES*

Reading: *PHK* INTRO; *PHK* I §1-24

In the *Three Dialogues*, Berkeley devotes the entire First Dialogue to a defense of the Ideality Thesis (sensible things are ideas) and the Collections Thesis (everyday items are collections of sensible things). By contrast, in the *Principles*, Berkeley's arguments in the *Principles* seem infuriatingly brief. Indeed, his arguments go by so fast one suspects he is assuming in advance what needs to be shown. In my view, there is something to this suspicion, although it is stated too starkly. One way to formulate the difference between Berkeley's strategy in the *Dialogues* and the *Principles* is in terms of *starting-point*.

In the *Dialogues*, Berkeley proceeds with the views of the philosophers. His aim is to reduce representational realism and philosophical materialism to skeptical absurdity. Yet in defending one's own views, it is not clear why one should always have to start with the views that are opposed to one's own and then attempt to defeat them. Rather than proceed defensively, one might begin by assuming, say, a more neutral starting point—defending one's own views positively (not critically) on the basis of that.

The problem, however, is that Berkeley's views are such a departure from standard ones, it is unclear how any starting point that doesn't accept basic tenets of his opponents can seem in any way neutral. It is correct to say, at any rate, that Berkeley proceeds with a specific "Berkeleian Framework" and then points to why, given this starting-point, the views of his opponents cannot be successfully developed. More needs to be said, then, about Berkeley's justification (or at least motivation) for proceeding in this way. I shall return to this issue at the end of this chapter.

In his Introduction to the *Principles,* Berkeley prepares for the arguments which follow in the main body of the text, by outlining his views on the meaning of general terms and by arguing that there is no such thing as an abstract idea. In the opening sections of the *Principles* (§1–24), Berkeley then defends his basic idealism. However, rather than emphasizing the fate of everyday items, Berkeley is mainly concerned to draw the conclusion that spirits are the *only* substances. That is, he defends his *spiritualism.*

Berkeley's argument for spiritualism and his related defense of immaterialism differ in important ways from his defense of basic idealism as found in the first of the *Three Dialogues*. In my view, Berkeley proceeds by *assuming* the Ideality Thesis. By this I mean Berkeley assumes that in sense-perception, the *contents* thereof are nothing but ideas (i.e., one only ever sense-perceives *ideas*). In the specific interpretation I have proposed, this means Berkeley assumes sense-perception is nothing but a form of essential consciousness and that the contents of sense-perception are nothing but subjective-objects.

However, as we saw in Chapter Two, Berkeley also aims to defend a stronger thesis. In this view, Berkeley is committed to "cognitive closure." Specifically, he thinks that all thought-contents (all the things that thought is *about*) are ideas. In the interpretation I advance, this means that all thought is a form of essential consciousness where thought-contents are nothing but subjective-objects. It is precisely by defending "cognitive closure" that Berkeley hopes to defend his spiritualist doctrine. Obviously, then, his argumentative strategy depends significantly on his views about intelligibility and his rejection of abstract ideas.

SECTION ONE: INTELLIGIBILITY AND ABSTRACTION

Berkeley's Philosophy of Language: The Intelligibility Constraint

In order to understand Berkeley's views about abstraction, one needs to understand their close connection to his philosophy of language. In my view, Berkeley inherits two very important and controversial semantic theses from Locke. According to the first thesis, one can separate the content of thought from the words used to convey that content. There is a mental *given* which is prior to and independent of human language. This was a dominant assumption in the early modern period, which came under serious scrutiny and wide rejection in the 20th century.[1] For Berkeley this means that prior to human language, one is conscious of oneself and one's various subjective-objects.

The second thesis is that categorematic terms derive their content from this prelinguistic given. This is certainly Locke's view according to which such words become meaningful through their use as signs for "internal conceptions" (i.e., ideas) (*E.* 3.2.1, 405). A speaker who uses a term without any internal conception that she is attempting to convey is no better off than a parrot who does not understand her own words. Thus, the significance of a term is given by a *prior* (i.e., prelinguistic) mental conception. Successful communication involves using terms to excite similar ideas in the auditor. Thus, a communication is understood only on the condition a similar internal conception is excited in the mind of the auditor. I call the thesis "the intelligibility constraint" since it requires that certain prelinguistic mental conceptions be annexed to words in order for them to be intelligible.

I claim that Berkeley accepts something like this intelligibility constraint. I need to be clear, however, that Berkeley's position seems less extreme than Locke's. Indeed, there are some areas in which Berkeley appears to abandon this constraint. So I want to explain his nuanced position to show that he still remains fundamentally committed to it.

Against Locke, Berkeley argues that the purpose of language is not always to convey a prelinguistic mental conception from the speaker to the hearer (*PHK* Intro §19–20). Sometimes a speaker may use words without prior ideas backing them up and still speak meaningfully and with understanding; sometimes an auditor may understand words without having prelinguistic ideas excited in her mind and still have full comprehension of what was said.

In order to support this claim, Berkeley provides some examples. First, he points to the use of symbols in algebra to stand for particular quantities (*PHK* Intro §19). In *Alciphron* he also mentions counters (or chips) used during card games to denominate specific sums (*ALC* VII §5). In both cases, Berkeley points out that one can use these devices perfectly well without, on every occasion of use, having an internal conception of the sum or the quantity before one's mind. Nor is the point of such deployments in algebra or during cards to convey internal conception from speaker to auditor. Instead, symbols can play a significant role in guiding one's behavior.

Berkeley also argues that terms such as "good," "rascal," and "danger" may be used without any idea before the mind of the speaker; without any idea being excited in the mind of the auditor (*PHK* Intro §20, *ALC* VII §5). At first, such terms indeed suggest specific ideas to an auditor. For example, in first learning to use the word "good," an idea of some pleasure (such as food) might be suggested. However, Berkeley argues, once a person is familiar enough with the words, a passion may be excited upon hearing a word without any specific conception being conveyed. Upon being promised some good thing, I might experience desire for that thing without having any specific conception of what it is. For example, when I am promised a good reward in the afterlife, instead of imagining singing in a heavenly choir, I may simply experience an intense longing for the promised reward without having a clear sense of what is in store for me. Yet while Berkeley allows that terms may be meaningfully used even though no internal idea is transmitted to an auditor, this does not show that he rejects the intelligibility constraint. In order to see this, we need only contrast his account of general terms with that of Locke.

For Locke, the difference between a general name which applies to many items (such as "human") and a proper name which refers to only one (such as "Socrates") is that the latter has a particular idea for its meaning, while the former has an abstract, general one. That is to say, names become general by standing for abstract ideas. Abstract ideas (as prelinguistic internal conceptions) constitute the meaning of a general term (*E.* 3.3.6, 410–11).

In his view, simple ideas come into the mind experientially—either through sensation or through reflection (a kind of internal sensation of one's own mental actions). The mind can then subject these simple ideas to various processes including compounding, comparing, and abstraction. Abstract ideas are formed by proceeding with similar particular ideas. For example, one proceeds with ideas of Peter, Paul, and Mary and then retaining what is similar, and leaving out the difference, yields an abstract idea of human.

For Berkeley, however, terms are general simply because they apply to a range of particular ideas. The term 'human' is significant not because it has an abstract idea assigned to it, but because it indifferently denotes many ideas of particular human beings (*PHK* Intro §18). Berkeley's view is that terms can *suggest* ideas to auditors (although they needn't), depending upon their use. For example, from my praising the dog as the philosopher's best friend, a particular idea of a dog may be suggested to you (e.g., your childhood companion). What makes the term *general* is that *any* idea of a dog can be suggested by it—it doesn't matter which. In this way, the significance of a general term is determined by the range of particular ideas it is apt to *suggest*. This means that while Berkeley can allow terms such as "good" and "rascal" do not always convey ideas, he does not deny the intelligibility constraint.

Berkeley also explicitly argues that certain significant terms do not have any ideas annexed to them *at all*. Yet Berkeley's major example of this is spirit itself (*ALC* VII §5); his point is that while one *does* have prelinguistic awareness of oneself, this is not an idea. In other words, spirits are not objects of thought (i.e., they are not subjective-objects). Yet this does not undermine Berkeley's commitment to the intelligibility constraint since terms such as "spirit" are given content by appeal to the prelinguistic awareness of one's self.

Finally, Berkeley gives examples of words whose meanings might appear to largely derive from their use—their capacity to help make successful predictions and calculations in science, or their ability to insight to certain actions. Examples of this type include scientific terms such as "force," Christian terms of mystery such as "grace," and psychological terms which purport to refer to specific mental operations such as "discourse" (*ALC* VI §9, VII §6–7). This has led some commentators to suppose that Berkeley rejects the intelligibility constraint, and maintains that some terms derive their content not from any prelinguistic mental content but from their use in inciting emotion, in motivating action, or facilitating mathematical calculation and scientific prediction.[2]

Yet even in these cases, Berkeley argues that such terms can be *defined* in terms of agent, subject, effects, and circumstances which *themselves* are given as prelinguistic mental content. His point is only that there is no mental content specifically answering to the action itself (the *modus operandi*). For example, one may have no mental content concerning the specific action of divine grace. Instead, one may only have a conception of God and the effects his action instill in human subjects. Consequently Berkeley does not reject the intelligibility constraint outright. While he allows that certain terms may be significant even though there is no prior mental content answering to them, he requires they be defined in terms which *themselves* are grounded in mental content. To this extent, Berkeley remains committed to the intelligibility constraint.

Berkeley's Antiabstractionism

Traditionally, Berkeley's rejection of abstract ideas has been found wanting. One of the reasons for this is that Berkeley doesn't seem to provide much argument for the position. In the *Principles*, he merely alleges that he cannot engage in this process of abstraction. Obviously Berkeley is not pointing to some idiosyncrasy on his own part. Rather, he believes nobody can frame such ideas. The question is *why*.

One traditional concern about Berkeley's professed inability to form an abstract idea is that he is assuming ideas must be *imagistic* in nature.[3] That is, he is assuming ideas are either sensory or produced by imagination (as one might, with some focus produce the idea of a particular unicorn upon closing one's eyes). In this view, the reason Berkeley finds he cannot produce the abstract general idea of a human is that imagination only ever involves imagining particulars things (such as particular humans). It isn't possible to imagine a human without imagining some one particular human.

If this reading is correct, then it would seem Berkeley is merely begging the question. Consider that Descartes distinguishes between imagination and pure understanding. It doesn't seem possible to imagine a chiliagon specifically (as opposed to a myriagon). Yet one may have an understanding of what a chiliagon is. This understanding, for Descartes, is not based in imagination but consists in pure intellection.[4] If Descartes is correct that we possess ideas of pure intellect, then Berkeley's rejection of abstraction based on the fact that he can imagine no such thing entirely neglects pure understanding rather than arguing against it.

However, Berkeley's denial that he can frame abstract ideas needn't be based on his inability to imagine something that is not particular. Instead, we should bear in mind the relation between Berkeley's rejection of abstract ideas and his philosophy of language. What Berkeley is rejecting are abstract ideas which are *prior* to language. They are the entities that are alleged (by Locke) to constitute the significance of general terms. Thus, we can fine-tune the challenge: If such abstract ideas exist, then it ought to be possible to form an abstract idea or internal conception *without using language at all*. The challenge, as I understand it, then, is to formulate an abstract idea without using words.

In order to understand this challenge more deeply, I want to distinguish between two different types of procedures. In what I shall call *division*, one is supposed to conceive of the abstracted feature separated from the features that are left out; viz. one is supposed to conceive of a feature existing actually separated from the rest. By contrast, in the case of *consideration*, one only attends to certain features without attending to the others. One might think of the triangularity of a particular triangle without thinking of any of the specifics which makes it unique. But in focusing only on triangularity to the exclusion of the other features, one needn't actually conceive of triangularity as existing separately.[5]

While this is highly controversial, Locke has been interpreted by some to endorse abstraction of the second variety.[6] This has the benefit of avoiding the view that when we abstract, we conceive of things that are impossible in reality. For example, given that motion cannot exist without extension, it would not be required that one conceive of motion occurring without any extension at all. Instead, one would simply attend to the motion without attending to the extension. Locke minimally requires this kind of procedure, and he requires it to occur prior to language.

The process of *mental* consideration (as I shall call it) can be viewed as a kind of "funneling" by which the mental content is contained and diverted into the semantic content of a given term. For example, while it might be impossible to conceive of color existing without shape, it might be possible to mentally consider only the color (while leaving out the extension). As a consequence, the aspect of color can be "funneled" into the semantic content of a term such as "orange" without there being any unrelated content included therein.

In rejecting abstraction Berkeley *rejects* mental consideration. Instead, he endorses another kind of consideration we can call *discursive* through which one *mentions* certain aspects while *failing to mention* others. For example, one might *mention* the color of a patch without *mentioning* its shape. This differs from mental consideration which involves focus upon certain aspects of ideas to the exclusion of others *without using language at all*.

Locke requires mental consideration in order to explain how terms acquire their semantic content. In order to generalize from several different particular human beings, one must be able to mentally consider the similarities in order to provide the term "human" with content. In doing so, one mentally "funnels" the similarity into the semantic content of "human" while excluding all the differences from it. In Berkeley's view such "funneling" is impossible. Consequently, general terms like "human" must include the differences as well as the similarities. In effect, they must apply to a range of resembling particulars rather than a pure abstraction of the similarities.

However, caution is required. The fact that one cannot mentally consider some orange without considering its extension, had better not lead to the stronger view that an idea of some orange patch doesn't have at least two aspects—namely its color and its extension. Certainly, one can compare the difference between a small patch of orange and a large patch of orange. They are similar in color, but different in extension. So, there are two aspects for comparison.

What Berkeley is denying is that there are distinct aspects which one can mentally attend to *inherent in any idea itself*: While one can compare and contrast two patches of orange with regard to their extension, one cannot mentally attend to color without extension given some *isolated* patch of orange. This means that in accepting comparison between several ideas while rejecting mental consideration of single ideas, an account of general terms is required that fundamentally involves resemblances among a *plurality* of ideas. One idea of orange alone cannot provide the term "orange" with semantic content. Rather, the *similitude* between two ideas with different shapes and the same orange is necessary to provide the term with its content.

One of the consequences of Berkeley's rejection of abstraction (coupled with his commitment to the intelligibility constraint) is that a much stricter view of necessity and impossibility moves to the fore. In Locke's view, while it is impossible for color to exist separate from extension (and impossible, therefore, to conceive of color existing without extension), it is nonetheless coherent and intelligible to speak of color existing without extension. This is because, through a process of mental "funneling" extraneous details can be omitted from the semantic content of terms such as "extension" and "color."

In Berkeley's view, however, "funneling" is impossible. Consequently, any appeal to (visible) extension which has been singled out from color is illicit. It is therefore either contradictory or unintelligible to speak of a color which has no particular extension. Because mental "funneling" is rejected, the "extraneous" details in the mental content cannot be excluded from the semantic content (just as unmarried cannot be excluded from the semantic content of "bachelor"). Just as "married bachelor" is a contradiction, so is "extensionless color."

SECTION TWO: THE EXISTENCE ARGUMENT

The Objects of Knowledge and the Knowing Spirit (§1–2)

In §1 of the *Principles* Berkeley begins by listing all the "objects of knowledge." Recall that the word "idea" is used by early modern philosophers in different ways. In one use, it is a *synonym* for "object of knowledge." In both this section and the following one, Berkeley writes as if his intention is to use it in this way. If so, however, there is no reason to suppose ideas are mind-dependent: The tree in my backyard may be an object knowledge (an idea), but there is no reason to think it cannot exist unperceived.

Berkeley produces a list of "objects of knowledge" (ideas) such as colors, hard, soft, heat, cold, motion, resistance, odors, sounds, and tastes. He also includes "ideas" formed by memory and the imagination which represent ideas received by sense, compounding and dividing in various ways. What is peculiar, however, is that at §2 he excludes spirit from this list and then claims that ideas cannot exist unperceived. If Berkeley means to treat "ideas" as synonymous with "object of knowledge," however, there is no reason to exclude spirits from his list. Nor is there any reason to allege that ideas cannot exist unperceived!

Berkeley is assuming that to think is to be essentially conscious of oneself and one's objects of thought. In this view, all immediate thought-contents are subjective-objects, so cognition is "sticky." And if cognition is "sticky" then it is clear that all immediate objects thereof, cannot exist unperceived. Moreover, it is clear why "oneself" (the spirit) is not an object of knowledge (or thought). While one is always conscious of oneself in thought, one is only ever conscious of oneself as the thinker of other objects. In affirming this view about the objects of knowledge, Berkeley is indicating his commitment to "cognitive closure." As we shall see, Berkeley goes on to defend this view in the sections that immediately follow. The point I want to make now is that by the end of §2, Berkeley has outlined his argument for spiritualism: The only objects of knowledge are ideas. These are dependent upon knowing spirits in the sense that ideas cannot exist independently of being perceived or thought of.

The Existence Argument (§3–6, §24)

At §3, Berkeley offers an opening argument which I think works well if we understand Berkeley as already accepting the Ideality Thesis.

1. It is generally recognized that passions and thoughts cannot exist unperceived.
2. So, it seems likewise evident that ideas imprinted on the sense cannot exist unperceived.

We can understand (1) as the claim that passions and thoughts cannot exist except as elements of essential consciousness. Berkeley is assuming (as an unstated premise) that "ideas imprinted on the senses" are on par with passions and thoughts. From this Berkeley concludes by parity "ideas imprinted on the sense" can likewise not exist unperceived. In assuming "ideas imprinted on the sense" are on par with thoughts, Berkeley is disregarding the view that "idea" refers to the content of a sensation, where the content is immediately$_w$ perceived by means of a mental state. Instead, he simply assumes that an "idea imprinted on the sense" is on par (i.e., likewise a variable element of consciousness), from which it indeed follows that the ideas of sense cannot exist unperceived. His point is that as objects of knowledge (i.e., as objects of essential consciousness), passions and thoughts cannot exist unperceived. Likewise, he argues, as objects of knowledge sensible qualities (such as colors and sounds) cannot exist unperceived.

Berkeley now goes on to provide a more elaborate argument that is probably as difficult to understand as it is important. Berkeley claims an "intuitive knowledge" of the mind-dependence of sensible things and everyday items can be obtained merely by attending to what "exist" means when it is applied to them. He claims, for example, "There was an odor" means "An odor was smelled" and "There was a sound" means "A sound was heard." Is this true?

If it is, it is doubtful it can be established just by quickly reflecting upon the meaning of "exists" when applied to sensible things. Certainly "When the tree fell in the forest, it made a sound heard by no one" doesn't seem self-contradictory, unlike "Tom is a married bachelor" which does. Yet while "unheard sound" or "unseen color" does not seem like an oxymoron, "invisible color" or an "inaudible sound" (with some plausibility) does. Indeed, Berkeley appeals to such an insight, as we saw, in the *Dialogues*. There he critiques the notion of a "philosophical sense" of "color" or "sound" in which they turn out to be invisible and inaudible respectively.

It seems, however, that Berkeley wants to make the stronger claim (the notion of an unseen color is an oxymoron) rather than the weaker claim (the notion of an invisible color is an oxymoron). This is clear since Berkeley concludes this section by stating of sensible things that their *esse* is *percipi* (to be is to be perceived). If he meant to make only the weaker claim *esse* is *posse percipi* (to be is to be perceivable), he would have said so.

However, Berkeley also starts this argument with a peculiar claim that does not seem to fit altogether well with what we have discussed up to this point. This is one of the reasons I think the argument is especially confusing. He says, "The table I write on, I say, exists, that is, I see and feel it; and if I were out of my study I should say it existed, meaning thereby that if I was in my study I might perceive it, or that some other spirit actually does perceive it" (*PHK* I §3). Here he discusses an everyday item (a table) rather than sensible qualities (such as sounds). And rather than providing an analysis which requires the actual perception of the table, he allows an option of actual perception or "counter-factual" perception (if I were in my study I would perceive it).

Fortunately, the simplest reading runs as follows: The analyses "some other spirit actually perceives the table" and "I would perceive the table if I were in the study" are compatible. To be sure, while the latter proposes only the perceptibility of the table (to me), the former requires actual perception. Yet according to Berkeley, only ideas are objects of perception, so there is only perceptibility in case there is actual perception. Consequently we can avoid reading the complex analysis as a peculiar disjunctive analysis, and read it as a disjunction between two possible (synonymous) analyses. This leaves us with no difference in analyses between sensible qualities and everyday items thereby cleaning up a rather muddy passage quite nicely.

Yet this leaves us with the problem of an argument that seems very hard to fathom. Berkeley wants us to see that like passions and thoughts, sensible things are mind-dependent. He claims an "intuitive knowledge" of this can be secured by attending to the meaning of "exist" when applied to sensible things. But the best common usage can give us is the claim that "invisible color" is an oxymoron and, more generally, that sensible things are inherently *sensible*. To say a sensible thing exists is to say something is sensible. But this does not yield the stronger claim that something is *actually* sensed. The move from the weak to the strong claim presupposes the Ideality Thesis that we sense-perceive only mind-dependent ideas. But if so, it is unclear how this attempt at analysis of the term "exist" has in any way helped us.

The answer can be found at §24. Berkeley claims "the absolute existence of sensible objects in themselves, or without a mind" is either an outright contradiction or else void of all meaning whatsoever. This is what Berkeley means when he claims at the end of the Existence Argument, "For as to what is said of the absolute existence of unthinking [sensible] things without any relation to their being perceived, that seems perfectly unintelligible." In other words, when Berkeley claims that the existence of sensible things unperceived is unintelligible, he means that it is either a contradiction in terms or else void of meaning. The Existence Argument therefore continues in the three subsequent sections. At §4, Berkeley argues for the claim that the absolute existence of sensible things is self-contradictory. And then at §5 and §6 he argues that attempts to escape this contradiction depend illicitly on abstraction and yield uses of expressions that are void of meaning.

What should be clear at this point is that the reasoning behind the Existence Argument neither draws on the views of the vulgar nor involves an appeal to ordinary language. Unlike Berkeley's systematic appeal to both in his *Dialogues* defense of the Ideality Thesis, in the *Principles* there is a far more abstruse appeal to the nature of abstraction and the meaning of general terms. That is, while Berkeley's argument for the Ideality Thesis involves an overt appeal to the vulgar, Berkeley's argument for spiritualism involves a direct assault on the philosophers and their reliance on abstraction.

The Contradiction Argument and the Abstraction Argument: (§ 4–6)

Berkeley's argument for the claim that "Sensible things can exist unperceived" is a contradiction is fairly straightforward:

The Contradiction Argument (§4):

1. Sensible things are ideas (Ideality Thesis).
2. It is a contradiction to say that ideas exist unperceived (definition).
3. So, it is a contradiction to say that sensible things exist unperceived.

As it stands, however, the argument is invalid. Consider the following:

4. Philosophers are unhappy people.
5. It is a contradiction to say that an unhappy person is happy.
6. So, it is a contradiction to say that philosophers are happy people.

Even if (4) happens to be true, this is not enough to yield the conclusion that its denial is self-contradictory.

In order for the contradiction in (2) to "transfer" to sensible things, "being an idea" must be part of the very notion (or definition) of "sensible thing." This, of course, is a *very* strong claim. If, however, Berkeley is right that we can only ever sense-perceive ideas, then his point is that the expression "sensible thing" derives its meaning from this given insofar as it is applied to it (only).

The question now, is why he thinks premise (2) is true. It is not enough to say that by definition ideas cannot exist unperceived. Since Berkeley is grounding the content of "sensible thing" *in the given* (if you will), there must be something about the *given itself* (rather than the mere words applied to it) which yields the view that ideas cannot exist unperceived.

According to Berkeley, a subjective-object (such as a patch of orange) is characterized by the fact it is always attended by an "I." As the Master Argument aimed to show, one cannot conceive of a sensible thing without thereby being aware of a perceiving self. This is grounded in the reflexivity of thought, the fact that subjective-objects cannot exist except as elements of conscious awareness. Because the "I" is a required component of essential consciousness, subjective-objects cannot exist unperceived. As a consequence, one cannot coherently affirm the existence of a sensible thing while deny-ing that there is a spirit perceiving it. Such a position is analogous to affirming the existence of married bachelors.

The Contradiction Argument, it seems, is primarily meant to address the vulgar. For according to them, the items we immediately$_s$ sense-perceive are capable of existing unperceived. What they do not recognize, however, is that sensible things are subjective-objects (just like thoughts and passions). But, just as it is a contradiction in terms to speak of an unperceived thought or an unfelt pain, so too, it is a contradiction to speak of unperceived colors or sounds.

The philosophers, by contrast, believe that a distinction can be drawn between the intelligible existence of a sensible thing (i.e., its existence in the mind insofar as it is represented content of a mental state) and its real existence (i.e., its existence insofar as it is an acci-dent which inheres in a material substance). It is precisely this distinction, Berkeley argues, which opens up the door to all kinds of skepticism. It relies, however, on an illicit abstraction:

The Abstraction Argument (§5–6):

1. A sensible thing is an idea (Ideality Thesis).
2. The existence of an idea cannot be separated or distinguished in thought from its being perceived (Antiabstractionism).
3. So, the existence of a sensible thing cannot be separated or distin-guished in thought from its being perceived.

Sensible things are nothing but subjective-objects, and the exis-tence of subjective-objects consists in being perceived: The existence of a thought cannot be distinguished from its being an object of conscious awareness. So, this is true also of sensible things. One may not mentally attend to only the subjective-object and thereby isolate this mental content to provide "sensible thing" with meaning in a way that excludes its connectedness to the perceiving spirit.

Recall that according to the Master Argument, subjective-objects are represented *as* perceived insofar as there is a perceiving "I." The philosopher who aims to conceive the existence of color that is abstracted from being perceived, must thereby somehow form an idea which does not include the "I." But this is impossible, according to Berkeley. To eliminate the "I" *requires eliminating the subjective-objects themselves.* As a consequence, one will be left with no semantic content *at all* for terms such as "color." This is to say, "unperceived color" if not an oxymoron is entirely *unintelligible.*

SECTION THREE: AGAINST PHILOSOPHICAL MATERIALISM

In his subsequent argument against material substance, now Berkeley takes up philosophical theories of perception explicitly (the view of "the philosophers"). He first provides a refutation of the representational realist view that our vehicles of sense-perception are resemblances of the sensible things themselves which can exist mind-independently. This refutation of what he sees as the canonical philosophical position on perception is deeply bound up with his explicit refutation of philosophical materialism. We should recognize, however, that representational realism is already under attack in the Abstraction Argument. In Berkeley's view, the representational realist's attempts to distinguish between a sensible thing as it exists in the mind and a sensible thing as it exists in the material substance involves an illicit abstraction.

The Refutation of Philosophical Materialism

At §7, Berkeley offers the first formulation of his attack on philosophical materialism. Given our discussion of this in the *Dialogues,* we should not be surprised:

1. Sensible qualities are ideas.
2. Ideas can exist only in a perceiving thing.
3. Material substance is an unperceiving thing.
4. So, sensible qualities cannot exist in material substance.

However, the argument is not fully developed until §9. There Berkeley argues:

1. Extension is an idea.
2. Ideas can exist only in a perceiving thing.
3. By definition, a material substance is an unperceiving thing in which extension exists.
4. So, the notion of material substance involves an inconsistency (since material substance is an unperceiving thing in which something that can only exist in a perceiving thing exists).

Berkeley now considers the possibility that rather than ideas, resemblances of ideas exist in material substance. Here, he considers a representational realist account of perception. He argues that since ideas can only resemble other ideas, the same inconsistency is preserved. His attack on representational realism at this stage therefore, should be understood as specifically geared to undermine this attempt to escape the argument that "material substance" is a contradiction in terms.

In taking up the representational realist view that our vehicles of sense-perception are resemblances of the sensible things themselves which can exist mind-independently, Berkeley provides the following argument:

1. Ideas can only resemble other ideas (The Likeness Principle).[7]
2. Ideas are mind-dependent things (The Substantiality Thesis).
3. So, ideas can only resemble mind-dependent things.
4. So, the thesis that ideas resemble things that exist independently of the mind is false.

The argument is obviously dependent mainly on the first premise. So what is the basis for Berkeley's "Likeness Principle"? Winkler proposes the following "verificationist" interpretation of the argument.[8]

1. Only ideas are immediately perceived.
2. So, an idea and an external thing cannot be compared.
3. So, it makes no sense to say that an idea and an external thing are alike.

The contentious premise is (2). One response that the representationalist might make is to say one *can* compare an idea (immediately perceived) and an external thing ("mediately" perceived). As Winkler observes, however, it seems impossible that our comparison should ever yield the result that the idea and external thing are unlike. If so, how is this a genuine comparison? The issue between the representationalist and Berkeley in this reading is that while the former allows for a resemblance (despite the fact that it cannot be verified), Berkeley dismisses this possibility on the grounds there is no way, in principle, to verify it.

However there is a difficulty with this interpretation of Berkeley's Likeness Principle. In formulating his argument at §8, Berkeley says that a color can only resemble a color, a sound can only resemble a sound, and so forth. Yet these claims, which seem to be related to the Likeness Principle, are not claims about verifiability. One can immediately perceive both a color and sound; and if the preceding claims are true, a color cannot be like a sound. This, quite clearly, *can* be verified. If these claims about colors and sounds are supposed to motivate the Likeness Principle, then it isn't clear why the Principle should be motivated by concerns about verifiability.

So let us turn instead to consider the formulation of the argument that Berkeley provides at §8. It runs as follows:

1. An idea cannot resemble something unperceivable (i.e., a color cannot resemble something invisible, a sound cannot resemble something inaudible).
2. Only ideas are perceivable.
3. Either the supposed originals are perceivable or not.
4. If they are perceivable, they are ideas.
5. If they aren't perceivable, then they can't resemble the ideas (how can a color resemble that which is invisible, a sound that which is inaudible?).

As Winkler observes, this argument appears to beg what needs to be shown. In particular, premise (2) excludes the possibility that external things can be perceived "mediately" through ideas themselves immediately perceived. If external colors and sounds can be perceived by means of idea, then there is no reason they can't be "mediately visible," "mediately audible," and so forth. So, as formulated, it is not clear why we should accept premise (2). However, if (2) is weakened to the claim that only ideas are immediately$_s$ perceivable, then this is not enough to show that external things can't be ("mediately") perceivable, and then it cannot be shown that external things can't resemble ideas, and it is not clear why we should accept premise (1).

Yet perhaps the argument is better than it initially appears. It is the similitude between ideas and their alleged originals which is supposed to allow the originals to be "mediately" perceived. Thus, the similitude is theoretically prior to the "mediate" perception (and hence the "mediate" visibility, audibility, and so forth). But if the similitude is theoretically prior to (and itself is supposed to facilitate the "mediate" perceptibility), then one cannot appeal to "mediate" perceptibility as an aspect of similitude which facilitates "mediate" perception. Such an account is circular. Hence, it is not enough for the originals to be "mediately" visible and the like: They must to be immediately$_S$ visible, audible, and so forth. In a word, they must be ideas.

Now obviously this reasoning requires a prior commitment to the Ideality Thesis that colors and sounds are immediately$_S$ sense-perceived subjective-objects. This is required, I claim, since the reasoning presupposes that colors and sounds look or sound like something *immediately$_S$* It is only because they do so, that similitude through sounding or looking becomes salient in determining similitude between the representation and the original. If the representations were *not* immediately$_S$ sense-perceived, then they wouldn't look or sound like anything at all.

Berkeley's Likeness Principle clearly flows from the claim that colors can only resemble colors, sounds can only resemble sounds. Presumably what Berkeley means by this is that colors resemble insofar as they *look* the same, sounds resemble insofar as they *sound* the same. Consequently a sound cannot resemble a color since the former doesn't look like anything at all, and the latter cannot resemble the former since the latter doesn't sound like anything at all. Thus, while two colors may be very different in that they look unlike, they can at least by compared in terms of how they look. By contrast, a color and sound cannot be compared in the same way: They don't have the same relation of comparison at all, if you will. But if "looking alike" is essential to a resemblance between a color and something else, then this is the kind of similitude that must obtain between the color immediately perceived and the external color "mediately" perceived. But the fact that the external thing hypothetically "mediately" looks like something cannot be used to secure the prior resemblance. The visible idea and the external thing need "to look alike" in order for the external thing to be "mediately" perceived, so its looking like something as a consequence of "mediate" perceptibility cannot be appealed to in order to secure this similitude. The basis of the argument is that relations of resemblance among ideas are specific (ideas must "look alike," "sound alike," "smell alike," and so forth). Any more general claims about the resemblance of ideas would presumably involve generating a notion of similitude that abstracts from the sensible conditions thereof. In effect, they would require mentally considering the similitude without considering the modality of similitude.

One objection to this reading is this: If it is true that colors can only resemble other colors, then one wonders how it is possible for ideas to resemble each other more generally. Surely Berkeley wants to admit that colors and sounds can resemble each other at least insofar as they are both ideas. But how can Berkeley allow this given the preceding?

One possible answer is that any further resemblances between ideas do not concern any positive commonality, but rather a similitude involving the absence of some positive feature or else a similitude in relation. For example, while a sound does not look like anything and a color does not sound like anything, they both lack any agency or causal power (i.e., they are both passive). Moreover, both enter into the same relation with spirit (i.e., both are dependent upon spirit for existence). Consequently, both enter into relations which are themselves analogous. Neither of these admissions, however, undermines the view nothing can resemble a color (*qua* color) except by *looking like* something and nothing can resemble a sound (*qua* sound) except by *sounding like* something.

In closing off the attempt to escape the argument that it is contradictory to suppose that extension (an idea) exists in a material substance by claiming that mind-independent resemblances of ideas exist in material substance, Berkeley takes himself to have shown that the notion of material substance is either contradictory or unintelligible.

Instead, spirits are the only substances. Anything that can be known (all objects of knowledge) are dependent upon spirit for their existence. That is, they cannot exist independently of their being thought of. Given cognitive closure, the thesis is very strong: Any reference to sensible things that are not dependent upon spirits for their existence is either a contradiction or else void of meaning. Both the vulgar and the philosophers are guilty of maintaining incoherent positions. Consequently, neither the vulgar notion of matter nor the philosophical one can be objects of knowledge. Any reference to a substance that is neither a spirit nor an idea is void of meaning. Indeed, any reference to anything at all that is neither spirit nor idea is void of meaning. In this way, Berkeley defends his spiritualism.

Against the Theory of Materialism

After arguing against the representation realist's attempt to escape the argument that the notion of material substance is a contradiction in terms, Berkeley goes on to consider the modern distinction between primary and secondary qualities. He uses many of the arguments already discussed (as found in the *Dialogues*): (1) The argument that the relativity considerations which apply to secondary qualities apply likewise to primary ones, (2) primary qualities cannot be abstracted from secondary ones, and (3) material substratum is vacuous.

However, Berkeley clearly sees this discussion as a digression. They are certainly not necessary to his central arguments in the *Principles* (whereas they are pivotal in the *Dialogues* strategy). So there is no need to discuss them again. Berkeley concludes his attack on the philosophers by considering theoretical arguments in favor of materialism. I will treat this briefly because it captures the reasoning which is often attributed to Berkeley and (falsely) assumed to be his *main* reasoning. It also sheds some more light on Berkeley's decision to presuppose his own account of sense- perception.

Berkeley concludes his argument against philosophical materialism, by raising concerns about the theory of materialism. He begins by arguing that it is not a theory we can know to be true. Since we perceive only ideas, according to Berkeley, sense-perception cannot help establish the existence of material things. So we must establish their existence on the basis of reason. However, Berkeley argues, there is nothing that requires a necessary inference to material things from the occurrence of sense-perception. We can have dream-experiences qualitatively indistinguishable from our waking-experiences. But those dream-experiences are not produced by material objects they might be taken to resemble. Indeed, argues Berkeley, it seems possible that we have dream-experience with no material objects at all. Why not in waking life, too? If so, argues Berkeley, there are no necessary grounds for concluding the existence of material things from the sheer occurrence of our sense-perception.

Yet perhaps it is too much to expect a deductive relationship between sense-perception and the external (material) world. Another possibility is that materialism is simply a good theory that has some probability of being true. One might point to the explanatory power of the theory in accounting for how our sensations are caused in us. Here, Berkeley makes a crucial intervention: He observes that given that materialists' inability to explain the causal relationship between mind and body (and in particular, to explain how sensations are caused by material things), this explanatory boast is hardly impressive. In other words, given what is sometimes called "the mind-body problem," the materialist has no claim to explanatory power until she solves it.

Such considerations, especially the first one (that we cannot know there are material things), are sometimes cited as the chief reason Berkeley adopts his idealist position: Given the problem of skepticism with regard to the external (material) world, Berkeley simply eliminates any appeal to it whatsoever. The danger with this emphasis is that it neglects what are more properly viewed as Berkeley's key arguments. He does not merely reject material substance since it cannot be known to exist. Rather, he positively concludes that material substance *cannot exist* on the grounds that the notion is incoherent. Berkeley thinks that matter can be known to not exist (just as a round square can be known to not exist).

That said, I think that these theoretical considerations indicate something important about Berkeley's attitude (especially in the *Principles*). One of the reasons I think Berkeley assumes the Ideality Thesis, is that putting traditional philosophy aside, this is what one finds when one "peals away the curtain of words" (namely, a spirit and its own ideas). Philosophical theories (philosophical materialism and representational realism) depart from the given by an illicit process of abstraction. The point that Berkeley is making here, however, is that as *theories* they require arguments. And even if a theory of sense-perception (such as direct realism) does not require that any perceiver *herself* engage in reasoning when she sense-perceives some object, the theory itself must nonetheless be grounded on a reasoning which moves us from the given to the material things. Once representational realism (with philosophical materialism) is treated as a theory, however, its grounds start to look less far compelling, especially in light of its failure to explain causal interaction between body and mind. While these concerns are not a defense of Berkeley's starting-point in the *Principles* (as he *does* defend it in the *Dialogues*), they nonetheless help illuminate Berkeley's strategy in proceeding from a wholly Berkeleian framework.

PART THREE: THEOCENTRIC IDEALISM

CHAPTER SEVEN

DIVINE GOVERNANCE

Reading: *PHK* I §25–33, §145–49; *ALC* IV §1–15

Also: *3D* II and *Essay Towards A New Theory of Vision*

In moving beyond one's own ideas and one's own self, Berkeley needs to demonstrate the existence of God. Likewise, Berkeley needs to show how one can infer the existence of other human spirits who partake in this shared world. God is, if you will, the spine, and human spirits are the connected bones upon which the muscle and flesh of the public work is to be hung. Without God to secure a world that is independent of one's self, and without other human spirits who also partake in it, it is scarcely credible that Berkeley has secured a commonsense view of the world. Berkeley's first move in establishing a shared world, then, is to prove the existence of those who share it: The frame of the world, for Berkeley, is a community of spirits in discursive intercourse with each other and with a Divine Governor through whom all communication is mediated.

In this chapter, I look at the main argument (Causal Argument) for God's existence found in the *Principles*, as well as his reason for concluding the existence of other human spirits. I also include a second argument for the existence of God which comes not from the *Principles,* but from *Alciphron.* I include this since it is the natural extension of Berkeley's discussion of other human spirits, and since it sheds further light on Berkeley's notion of divine language in the Principles. In elaborating this argument, I additionally draw on

Berkeley's defense of his theory of vision (as outlined in his *Essay*). My goal in doing so is to elaborate Berkeley's account of divine language, and to further illuminate his account of everyday items.

I should be clear that in neither the *Essay* nor *Alciphron* does Berkeley assume his immaterialist and idealist positions. As a consequence, his argument for the existence of God in *Alciphron* is supposed to operate independently of specific immaterialist and idealist commitments. Because of this, my integration of Berkeley's arguments from *Alciphron* and the *Essay* is by no means unproblematic.

SECTION ONE: THE CAUSAL ARGUMENT (GOD AS SOURCE OF REALITY)

The Argument from Causation begins early in the *Principles,* running from §24–33:

1. Sensible ideas must be caused by some spirit or other.
2. I am not the cause of my sensible ideas.
3. So, there must be some other spirit which causes my sensible ideas.
4. This spirit is God.

Premise (1) is established through a process of elimination. Berkeley takes for granted that sensible ideas must have some cause or other (i.e., he assumes a version of the Principle of Sufficient Reason), and then considers the following possible causes: ideas themselves; material substance; and spiritual substance. After summarizing the Existence Argument at §24, Berkeley initiates the Argument from Causation, by first defending the view that ideas themselves are entirely passive and inert. He alleges the passivity of ideas can be determined simply through the bare observation of them: He observes them, finds no power or activity within them, and concludes they are not causes.

This argumentative strategy relies on the view that beyond our perception of them, ideas cannot conceal anything: "For since they and every part of them exist only in the mind, it follows that there is nothing in them but what is perceived" (*PHK* I §25). This thesis (which Phillip Cummins dubbed "The Manifest Qualities Thesis") says that ideas cannot have any characteristics which they are not perceived to have.[1] This is precisely what we should expect in the view that ideas are nothing but subjective-objects. As elements of consciousness, their very existence consists in being perceived.

What does Berkeley fail to find when he goes looking for power within his ideas? I can certainly perceive an idea of a moving cue ball smashing into an eight ball, and I can then perceive the eight ball moving. Doesn't it seem we perceive the previous idea (of the moving cue ball) causing the following idea (of the moving eight ball)? Presumably one of the concerns Berkeley has in mind (inherited from Malebranche and then made famous by Hume) is that there is no necessary connection between any such ideas.[2] Consequently, it seems there is no reason to suppose one idea necessitates the next.

Having ruled out ideas themselves as causes, Berkeley then quickly discards material substance on the grounds it has already been rejected, and moves on to the view that the cause must be a spiritual cause. However, it is worth pausing to consider that in the Second Dialogue, after Philonous argues that God is a perceiver and the cause of the sensible world, Hylas attempts to rehabilitate the notion of matter by claiming that it is a secondary or subordinate cause—despite the fact that God is the ultimate cause. His view is that while matter is not an agent, it can still be viewed as a subordinate cause which operates only with the concurrence of God.

Philonous forces Hylas to agree that matter-as-cause is not immediately perceived by the senses; Hylas admits that he infers its existence since "I find myself affected with various ideas, whereof I know I am not the cause; neither are they the cause of themselves" (*3D* II 216). Philonous' first criticism is that material substance has already been shown to be a contradiction in terms. He charges Hylas with changing the meaning of the word "matter" which he takes as *synonymous* with "material substance." Presumably Hylas leaves himself vulnerable to this charge by deciding to call *whatever* happens to be the cause of his ideas "matter" (regardless of what it turns out to be).

Philonous further objects to Hylas' account of matter-as-cause on the grounds that because motion is nothing but an idea, it cannot be a cause. Since motion cannot be a cause, it is a perplexing question what Hylas has in mind when he attributes causal efficacy to matter at all. The only other possibility seems to be the mental activity of which we are aware in ourselves. If not that, then what? And if the answer is "nothing," then what does "cause" even mean in such a use? The argument Berkeley presses here is aggressive. The suggestion is that just as material substance is a contradiction in terms, so too is the notion of a nonspiritual cause. Such a forceful argument is found in the *Principles*. After having quickly dispensed with material substance at §26 of the *Principles*, Berkeley provides a more detailed introduction of his conception of spiritual substance at §27. Then, at §28, he explains how he can find a conception of agency within himself:

> I find I can excite ideas in my mind at pleasure, and vary and shift the scene as oft as I think fit. . . . This making and unmaking doth very properly denominate the mind active. . . but when we talk of unthinking agents, or of exciting ideas exclusive of volition, we only amuse ourselves with words.

While a conscious, willing agent (such as oneself) provides the term "cause" with semantic content, nothing else can. To use "cause" in a way that departs from this is to "only amuse ourselves with words." Here Berkeley is plainly appealing to "cognitive closure." Since the only things available in consciousness are passive subjective-objects and oneself (an agent), the only intelligible and consistent notion of "cause" is a "perceiving, willing spirit."

Since the conception Berkeley acquires of his own agency is essentially bound up with consciousness (i.e., consciousness of one's activity in producing and destroying ideas), it is also fairly clear why Berkeley thinks he can rule out the possibility of his own production of sensible ideas unbeknownst to himself: Again, this would require using "cause" in a way that departed from anything that could be conceived by us. So premise (2) is fairly quickly established as well. Thus, at §29 Berkeley observes that he is not responsible for the production of sensible ideas, and concludes that some other spirit must have produced them.

What remains a pressing problem, however, is how Berkeley can move from the claim that his sensible ideas are caused by some spirit other than himself, to the claim they are caused by *God*. More specifically, Berkeley wants to ascribe certain attributes to this spirit—namely, omniscience, omnipotence, all-goodness, eternality, and so forth. Yet it is scarcely clear how this follows from a sheer observation of the sensible ideas produced by some other mind. To be sure, "the constant regularity, order, and concatenation of natural things, the surprising magnificence, beauty, and perfect of the larger, and exquisite contrivance of the creation, together with the exact harmony of the whole" (*PHK* I §146) might help establish the existence of some very powerful and knowledgeable mind. But how does Berkeley move the stronger claim that this mind is all-powerful and all-knowing? Berkeley suggests that we need only attend to the meaning of the words "one," "eternal," "infinitely wise," "good," and "perfect" (*PHK* I §146) to make this conclusion. And while this suggestion is scarcely clear, there are indeed considerations to which Berkeley can appeal.

Between §30–33, Berkeley points to key differences between ideas received by the senses and ideas produced by the imagination. His main reason for doing so is to show how the appearance/reality contrast can still be drawn. The worry is that if sensible things are nothing but ideas, it is hard to see how there *is* any contrast between appearance and reality. Recall that Berkeley has already rejected the distinction between the intelligible existence of sensible things (as they exist as perceived in the mind) and the real existence of sensible things (as they inhere as accidents in material substance). How then can he draw an analogous distinction?

Aside from the fact that sensible ideas are produced by God while imaginary ideas are produced by oneself, there are a couple of differences between sensible and imaginary ideas Berkeley points to. First, while sensible ideas are both strong (forceful) and vivid, ideas of the imagination are weak and faint. Second, sensible ideas are connected together in a coherent, regular way. By contrast, imaginary ideas are not connected to sensible ideas in the same way, nor are they connected to each other with the same sort of order and coherence. According to Berkeley, the regularity and "admirable connection" between the sensible ideas constitute the very Laws of Nature.

Berkeley uses these features to draw a distinction analogous to the contrast between intelligible and real existence. The sun, for example, insofar as one sense-perceives it is real. By contrast, the sun insofar as one imagines it exists only in one's own mind. Berkeley claims while the former ideas are the real things (the originals), the latter are mere thoughts (copies) of the original ideas. Moreover, while Berkeley allows that the imaginary sun in some sense exists (in one's own mind), it has *less* reality than the sensible sun insofar as the ideas are less forceful, vivid, orderly, and coherent (i.e., it is not governed by the Laws of Nature). In this way, the Causal Argument for God's existence helps elucidate Berkeley's strategy in drawing the appearance/reality contrast insofar as he grounds the very nature of sensible reality in the Laws of Nature which are instituted by God.

For Berkeley, one of the important features of the Laws of Nature is that they give us a foresight about how to negotiate our actions in the world for the benefit of our lives. Without such laws "we should be eternally at a loss: we could not know how to act anything that might procure us the least pleasure, or remove the least pain of sense" (*PHK* I §31). Given this, Berkeley has some reason for concluding the goodness of this divine cause. And given that the *very Laws of the Natural World* (and therefore sensible *reality*) are grounded in the causal power of this mind, one has a decent case that he is all-powerful at least within the natural world itself (since he is the one who *writes* the rules). Moreover, since everything God causes must be ideas which also exist in his own mind (otherwise, how could God know what he was doing?), God likewise has all the ideas of everything that was in time and everything that will come to be in time (Berkeley calls this "the Course of Nature"). Since the Course of Nature (effectively, sensible reality in its entire historical dimension) exists entirely in the mind of God, he is likewise all-knowing at least with respect to the natural world. Moreover, he is eternal at least insofar as he perceives all events which occur over the Course of Nature.

That said, it remains unclear how Berkeley can move from the apparent goodness of God (attested by the usefulness of the Laws of Nature) to his all-goodness, given that evil things also appear to be the consequence of these laws. It is also unclear why Berkeley feels entitled to conclude the existence of only one mastermind instead of more. Are the regularity and uniformity of sensible ideas sufficient to establish this unity? While nature is in many ways uniform, it is hardly homogeneous.

SECTION TWO: OTHER HUMAN SPIRITS

At §145–49 Berkeley is interested in comparing our knowledge of other (human) spirits with our knowledge of God. He begins by arguing that we do not immediately sense-perceive other human beings; rather we perceive only the visible (and tangible) effects they produce. Berkeley makes it plain a human being is nothing more than a spirit, the visible body is nothing but a kind of sign or visible badge; he claims our knowledge of other humans is nonimmediate insofar as it involves the intervention of ideas. On the basis of sensible effects, we infer the existence of a spirit which is responsible for those effects; and the effects together constitute something like a visible sign of a human spirit. Apparently we use the rationality indicated by the set of effects to infer a center of rationality. And we use our own consciousness of self as a model to understand just what this center must be like. Consider, for example, that one finds various different stones arranged in a pattern. The fact that this arrangement is not random suggests there is some sort of intellect or center of rationality involved. And the nature of the arrangement gives us information about the particular intellect itself. After all, it may be that a different intellect may have organized the stones differently.

Berkeley argues that our knowledge of God is quite similar to our knowledge of human spirits. Just as we do not, strictly speaking, *see* a human being so we do not *see* God. Rather, the human spirit is represented by signs (visible effects) which bespeak a unique center of rationality. Similarly, God is represented by a great many signs—sensible effects of a mighty agent abound. The difference is that we know God demonstrably (and there are far more effects which bespeak the existence and rationality of God than the effects which bespeak the existence of any one human spirit).

Unlike the inference to God (which Berkeley takes to be necessary and hence demonstrative), the inference in cases of human spirits is merely probabilistic. The evidence in the effects may give probable reason to suppose a distinct center of rationality, but this does not follow with necessity. Why? According to Berkeley, the existence of sensible ideas necessarily requires the inference to another spirit. Given that one doesn't cause the sensible idea, it necessarily follows that it is caused by some other spirit. By contrast, insofar as we conclude the existence of other human spirits on the basis of sensible effects (such as the motion of a human body), there is no necessary ground for concluding the existence of a human spirit, since it is entirely possible that God alone caused those effects.

The contrast, however, points to an important difficulty with Berkeley's account of our knowledge of human spirits. This view presupposes that human spirits are capable of causally producing the visible ideas which we ourselves perceive: These ideas are considered the effects of an agent, and attributed to a rational (albeit finite) causal principle. But visible and tangible ideas are sensible ideas, and according to Berkeley, God himself is the immediate cause of all sensible ideas. If this is the case, it would seem that God (not the human spirits) is solely responsible for the movements of the visible and tangible ideas. Consequently, the inference to finite spirit doesn't get off the ground, since no human spirit can have a causal impact upon the sensible world at all.

It also leads to the untoward view that God himself is the immediate cause of all ills in the world (even those we would have normally attributed to human spirits): When one human presses a knife into the chest of another, all of the ideas involved in this murderous transaction are caused immediately by God himself. Why, then, is God himself not a murderer? The problem is an extreme version of the problem of evil. One aspect of the problem involves the question of how and why God allows human beings to commit sinful acts. In Berkeley's own theory of worldly causation, however, the problem is far worse. It seems God is not merely *allowing* sinful action, but is the immediate cause of it.

Berkeley takes up this concern about human evil in the *Dialogues* and he has Philonous respond to Hylas in several different ways (we will discuss the last). Philonous explicitly *allows* that human spirits may have the capacity for outward action (i.e., movement): "this is very consistent with allowing to thinking rational beings, in the production of motions, the use of limited powers, ultimately indeed derived from God, but immediately under the direction of their own wills, which is sufficient to entitle them to all the guilt of their actions" (*3D* III 237). This fits well with a related claim Berkeley makes at the end of his reformulation of the Causal Argument in the *Principles*: "For it is evident that in affecting other persons, the will of man hath no other object, than barely the motion of the limbs of his body; but that such a motion should be attended by, or excite any idea in the mind of another, depends wholly on the will of the Creator" (*PHK* I §147).

How can we render consistent the claim that human agents can cause motion in their bodies with the claim that God is responsible for all sensible ideas? The only possibility is to allow that at least some ideas of motion need not be sensible ideas. Recall for Berkeley, sensible ideas are caused from without. We passively receive them. It may be that there are some ideas of motion (internal kinesthetic ideas) which we can cause ourselves. As such, they would not be received passively through the senses. Instead, they would be perceived through our activity in much the same way that our ideas of imagination are perceived.

The pressing question is how to distinguish these internal ideas of motion from the ideas we produce in imagination. Recall that the latter are supposed to be faint, weak, and indistinct. Moreover, they are not supposed to hang together in the same ordered way that sensible ideas do; instead they are mere copies or resemblances of sensible ideas. Yet the sheer fact these internal ideas of motion are produced by us does not rule out the possibility that they are vivid, strong, distinct, and fit within the causal order of nature. Indeed, it seems they *do* fit within the causal order in Berkeley's view, since an internal motion of the body is regularly attended by visible ideas produced in one's own mind as well as the minds of others.

This reading requires separating the activity/passivity distinction (on the one hand) from the vivid/faint, strong/weak, orderly/erratic distinctions (on the other). The latter plays the key role in Berkeley's attempt to distinguish reality from mere fantasy or thought; the former plays a role only in distinguishing between passive perception (passion) and active perception (volition). The reading also requires the recognition of ideas other than imagined or sense-perceived ones: Kinesthetic ideas of motion (such as the idea of moving one's left pinky finger) are some of these ideas.

SECTION THREE: THE DIVINE LANGUAGE ARGUMENT

After deploying an argument very similar to the one outlined in the preceding section, Berkeley makes the free-thinker Alciphron decide that the visible effects of a body moving (regardless of any rationality that may be exhibited through it) are insufficient to establish the existence of a person causing the effects. By contrast, Berkeley thinks that the deployment of language *does have such a necessary connection.* He explicitly denies that such language use can in any way be explained by appeal to "laws of motion, by chance, by fate, or the like blind principles" (*ALC* IV §14). Alciphron thinks that what truly convinces one that some other agent exists is the use of language. He therefore requires that one of Berkeley's protagonists (Euphranor) prove that we know God's existence in the same way we know the existence of a human person (namely, through speech).

Alciphron begins by outlining what he takes as the two hallmarks of language. First, language involves the use of sensible signs to stand for other things, and this connection is arbitrary. For example, that the visible mark *dog* denotes various canine animals is entirely arbitrary; the visible mark *hat* might have just as easily done the job. Specifically there is supposed to be no necessary connection between sign and signified (one cannot with necessity infer the one from the other), and no resemblance. The second hallmark of language, according to Alciphron, is that these signs are used to suggest various things, to inform, and to direct action. More strongly, they should be capable of directing action with regard to things that are distant in time and place as well as things present.

Ultimately, Euphranor adds a third hallmark of language to Alciphron's list (to distinguish between a mere sign and a sign which is part of a veritable language). According to him, what characterizes a language is "the articulation, combination, variety, copiousness, extensive and general use and easy application of signs" (*ALC* IV §12). While an animal cry may indicate a pain, it is not part of a veritable language in the way that the word *stop* is. Part of what Berkeley may have in mind here is that a veritable language involves generative powers through rules of combination, whereas simple signals do not. Berkeley may adopt a Cartesian position which insists that this capacity for infinite generation and adaptability is the hallmark of rationality, utterly inexplicable on simple mechanistic principles.[3]

We can begin by noting, that in Berkeley's immaterialist universe, since no sensible thing is a cause (and since God is the cause of all sensible things in nature), there is a bit of a puzzle concerning the constant correlation among various sensible things. For example, upon seeing a fire, one will always experience burning heat by moving one's hand into the center of it. Upon hearing a rumbling sound, one can expect to see a motorcycle. Yet, since no idea we perceive *is* a cause, the relation between correlated ideas needs some other explanation.

In Berkeley's view, what are (mis)taken for causal relations, are in fact semantic in nature. Thus, a particular aroma may *suggest* fresh-baked cookies, the audible sound of rumbling may *suggest* the eventual visible appearance of a motorcycle. In both cases, the former are *signs* which represent the latter. In both cases, Berkeley claims, relations between sign and signified involve neither necessary connection nor resemblance—they are arbitrary in the way conventional signs are arbitrary. Moreover, in both cases the signs play a role in guiding our behavior with regard to things that aren't present—either spatially or temporally: The odor directs us to follow our nose (and find the cookies in the kitchen). Likewise the sound lets me know that were I to go outside I would see a motorcycle: A motorcycle rider races at some distance from me. Yet for Berkeley, the relationship between visible ideas and tangible ones is especially important. Given "the articulation, combination, variety, copiousness, extensive and general use and easy application of signs" involved, he thinks that vision constitutes a veritable divine language (unlike other sensory modalities).

In order to understand Berkeley's positive account, we can begin by distinguishing between what he calls visible and tangible magnitude. One's thumb (visibly perceived) and a human head (visibly perceived) can have the same visible magnitude despite the fact that one has a much larger tangible magnitude than the other. (Try it yourself!) Berkeley frames this by saying that visible magnitude is determined by the number of visible points it contains (*minima visibilia*), and that the tangible magnitude is determined by the number of tangible points it contains (*minima tangibilia*) (*NTV* §54). A minimum is the smallest degree one can perceive before nothing is perceptible at all (it's a kind of minimal threshold). So a *minimum visibile* is the smallest color dot one can perceive before one perceives nothing at all.

In Berkeley's view, while any given everyday item (such as a head or a thumb) has a more or less fixed tangible magnitude, it has multiple visible magnitudes which alter depending upon the circumstances. It is, of course, the tangible magnitude which is what people normally have in mind when they assign a particular fixed magnitude to an entity. Likewise, an entity can visibly appear to have different shapes (depending upon the circumstances): A tower may look round from a distance and square when it is near. Again, despite this variability in visible shape, the tangible shape remains constant.

Now the sensible things we (immediately) see are diversified according to colors and light (i.e., brightness). However, some of the things we immediate see can appear faint, blurry, confused, or indistinct. Moreover, in using our eyes, we can experience various bodily sensations which attend the movement of our eyes and our head, as well as the strains which sometimes accompany the attempt to see certain objects. All of these features matter, for Berkeley, in an explanation of how we see distance, magnitude, figure, and situation. For in his view, we do not *immediately* see objects as spatially located at a distance. Nor do we immediately see their magnitude, figure, and situation of those entities (which is determined strictly by the tangible). Instead, we only *mediately* see objects at a distance, with a (tangible) magnitude, (tangible) shape, and (tangible) situation.

According to Berkeley, this mediate vision of distance, magnitude, figure, and situation is (like his account of language in general) accommodated by *suggestion*. After enough experiences of correlations among changes in visible magnitude, faintness, confusedness, etc. as well as some of the accompanying bodily sensations discussed above, certain tangible ideas are, by habit, *suggested* to one's imagination. Thus, when I immediately perceive a visible tower which has an exceptionally small visible magnitude, and which is also very faint (and I experience a strain in my eyes), a great distance will be suggested to me. In particular, it will be suggested that upon a great many movements of my legs, I will come to experience certain tangible sensations (as, say, when I slap the tower itself). Similarly, based upon a large visible magnitude which is blurry, a small tangible magnitude (and a short distance) can be suggested to my mind.

The insight driving Berkeley here, derives from the famous question posed by William Molyneux (1656–98) to John Locke (in a letter dated July 1688), whether a man born blind who had learned to distinguish and identify a globe and cube by touch would be able to do the same by vision alone if he were suddenly made to see. Berkeley answers in the negative. There is nothing in the visible ideas themselves which give any information about how to coordinate visible qualities with tangible ones. Instead, the newly sighted man would need to learn how to coordinate vision and touch through experienced associations between visible and tangible qualities. Only after having acquired the experience and the habit, would this man be able to distinguish and identify a cube and a sphere by vision alone.

Berkeley begins his account of vision in his *Essay* by arguing that we do not immediately perceive distance through vision. In vision, we only immediately perceive color and light which themselves have various visible magnitudes; and which come in degrees of vividness and distinctness. While a decrease in visible magnitude may often suggest an increase in distance, this does not mean we immediately see distance itself. The way in which Berkeley argues for this point is to claim that distance itself is a line turned endwise to the eye. Regardless of the distance, then, there is only a single point to be perceived by the eye. And since this single point is consistent with any distance whatever, distance itself cannot be immediately perceived through vision.

Instead, Berkeley argues we (mediately) see distance only by learning to associate the visibly extended colors we immediately perceive with tangible distance (constituted by the number of motions of one's limbs over time). According to Berkeley, our visible (and bodily) experiences have no necessary connection with distance, nor do our visible experiences of objects resemble objects at a distance. And since the connection between what we (immediately) see and the distance involve neither necessary connection nor resemblance, the correlation is arbitrary in nature.

Berkeley also denies that what we immediately perceive by vision resemble the objects themselves at a distance. This is to say: We do not immediately see objects *as* located at a distance. What Berkeley is denying here is that our visible experience involves any representation of objects spatially located at a distance, or (as he puts it) whether the "outness" of objects is manifest in our immediate visible experience. The objects we immediately perceive by sight (i.e., colors) change in visible magnitude as we approach or recede from the object which is at a distance. Berkeley concludes from this that we do not immediately see the object itself which is at a distance, nor does what we immediately see resemble that which is at a distance. He writes:

> Suppose I perceive by sight the faint and obscure idea of something which I doubt whether it be a man, or a tree, or a tower, but judge it to be at the distance of about a mile. It is plain I cannot mean that what I see is a mile off, or that it is the image or likeness of anything which is a mile off, since that every step I take towards it the appearance alters, and from being obscure, small, and faint, grows clear, large, and vigorous. (*NTV* §44)

Obviously, the considerations about relativity we saw at work in Berkeley's arguments in the *Dialogues* are also at work here. One natural supposition is that just to see the faint idea of something, is to see the object at a distance itself. In such a view, one might immediately$_w$ perceive that actual object by sight. However, in pointing to the breakdown in resemblance, Berkeley is thereby showing why a direct realist account can't work. Given a failure in resemblance, the Aristotelian account, for example, is out of the running. To be sure, Berkeley does not here consider the other options discussed in the *Dialogues*. However, both the equivocation Theory and Power Theory were deployed only to salvage secondary qualities. Given that this discussion concerns the primary qualities (which really are supposed to be reflected in the world), the failure in resemblance is significant. The upshot is that there is neither a necessary connection nor a resemblance between the visible ideas and the tangible ones they suggest. This is to say: the connection is arbitrary.

Berkeley deploys a similar argumentative strategy in the case of magnitude. He argues that we do not immediately perceive magnitude by sight on the grounds that visible magnitudes can vary per the same tangible magnitude, and indeed that the same visible magnitude can be assigned to different tangible magnitudes. Because such considerations again, indicate that any resemblance is out of the running, and therefore a direct realist conception of the perception must fail, Berkeley can deny that (tangible) extension is immediately seen.

Moreover, he argues there is nothing in what we immediately see by sight which has a necessary connection with tangible magnitude. Certainly, there is no such connection between faintness or confusedness. Nor, even is there any necessary connection between visible magnitude and tangible magnitude. Berkeley defends the last claim, by pointing out our eyes may have been constituted such that we only see objects much smaller than we can touch (e.g., suppose we have microscopical eyes which enable us only to see molecules). In such a case, there would be a complete lack of coordination between what we saw and what we felt—there would clearly be no necessary connection between visible and tangible magnitude. Moreover, Berkeley argues, in truth the very same visible magnitude can be referred to different tangible magnitudes, depending upon the circumstances. If so, there is no necessary connection between the two. Indeed, Berkeley quite radically claims that small visible magnitude might very well have been coordinated with objects of large tangible magnitude.

So these are the types of arguments Berkeley deploys to establish that the ideas of vision bear neither a resemblance nor a necessary connection to the tangible ones. Rather than consider other arguments (concerning situation, in addition to distance and magnitude) to the same effect, I want to now consider the second and third hallmarks which Berkeley assigns to language (namely its utilization to direct behavior and its combinatory, generative capacities) in order to see whether he can make the case for his optic language, and to what degree his argument is successful.

Certainly Berkeley seems right to suppose that visible ideas provide information about how to navigate the world with respect to our pursuit of pleasure and our avoidance of pain. Recall, earlier that in his Causal Argument, Berkeley points to the use of the Laws of Nature to enable us to negotiate the world as evidence of God's beneficence. Putting these two points together, it appears that if God is speaking to us through a kind of optic language, then his end in using this language is to simply guide us away from harm and into pleasure. According to Berkeley, this can show not only that God exists, but also that he is a Divine Governor who is constantly guiding and directing our actions through the Optic Language.

Let's consider the third hallmark of language. While Berkeley refers to "the articulation, combination, variety, copiousness, extensive and general use and easy application of signs" he does not say much to make us see why this alleged language really does involve generative capacities. However, consider the examples provided by Alciphron: "Smells and tastes, for instance, are signs that inform us of other qualities to which they have neither likeness nor necessary connection" (*ALC* IV, §12). Here we seem to merely have the assignment of a kind of primitive vocabulary (this aroma stands for cookies, this taste stands for milk). However, there is no rule involved which allows for the generation of new signs. By contrast, the correlation between a decrease in visible magnitude (and vividness) with increase in tangible distance, is a rule that is applicable to any species of visible idea (any color of any visible magnitude). It is therefore capable of responding to a potentially infinite number of visible ideas by generating information about distance. In this way, Berkeley does seem to make the case that vision affords "an extensive and general use of signs."

Curiously, however, this is insufficient to count something as a language. Consider the relation between the sound of a motorcycle and the motorcycle itself. There *does* seem to be a general rule which concerns distance and loudness. With the right background experience, an increase in the sound (of a motorcycle) will generally suggest its spatial approach. This rule is applicable to a great many sounds (and attendant entities), so there does seem to be "a general use of signs." Why does Berkeley not allow this as a case of language?

Vision not only has rules which facilitate the perception of distance, but also magnitude, shape, and situation. In effect, visible ideas enable us not only to assess the distance of a tangible object, they also enable us to determine the intrinsic features of the tangible object itself. While the smell of a cookie might be correlated to a cookie (on the basis of experience), there is nothing in the smell itself which can provide information inherent to the tangible object, unlike a visible idea which can provide information about the magnitude, shape, and situation of the cookie. Vision involves a kind of sophisticated structure which sounds and smells lack (i.e., vision involves *articulation*), and objects of vision can be combined to form more complex objects while this seems largely untrue of odors and tastes.

One way to see this point is to consider Berkeley's recognition that some visible ideas are "fitter" to represent tangible ideas than others (despite the lack of resemblance). He gives the example that the visible word "adultery" may be fitter to represent the audible word "adultery" because the eight visible marks can correspond to the eight audible sounds. Similarly, he thinks, a visible square may be fitter to represent a tangible square since the four visible angles can correspond to the four tangible angles. But just as the visible word adultery is arbitrarily assigned to the audible word, so too, the assignment of the visible square to the tangible square is arbitrary (although more fitting than other possibilities). The point is, however, that visible ideas exhibit a kind of complex structure that admits of combinatorial possibilities that are not evident in the cases of smell and taste.

With the argument firmly in mind, I would now like to assess its overall strength. There are two major concerns. First, while Berkeley might be right (along with Descartes) that linguistic behavior cannot be accommodated by the simplistic mechanism of their day, it does seem to be now generally recognized that complex linguistic behavior can be accommodated in a materialistic theory.[4] If this is right, Berkeley could not rule out this possibility with his argument (which is supposed to work independently of his own immaterialist theory). That said, it is worth noting that while a materialist account is not ruled out, neither is Berkeley's claim that there is a necessary connection between linguistic behavior and rationality. For one way to describe such a situation is to recognize material entities capable of such linguistic behavior as rational beings.

A second concern, it seems to me, is while the hallmarks of language Berkeley outlines are necessary conditions for a language, they may not be sufficient. The fact that there is neither necessary connection nor resemblance between visible and tangible ideas, for example, does not show the relation is semantic in nature. Moreover, it does not seem right that the sheer fact that visible ideas can help us negotiate the tangible is enough to establish the relation is semantic. Nor do the features of general applicability, structure, or combinability. Nor do these features when taken altogether. What is further required is that this system be used *intentionally* by minds in order to communicate information, direct action, and so forth. Yet, this is not something that Berkeley can assume from the beginning. Rather, this is supposed to be the conclusion of the argument. For the difficulty is that this is not a language with which we are well familiar (and which human spirits use to communicate). Instead, the only one to use this language to communicate is God. Consequently, it seems necessary to first assume that God uses the system intentionally in order to establish that it is a language.

In order to see this concern more sharply, consider the possibility that such correlations between our tangible and visible ideas developed as a consequence of natural selection. The constant correlation serves an adaptive function which enables us to negotiate and survive in the world. Thus, the fact visible ideas provide information about tangible ideas and thereby direct our behavior doesn't require a Governor as part of the explanation. And certainly the further fact that the relation between tangible and visible ideas involves neither resemblance nor necessary connection, nor the fact that visible ideas have structure and can be combined in regular ways to communicate information about tangible ideas suffices to establish that a Great Communicator is required. Of course, this appeal to the biological notion of natural selection as an objection to Berkeley may be fairly described as anachronistic. However, it still points to the insufficiency of the three hallmarks. This means that Berkeley's claim that the visual system he describes is a language can now only be defended (at best) as an inference to the best explanation.

If the first Causal Argument Berkeley provides is successful, then he can independently establish the intentionality involved in the production of sensible ideas. As a consequence, this argument from the Divine Language would now be dependent upon his idealistic and materialistic conception of the universe—and it is clear that his deployment of the Divine Language Argument in *Alciphron* is not intended to be dependent upon Berkeleian metaphysics.

SECTION FOUR: EVERYDAY ITEMS
IN THE DIVINE LANGUAGE

Heterogeneity Theses

Before I conclude this chapter, I want to briefly examine some consequences of Berkeley's Theory of Vision with respect to his account of everyday items. As I argued earlier, the variability of the visible magnitude with respect to tangible magnitude, undermines the view that one immediately$_w$ perceives (by sight) the thing that exists at a distance. In *Alciphron*, Euphranor avers, "Is it not plain, therefore, that neither the castle, the planet, nor the cloud, which you see here, are those real ones which you suppose exist at a distance?" (*ALC* IV §9). However, this consequence raises the problem that the content of vision is "restricted" to the representational content alone, suggesting we perceive nothing but false appearances. Alciphron raises this worry: "What am I to think then? Do we see anything at all, or is it altogether fancy and illusion?"

Euphranor's answer to this is important: He claims colors (and lights) are the *proper* immediate objects of sight, denying that items at a distance *are*. Instead, the latter are supposed to be perceived only mediately by sight. The response is helpful in two ways. First, if we immediately perceive only colors by sight, then we can't be said to have a kind of false idea of extension, shape, and so forth represented to us by vision. For the proper and immediate content of vision is only color (and light). Second, nonetheless we can be said to accurately see the object itself at distance. We do so, however, not by means of resemblance but by means of what is tantamount to an optic language.

Part of the view, fully developed in the *Essay,* is that there are no ideas (such as extension, figure, and motion) common to both senses. Not only is it not the case that one immediately sees and touches the numerically same extension (and so forth) owing to relativity considerations, the visible extensions and the tangible extensions are of two entirely different types or species. This two-fold denial has been called the "The Heterogeneity Thesis": Berkeley's arguments in favor of this thesis are highly controversial in the literature.[5] However, the denial of numerical identity already follows from the claim that one does not immediately see the (numerically) same thing that one immediately touches which is itself driven by a failure in resemblance.

This second, more extreme claim, says visible extension (and so forth) and tangible extension (and so forth) comprise entirely different species or kinds. This thesis is important in answering an Alciphron-style concern that we see nothing at all—that it is all fancy and illusion. If the visible extension (and so forth) is of the same kind as the tangible extension (and so forth), then it seems we perpetually immediately see the *wrong* extension: The small visible magnitude we immediately perceive in perceiving the distant tower is an erroneous representation of the true (tangible) magnitude of the tower. If, however, the visible extension (and so forth) are of an entirely different species, then this concern does not appear to arise. To suppose one immediately perceives the wrong (visible) extension, presupposes that visible extension and tangible extension belong to the same kind of thing.

In order to defend the thesis that visible extension (and so forth) and tangible extension (and so forth) are of two distinct species, Berkeley begins by alleging that those who maintain they are of the same kind presuppose abstract ideas. In particular, they suppose that extension (and so forth) can be stripped of its sensible qualities to yield a conception of extension in general. Berkeley sees this as an illicit form of abstraction (from particular to general) and rejects it accordingly. Berkeley then provides several considerations in favor of the view that visible and tangible extension (and so forth) are of distinct species. To see his point, we consider only the following.

According to the Likeness Principle, a color can resemble nothing but a color, a sound can resemble nothing but a sound. Berkeley's point is that the proper objects of vision and touch comprise two distinct species because there are discrete relations of similitude (looking the same, feeling the same). Now Berkeley rejects the Lockean view that ideas of extension (and so forth) are common to both senses: Such a view involves an illicit abstract consideration of the primary properties to the exclusion of the secondary ones. Instead, extension which comes in through sight cannot be mentally considered without color, and extension which comes in through touch cannot even be mentally considered without properties such as hard, soft, etc. Since visible extension is inextricably blended with color, it must *look like something*, and since tangible extension is blended with sensations of touch, it must *feel like something*. They therefore belong to two difference species (i.e., relations of similitude). Indeed, given the incapacity to "mentally funnel" color must be included in the very semantic content of "extension" as it is applied in either the case of vision, but not in the case of touch. If so, it would seem the term "extension" has different semantic content when it is applied in the two cases and so is nonunivocal.

As a consequence of the fact that visible and tangible ideas belong to entirely different species, Berkeley can show why the immediate perception of variable visible extensions does not reduce to the mere experience of false representations of the actual tangible extension. Instead, one immediately perceives only colors (and light), which having a visible extension do not have extension in the same sense that tangible ideas do.

The apparent problem now, however, is that if one immediately sees only colors (and light), then when an oar appears bent in water, one does not misperceive the (visible) oar. Berkeley's answer is that while one does *not* misperceive anything immediately, one makes mistaken judgments about what one would tangibly experience in grasping the oar, or what one would see once it was removed from the water. Berkeley's account, more strongly, allows not only for mistaken judgment, but also misperception itself (when taken *mediately*). For in seeing the bent oar in water, the visible idea will suggest to the imagination certain (incorrect) ideas of tangible qualities. They are the wrong tangible qualities (of a bent oar) insofar as when one actually makes the appropriate bodily motions, one experiences quite different tangible ideas (of a straight oar).

The Collections Thesis

One of the most disconcerting Berkeleian theses is that, strictly speaking, we never see and touch the same thing. This seems to fly wildly in the face of common sense. However, some caution is required. Berkeley's point is that proper and immediate objects of sight are colors, while the proper and immediate objects of touch are hard, soft, hot, and cold objects. This leaves it open so that we can mediately see and touch the same everyday item (i.e., collection of sensible qualities). For example, while we immediately see only various colors, given the right experience, we may mediately perceive a table (of a particular tangible size, shape, and situation). Again, while we may only immediately touch objects such as hard or soft, given the right experience, we may mediately perceive a table (which has a brown color). Consequently, while we cannot immediately see and touch the same object, we can nonetheless mediately see and touch the same object (which is nothing but a collection of various ideas that are visible, tangible, audible, odorous, etc).[6]

One difficulty with this view, however, is that it seems to make Berkeley depart from common sense in an important way.[7] Recall Berkeley explicitly accepts a core tenet of the vulgar, namely that we immediately sense-perceive the real things. If so, it seems to follow from this account of perception that everyday items (such as rocks and trees) are *not* real things

Another difficulty with this reading, however, is that there are several passages (especially in the *Three Dialogues*) where Berkeley alleges that everyday items themselves are *immediately* perceived. Consider the following:

> Wood, stones, fire, water, flesh, iron, and the like things, which I name and discourse of, are things that I know. And I should not have known them, but that I perceived them by my senses; and things perceived by the senses are immediately perceived; and things immediately perceived are ideas. (*3D* III 230)

How should such passages be accommodated? One view is that when Berkeley claims everyday items are immediately perceived, he is only "speaking with the vulgar." However, this view surely places Berkeley at odds with common sense.[8] Another view is that, according to Berkeley, we *do* immediately perceive everyday items as well as sensible things such as colors, sounds, and heat. If everyday items are nothing but a collection of various sensible things, then in immediately perceiving one of those sensible things one immediately perceives what is a constituent of the everyday item. In doing so, one immediately perceives the everyday item itself. The thought is that just as one can immediately perceive a physical item (such as a television set) without perceiving *all of it* (i.e., its front, back, sides, top, bottom, insides), so too one can immediately perceive everyday items by merely immediately perceiving various constituents thereof.[9]

Although this interpretation is attractive because it has Berkeley agree more deeply with a commonsense view, it also runs into some exegetical difficulties. In raising the worry that one merely has visual appearances which fail to represent that actual (tangible) object at a distance, as we have seen, Berkeley's response is that the proper objects of sight are light and colors, which mediately suggest to us the objects at a distance.

To be sure, one may point out that this denial only concerns the *proper* immediate objects of sight and therefore leaves open the possibility that everyday items are nonetheless immediately seen.

The difficulty with this response, however, is that it does not make good sense of the exchange between Euphranor and Alciphron. Euphranor is not merely claiming that proper objects of touch can only be mediately perceived by vision. Rather, he seems to be claiming (more strongly) that the (tangible) rock can only be mediately perceived by vision. Alciphron says, "I see, therefore, in strict philosophical truth, that rock only in the same sense that I may be said to hear it, when the word *rock* is pronounced" (*ALC* IV §11).

Moreover, in raising the worry that one merely has visual appearances which fail to represent the tangible objects at a distance, as we have seen, Berkeley's response is that the proper objects of sight are light and colors, which mediately suggest to us the objects at a distance. Yet if Berkeley allows that one can immediately see the everyday item, he still must deny that it is immediately seen at a distance. But then, the visual appearance of the item is, in an important way, a misrepresentation of the reality of the everyday item. So the issues on this tricky question are far from clear.

They are further complicated by Berkeley's surprising suggestion that there are actually *two* rocks, the tangible one and the visible one which represents it. This way of speaking can also be found in Berkeley's *Essay* where he distinguishes between the visible and tangible moon (*NTV* § 47) as well as the visible and tangible earth (*NTV* §111). On the face of it, this seems to completely undermine the Collections Thesis which says that everyday items are collections of sensible things (united under one term). For this distinction between the tangible and visible moon would mean that actually there is a kind of homonymy or equivocation contained in the term used to designate an everyday item. Rather than one everyday item, there would be at least *two*.

That said, this odd tension may very well suggest a solution to the question whether everyday items are immediately perceived or not. For it would appear that the tangible everyday item *is* immediately felt, while the visible everyday item *is* immediately seen. As it stands, of course, one could not immediately perceive *the same* everyday item. Instead, one could only be said to *mediately* perceive the same item (insofar as one could mediately see the tangible item and mediately feel the visible item).

The consequence of this view is that while everyday items *can* be immediately perceived (strictly speaking) this by itself does not yield the stronger view that one can immediately perceive one and the same everyday items through multiple sensory modalities. Rather, one immediately perceives distinct items (the visible rock, the tangible rock, etc.), and can only *mediately* perceive the same item through multiple modalities. This means that there can very well be an equivocation concealed in the terms which apply to everyday items. The term "tree" can refer to the visible appearance of a tree, and it can refer to the tangible appearance of one. Of course, this may be largely irrelevant to the vulgar, however, who use terms "merely for conveniency and dispatch in the common actions of life" (*3D* III 247). This is to say that the concealed disunity of the everyday item may be irrelevant to the vulgar who use the term only to negotiate the world effectively.

CHAPTER EIGHT

DIVINE PERCEPTION

Reading: *3D* III

In the previous chapter, I showed how Berkeley defends the existence of a community of spirits. Human spirits are in a communicative relation with each other and with God who directs their actions and sustains their interactions. Yet in attempting to move beyond basic idealism, by defending the existence of this interactive structure, Berkeley needs to say more about the sensible ideas which constitute half the population of the world. If Berkeley truly wishes to preserve some semblance of common sense, he needs tell a story about how sensible things can help constitute a legitimately objective world. To put it crudely, he needs to put the flesh and the muscle on the skeletal structure.

In this chapter, I examine some of the core issues surrounding the issues of publicity. One of my goals is to show the powerful motivation behind an important reading of Berkeley (namely that he is a phenomenalist), while finding both reason and strategy for resisting it in favor of a closely related view. I proceed with Berkeley's argument(s) for the existence of God in the *Three Dialogues* and then examine several issues concerning divine publicity. Before I proceed, however, I want to briefly introduce the phenomenalist reading of Berkeley.

PHENOMENALISM AND IDEALISM[1]

The distinction between a phenomenalist and an idealist reading of Berkeley's philosophy can be drawn by considering the question how (what I shall somewhat inaccurately call) "unperceived sensible things" and "unperceived everyday items" can exist when no human spirit perceives them. The traditional idealist answer is that they really aren't unperceived at all: they continue to exist in God's mind.

Unfortunately, there are difficulties concerning the view that the sensible things perceived by us are likewise perceived by God (either because God perceives numerically the same idea or because he at least perceives something similar). One of the central difficulties, as we shall see, is that God's ideas seem so different from ours it is hard to see how there could be any resemblance, never mind an identity. Such considerations have tempted some commentators to adopt a phenomenalist reading of Berkeley.

In this view, the existence of unperceived items is explained, not by *identifying* the item with ideas in God's mind, but by appealing to counterfactual statements about what a human spirit *would* perceive under certain circumstances. For example, to say the table exists in the room is to say a human spirit *would* perceive the table *were* she actually in the room. Such statements can be grounded in facts about the various sensible ideas one would experience under certain circumstances. Aside from avoiding some serious difficulties with Berkeley's account, this interpretation has the benefit of linking Berkeley to a fairly historically reputable and important philosophical theory that has often been endorsed when representational realism has seemed to fail.

The obvious difficulty with this interpretation of Berkeley, however, is that it runs in the face of Berkeley's dictum *esse* is *percipi*. It appears one has to expand the principle to allow for mere possible perception: *esse* is *percipi aut posse percipi.* Yet this is not Berkeley's view. In order to ground the possibility of perception, therefore, one needs to appeal to an *actually* perceived idea, not an object of possible perception.

Yet there are more sophisticated versions of phenomenalism. Winkler has argued that Berkeley accepts "the denial of blind agency." In this view, in order for a mind to cause anything, the mind must know what it is doing and have some idea of the intended effect connected with its will. Given this, a divine idea will always be involved in God's volitions. Consequently, one can accommodate unperceived entities in terms of counterfactual statements about God's will, while allowing this accompanying idea to defeat the preceding concerns.[2]

What remains important in a phenomenalist reading, however, is that unperceived entities *not be identified* with God's ideas.[3]

SECTION ONE: ARGUMENTS FOR THE EXISTENCE OF GOD

In the *Dialogues*, Berkeley again offers the Argument from Causation in order to defend the existence of God. However, he also provides a new argument which we can call the Argument from Perception.[4] It runs as follows:

The Argument from Perception

1. Sensible things cannot exist unperceived.
2. Sensible things exist independently of my perception of them.
3. So, there must be some other spirits which perceive my sensible ideas.
4. This spirit is God.

The first claim in this argument depends upon Philonous' arguments in the First Dialogue that sensible things are mind-dependent. However, it is an interesting question how Berkeley thinks he can defend the second premise. It has been traditionally connected to a concern about Berkeley's position, namely the problem of intermittent existence: If objects of sense-perception are nothing but subjective-objects, it would seem that they disappear whenever one stops perceiving them. In such a view, the tree would not make a sound in the forest if there was nobody around to hear, since the tree itself wouldn't exist then.

One way Berkeley appears to avoid this problem, is to conclude that God perceives sensible things when we do not. Thus, the tree is kept in existence because God himself perceives it. In such a view, the second premise (sensible things can exist without being perceived by me) is either identified with or derived from the commonsensical view that sensible things do not disappear just because one stops perceiving them. There are a couple of difficulties with the reading.

One obvious concern is that trotting out God to save the day seems entirely *ad hoc*. Berkeley seems to be unfairly transforming a problem within his system, into a novel argument for the existence of God. In fairness to Berkeley, however, it is worth noting that if sensible things cannot exist unperceived, then we seem to be faced with the following dilemma: Either we fly wildly in the face of common sense by denying sensible things exist when one does not perceive them, or else we abide by common sense and conclude the existence of some other mind which keeps them in existence when we do not. Given the existence of God is a relatively common belief, it is more reasonable to believe it than to deny that sensible things exist when we don't perceive them.

Yet the feeling of the "ad hoc" does not dissipate quickly. Nor does such a view really give a good rational basis for believing in the intermittent existence of sensible things. While it may be commonsensical, this belief *could* be false (as commonsense beliefs sometimes are). Notably then, Berkeley does not seem to appeal to the actual intermittent existence of sensible things in order to conclude the existence of God (via the principle that sensible things can't exist unperceived). Instead, he insists one can know *by experience* that sensible things exist independently of one's own perception of them. In order to defend this view, he appeals to the premise that one is not the cause of one's sensible ideas and concludes from this that they exist independently of one's perception of them. The difficulty, however, is that the inference is dubious. Why should the causal independence of one's sensible ideas lead to the view that they are perceptual independent?[5]

One way to answer this problem is to see Berkeley as already accepting the following two assumptions: (1) Only spirits can cause ideas; (2) If a spirit causes an idea, then that idea is perceived by that spirit (i.e., a spirit always perceives the idea it causes).[6] The first claim is defended by Berkeley later in the Second Dialogue and also in the *Principles* (as we saw last chapter). The second claim derives from the view that in causing something, spirits have an idea of that thing they are causing. This has been called "the denial of blind agency." If it's true that I am not the cause of my sensible ideas, then some other spirit must cause them. But if some other spirit causes them, then they can exist unperceived by me (i.e., they can exist "without my mind").

While this does successfully establish the premise that sensible things can exist independently of my perception of them, however, it does so only by preempting what is distinctive about the Perception Argument. This argument purports to rely heavily on Berkeley's claim that sensible thing are mind-dependent ideas. Berkeley concludes the existence of some other mind (God) because sensible things exist without being perceived by me and because they cannot exist unless perceived by some mind or other. Yet in the proposed solution, the former is shown in such a way that appeals to the Causal Argument, making any reliance on the latter unnecessary, thereby diverting the Perception Argument into the Causal Argument.

While this worry about the diversion of the Perception Argument into the Causal Argument does not necessarily defeat an idealist reading of Berkeley, it certainly helps pave the way for a phenomenalist one. The structure of the Perception Argument requires an idealist position that the "unperceived" sensible things are ideas (which must be perceived to exist). The continued existence of these ideas thereby argues for another perceiver. Yet, it seems that the only basis for assuming the intermittent existence of sensible things is the Causal Argument itself which effectively bypasses the need to appeal to "unperceived" ideas in the first place. Hence, room is opened up for a phenomenalist reading of Berkeley.

SECTION TWO: THE PROBLEM OF PAIN

Berkeley objects to the modern view that the world does not resemble how it seems to us. He has Philonous explain at length how beautiful the world seems to be and deride the view that such scenes are not real. If God's perception of sensible things is supposed to secure their independence of any one human spirit's perception of them, then it would seem that what God perceives had better, in the very least, *resemble* what we ourselves perceive.

One way to understand this is to see Berkeley as offering a kind of replacement of the Aristotelian theory. In this view, something like the quality orange exists in a cat as an accident, and it exists in the soul as the sensible species: there is a resemblance between the accident and the sensible species. In Berkeley's view, it should seem that the orange exists in the mind of God and also exists in the mind of human sentient: There should be a resemblance between what God perceives and what the human perceives. Otherwise, it is hard to see how Berkeley can claim that the world is how it seems to us.

There is however, a serious difficulty with Berkeley's position. Later in the Third Dialogue, under pressure from Hylas, Philonous claims that God cannot suffer pain (and cannot experience pleasure, either) (*3D* III 240–41). To suffer pain (and to experience any passion whatever) is, in Philonous' view, an indication of imperfection; but God is perfect. Alas, the Pain Argument, a pillar of Berkeley's argument for the Ideality Thesis, hinges on the claim that intense heat simply *is* a pain (and warmth simply *is* a pleasure). How, then, can God perceive intense heat? How can it exist in his mind? Indeed, how can what God perceives so much as resemble what we sense-perceive given that many of our objects of sense-perception are pleasures and pains?

One answer to this problem is to adopt a phenomenalist reading of Berkeley.[7] In such a view, while God's idea may be involved in his willfully producing various sensations in us, there is no reason to require any resemblance. Rather, claims about the existence of sensible things independent of human perception of them simply reduce to counterfactual claims what one would sense-perceive under certain conditions. For example, independently of human perception, there is nothing resembling what we perceive when we perceive a table. Rather, to say this table exists unperceived (by us) in the room is to make a claim about what we would perceive were we to enter the room. Such an account is grounded in an appeal to God's will, and while requiring the existence of divine ideas, does not require anything resembling what we ourselves perceive.

One concern is that this does not stay true to the spirit of Berkeley's philosophy. If Berkeley is trying to preserve the commonsense view against the modern philosophers that the world is how it appears to us, then the preceding account does not accomplish this. At best, it preserves an account very similar to that of Locke's power theory. While there is nothing resembling our perception of secondary qualities existing in the entities themselves, there are independent powers to produce those sensations in us. To be sure, in Berkeley's view the ideas of God are implicated in this account. However, since they do not resemble our own, they do very little work in the overall account. It seems odd, therefore, that Philonous makes such a speech about how it is a departure from common sense to deny the reality of sensible things, if it should turn out that even in his own view nothing even resembling our own sensations exists independently of human perception.

There is an even stronger argument against this claim of nonresemblance. According to Berkeley, we understand other spirits by looking to ourselves. Because we have an immediate consciousness of our own existence, we can use this to conceptualize other minds.

According to Berkeley, this is how we conceptualize God's mind as well. Similarly, according to Berkeley, we understand the ideas of other minds by looking to our own ideas as models thereof. Consequently, it seems that in order to conceptualize God's idea we must use our own. But then it seems that in order to conceptualize them *at all* we must conceptualize them as resemblances of our own. But if so, we *must* understand them as resemblances. But if so, how can God perceive ideas which resemble our own when he does not experience pain or pleasure?

There is, I think, a powerful solution to this dilemma which can preserve the view that what God perceives does resemble what human beings perceive. According to Berkeley, the ideas that we produce in the imagination can resemble the ideas that we receive by sensation. Yet the ideas we produce in the imagination do not involve pain or pleasure. There is a great difference between imagining burning agony and actually experiencing it. And there is a great difference between imagining a glorious pleasure and actually experiencing it. The latter may involve anticipation, but it does not constitute the pleasure itself. Otherwise simply *imagining* the taste of chocolate would alone suffice. Given that Berkeley allows this, however, it seems while the content of imagination and sensation can be the same, whether there is an actual experience of pain/pleasure depends. Upon *what* does it depend?

As I explained in the previous chapter, there are three key types of differences between ideas of sensation and imagination. One is that while ideas of sense are strong and vivid, ideas of imagination are weak and faint. Another is that ideas of sense hang together in a way that is far more coherent than that of imagination. A final difference is that while ideas of sensation are caused from without, we ourselves cause our own ideas of imagination. The first difference plausibly explains why imagining intense heat does not hurt while experiencing it does. In such a view, whether there is pain/pleasure depends upon the strength and vivacity of the idea. However, it is implausible to suppose that God's own ideas are faint and weak. Indeed, Berkeley takes this contrast between weak and faint ideas of imagination with strong and vivid ideas of sense to indicate a difference between the relative powers of a human spirit and God. In this view, since God's own ideas must be conceived as strong and vivid, we would have to conceive of him as susceptible to pain and pleasure anyway. The distinction doesn't help.

The second distinction does not concern any specific idea itself so much as the relationships among a network of ideas. Consequently it does not seem a plausible way to distinguish imagined pains (which do not hurt) from experienced pains (which do). The last distinction, however, does seem viable. It is doubtful that one could ever come to experience an intense burning sensation simply through vividly imagining it. Such an account has the advantage of explaining why God never could experience pain or pleasure: God never passively perceives ideas caused by another spirit; he is always active in his perception and hence never undergoes pleasure or pain.

This appears to be Berkeley's own preferred position. He has Philonous respond to Hylas' objection that if sensible things exist independently of human perceivers, then God must experience pain and pleasure:

> We who are limited and dependent spirits are liable to impressions of sense, the effects of an external agent, which being produced against our wills, are sometimes painful and uneasy. But God, whom no external being can affect . . . can suffer nothing, nor be affected with any painful sensation, or indeed any sensation at all. (*3D* III 240–41)

This reading leads to an important result.[8] We must distinguish between pain/pleasure as a state which one is in and pain/pleasure as the content of immediate perception (i.e., as a subjective-object). In this view, one can perceive a painful or pleasant subjective-object without it being the case that one is actually in a state of pain/pleasure. Just as humans may imagine a painful or pleasant subjective-object without experiencing it, so God may perceive it without thereby experiencing pain/pleasure. In this view, to be in the state of pain is to perceive the painful subjective-object *passively*, to be in pleasure is to perceive the pleasant subjective-object *passively*. Thus there is *more* to a pain (or pleasure) than the subjective-object itself: The painful subjective-object doesn't *actually* hurt unless it is perceived in this special way. The painful subjective-object itself should therefore not be viewed as an actual pain unless it is passively perceived.

This seems to be at odds with Berkeley's TPA—which yields the *identification* of intense heat with pain. But it is not, however. Recall that the important consequence of TPA is that the immediate perception of intense heat is all one with the immediate perception of pain.

As a result, the perception thereof turns out to be "sticky" since the pain/heat is nothing but a variable element of essential consciousness. *This* is the key point that Berkeley seeks to establish. And this solution to the pain/pleasure problem does not undermine that point.

SECTION THREE: PRIVACY AND PUBLICITY: THE PROBLEMS

By allowing that what God perceives resembles what human spirits perceive, Berkeley can allow for the commonsense view that the world as it appears to humans mirrors how it really is. The deeper question, however, is whether Berkeley adopts a position that squares with the vulgar or with the Aristotelians.

At first, it seems that Berkeley must accept a view more akin to the latter. Recall that in the Aristotelian account of sense-perception, the sensible accident (such as orange) causes a resembling sensible species to be received in the soul. While in one way the accident and the species are numerically distinct (individuated by the distinct substances in which they inhere), in another way the sensible quality is one and the same (existing in the two substances in different ways).

Given that for Berkeley, we only immediately perceive our variable elements of consciousness, it would seem that what any one human spirit perceives (and what God himself perceives) are numerically distinct ideas. If so, while what one perceives and what God perceives are qualitatively alike, they are numerically distinct.[9] To be sure, Berkeley *does* say what one immediately sense-perceives exists independently of one's own perception of it. But the majority opinion in Berkeley scholarship is that rather than taking this as a claim about numerically one idea existing in both one's mind and God's, Berkeley may be "speaking with the vulgar." Perhaps the mere resemblance between two numerically distinct ideas is sufficient to capture the vulgar insight.

Alas, accepting this view appears to commit Berkeley to intractable difficulties. Given that Berkeley endorses the Ideality Thesis that we immediately$_s$ sense-perceive *our own* ideas, he cannot allow for a modified direct realist view according to which we immediately$_w$ sense-perceive God's ideas in receiving our own. Consequently, if there is any perception at all of God's ideas, it must be "mediate." This leads Berkeley to a form of indirect (representational) realism. He has to say that we only indirectly perceive the real things (God's ideas). And this runs contrary to his endorsement of the vulgar view that we immediately$_S$ sense-perceive the real things! If, by contrast, he allows that we do immediately$_S$ sense-perceive the real things, then whatever God's ideas turn out to be, they are not "the real things" and their very role in Berkeley's system remains unclear.[10]

An alternative reading is to have Berkeley agree with common sense in a far deeper way. According to a minority opinion in Berkeley scholarship, Berkeley holds that God and human spirit can perceive numerically identical ideas. Indeed, it appears possible that multiple human spirits can perceive numerically one and the same idea. In this view, ideas are not numerically individuated per perceiver; and the sensible ideas perceived by us can exist independently of any one human spirit. While the view is a radical departure from the majority opinion, it does allow Berkeley to square with common sense in a much deeper way. For rather than ultimately rejecting the view of a public reality (immediately perceived by humans) and attempting to "speak with the vulgar" at a superficial level, Berkeley is literally endorsing the view that the objects of immediate$_S$ sense-perception are publicly available.

A serious concern about this reading, of course, is how Berkeley can make sense of the notion of ideas that can exist in the mind of more than one perceiver. At this point, I want to merely show that Berkeley does, at least, *allow* for this as a possibility. Consider this rehearsal of his Perception Argument:

> It is evident that the things I perceive are my own ideas, and that no idea can exist unless it be in a mind. Nor is it less plain that these ideas or things by me perceived, either themselves or their archetypes, exist independently of my mind, since I know myself not to be their author. . . . They must therefore exist in some other mind, whose will it is they should be exhibited to me. (*3D* III 214)

This passage shows Philonous as using "my own ideas" and "these ideas or things by me perceived" as interchangeable. And the pronoun "they" refers back to "my own ideas." Moreover, Philonous explicitly approves of the possibility that the ideas themselves exist independently of his own mind. Consequently, Berkeley explicitly welcomes, minimally, the possibility that our own ideas exist independently of our own perception of them.

One response to this represents Berkeley as insisting only that everyday items exist independently of any human perceiver insofar as each private idea is a member of a public collection which constitutes a public entity, or that public sensible qualities (taken as collection of private ideas) exist independently of individual perception. The difficulty with such an interpretation is that, as we have seen, Berkeley explicitly argues for perceptual independence on the basis of causal independence. *Anything* which is not caused by me, Berkeley argues, can exist unperceived by me. Yet this would seem to apply to the private ideas just as well as anything else.

However, this passage does point to a problem with the minority opinion: Berkeley takes very seriously the view that God's ideas are resemblances ("archetypes") of our own ideas. However, if God perceives numerically the same sensible ideas as any human spirit, then it is very hard to see how we can distinguish between archetype and copy. To be sure, Berkeley doesn't explicitly endorse the archetype view in this passage. Yet he does recognize its *possibility*. And the minority opinion *cannot* accommodate this possibility; it must deny that the archetype option is accepted by Berkeley.

Moreover, while Berkeley does appear to suggest on several occasions that the very sensible ideas we ourselves immediately perceive exist independently of our sense-perception of them, he also recognizes the archetype option at two other important junctures. At the first juncture, Hylas points out that materialists have a genuine archetype (the matter) to which all of our individual ideas are referred. Philonous responds that the same is possible in his own view: God's ideas can serve as the archetypes to which our own ideas have a reference (*3D* III 248). While Berkeley again only recognizes this position as *possible* in his view, refraining from explicitly endorsing it: he clearly takes it seriously as an option.

At the second juncture, Hylas presses Philonous on how he can make sense of the biblical (Mosaic) account of Creation ("A creation of mere ideas?!"); here his response ultimately relies on a distinction between an archetypal (eternal) and ectypal (temporal, natural) "state of things" (*3D* III 234). Given that Berkeley recognizes at least the possibility of the archetype option, and appears to assign it an important role in his theory, the minority account is on dangerous footing. Indeed, it seems that Berkeley wants to recognize *both* the view that the very things that we immediately perceive exist independently of our own mind (in the mind of God) *and* the view that God's ideas are archetypes. The best interpretation therefore, is one that makes good sense of this fact.

Such concerns generate considerable pressure to adopt a phenomenalist reading. This allows Berkeley to say that our own ideas are the real things, assign God's ideas a role in the account (they are the ideational content of God's willful production of our own sensations), while dropping any reference to divine ideas as the sensible things themselves (that exist unperceived by us). Happily, it can allow for "archetypes" in the mind of God (as ideational content of divine willing) while still allowing that what we immediately sense-perceive are the real things. While I think that this view also has its difficulties, I defer discussion of them until the following section. At present, I simply want to sketch out a *nonphenomenalist* response to these preceding difficulties.

SECTION FOUR: PRIVACY AND PUBLICITY: AN INTERPRETATION

To understand my proposed reading, begin with the Aristotelian account of sense-perception. In this view, while the sensible accident (which exists in the entity itself) and the sensible species (which exists in the soul) are numerically distinct, they nonetheless resemble each other. This resemblance is what allows direct perception of the sensible quality itself. In my proposed reading, while Berkeley analogously allows for a resemblance between what a human spirit perceives and what God perceives, he neither claims the ideas are numerically distinct nor claims they are numerically identical. Instead, his view is that beyond the (causally determined) qualitative resemblance between what the human spirit perceives and what God perceives, there is no fact of the matter how to individuate ideas and determine numerical identity or distinctness.[11]

Recall that the word "idea" can be taken as a synonym for "object of immediate perception." This use of "idea" is innocuous. It refers only to the content of perception. Thus, one can substitute "idea" with "that which is immediately perceived" and "my ideas" with "that which is immediately perceived by me." To be sure, for Berkeley immediate perception is nothing but the essential consciousness; immediate perception is "sticky." But the fact that Berkeley requires a radical conception of immediate perception does not prevent Berkeley from using "idea" in this innocuous way. Thus, while we may speak of "that which is immediately perceived" (ideas) and "that which is immediately perceived by me" (my ideas), it also remains true in Berkeley's view that "that which is immediately perceived by me" (and "that which is immediately perceived" more generally) cannot exist unperceived.

Consequently, if that which is immediately perceived by me is qualitatively identical to that which is immediately perceived by God, then it would seem that the content "is the same." What remains unclear is how to bring the question of numerical individuation to bear in this case. And Berkeley has no further ontological resources to answer that question. According to the direct realist, there are numerically discrete vehicles of perception (individuated per perceiver). In Berkeley's view, variable elements of consciousness are no longer viewed as mental states which bear such content. Instead, variable elements are nothing but the *content* of sense-perception itself (i.e., subjective-objects). Consequently this ontological basis for numerical individuation has been abandoned. According to the direct realist, each of the mental states involved in sense-perception represents some external accident which inheres in a material substance. However, in Berkeley's view the contents of sense-perception may no longer be viewed as "so many modes and accidents" which inhere in material substance. This basis for numerical identification has also been abandoned. To be sure, Berkeley does grant that the vulgar may regard such cases of qualitative identity as a stronger numerical identity. But this may only be a common way of speaking.

The issue is complicated, since it seems entirely possible for two human spirits to imagine qualitatively resembling unicorns. It hardly seems this resemblance alone suffices for publicity. One important difference is that in the case of sensible ideas, it is not arbitrary two spirits perceive the same thing. It is not a coincidence that God and a human spirit perceive the same thing (given the former causes the latter to perceive what it does) and it is not a coincidence that two human spirits perceive the same thing when God is causally responsible. By contrast, the fact that two human spirits have the same thought is in many cases entirely arbitrary. Perhaps most importantly, in the latter case but not the former, there are two distinct causes (i.e., the two human spirits). This itself provides a basis for numerical individuation. By contrast, in the case of sense-perception there is only one cause (God) and shared content between God and various human spirits. In such a case, there appears to be no clear ontological basis for further counting how many ideas there are.

Philonous and Hylas discuss the private/public distinction with respect to sensible and imagined ideas and both *accept* the view that the difference between (private) imagined and (public) sensible ideas is fundamentally causal in nature. Hylas says (and Philonous agrees):

> Pray are not the objects perceived by the senses of one, likewise perceivable to others present? If there were an hundred more here, they would all see the garden, the trees, and flowers as I see them. But they are not in the same manner affected with the ideas I frame in my imagination. Does not this make a difference between the former sort of objects and the latter? (*3D* III 246–47)

This suggests that if others *were* affected by ideas framed in one's imagination (at least in the sense that they were caused to perceive "the same thing") then these ideas *would*, like sensible ideas, be public. Consequently, what makes sensible ideas public in Berkeley's view is the fact there is a shared, single causal source and multiple perceivers with resembling ideas all affected by that agent.

In this way, the private/public distinction is very much related to the appearance/reality distinction. Both are grounded in the Laws of Nature. Imagined ideas are mere thoughts because they are faint, weak, and unregulated by the Laws of Nature. They are also private because they have no impact upon other minds. Likewise one's own bodily motions (i.e., internal kinesthetic ideas), although real, are private since they have no impact upon other minds (except insofar as God causes other minds to experience sensible ideas in coordination with one's movements). Sensible ideas are public, by contrast, because while there is a single causal source (namely God), there are diverse human spirits which receive them.

Such a reading affords a way to accommodate both Berkeley's claim that the very things immediately sense-perceived by me can exist unperceived and his claim that God's ideas are archetypes without appealing to phenomenalism. There is a resemblance between what I perceive (my ideas) and what God perceives (God's ideas), so the latter can constitute the archetypes which my own ideas represent. This causally determined qualitative resemblance is sufficient for the vulgar view that the same idea (that which is perceived) can exist in multiple minds. However, when considered philosophically, there is no fact of the matter how to count ideas in cases of (causally determined) qualitative resemblance. This eliminates the problem whether God's ideas are numerically identical to our own, and therefore eliminates the question that subsequently arises whether God's idea are immediately$_S$ perceived or only "mediately" perceived. If we accept the vulgar view that the same idea can exist in multiple minds, then we can allow that in this sense we immediately$_S$ perceive God's ideas. This is compatible with the view that God's ideas are archetypes, since it is the very (causally determined) resemblance between what God and human spirit perceive that allows the vulgar claim of numerical identity to be made in the first place.

This reading is an entirely different account of Berkeley's relation to the philosophers and the vulgar than both the majority and minority readings. In the majority reading, Berkeley is taken to have deep philosophical views about mental privacy which are at odds with the vulgar views about publicity: He merely "speaks with the vulgar." In the minority view, Berkeley's deep philosophical views about the publicity of ideas are in complete conformity with the vulgar. In this view, Berkeley's deep philosophical position is reflective of his negative philosophical project: There is no fact of the matter how to numerically individuate sensible ideas. Thus, he agrees with the vulgar superficially, while maintaining that any deeper view involves nothing but abstraction.

Arguably, Berkeley explicitly endorses just this position. Hylas presses Philonous on the question how to numerically individuate ideas. He argues:

1. We perceive only the ideas existing in our minds.
2. The same idea cannot exist in more than one mind.
3. So, no two spirits perceive the same thing.

Yet while Philonous accepts (1) he does not accept (2). Philonous says, "If the term *same* be taken in the vulgar acceptation it is certain . . . that different persons may perceive the same thing; or the same thing or idea exist in different minds" (*3D* III 247). He then says "If the term *same* be used in the acceptation of the philosophers, who pretend to an abstracted notion of identity, then, according to their sundry definitions of this notion . . . it may or may not be possible for divers person to perceive the same thing" (*3D* III 247). While Philonous does not explicitly say that the question whether the (philosophically) same idea can exist in more than one mind admits of no factual philosophical answer, it seems reasonable to believe this is his implicit point since he treats the question whether we perceive the same thing as tantamount to the question whether the same idea can exist in different minds. Indeed, in the reading of "idea" as mere "object of perception" the two questions are effectively synonymous. Philonous then goes on to claim that he does not understand the "abstracted idea of identity" (*3D* III 238) and that the debate itself is purely verbal.

However, one concern with this reading, despite its textual support, is that since immediate perception is essential consciousness itself, the variable objects thereof must be private (i.e., must be individuated per conscious perceiver). Pain, for example, is an object of essential consciousness and it is clearly private to the individual. Again, when one willfully produces the imagined idea of a unicorn, the imagined unicorn is private to the individual. Given that sensible things such as heat, colors, and sounds are themselves objects of essential consciousness, it would appear they, too, must be private.

Recall, however, our earlier distinction between *what* one perceives in perceiving pain and the *state* of being in pain. What is generally thought to be inherently private to consciousness are one's own mental states. However, Berkeley does not view variable elements of consciousness as mental states. Instead the *state* of being in pain involves an individual spirit's passive perception of a painful subjective-object. Yet any spirit's passive perception of a subjective-object is individuated per perceiver (and is hence private). Subjective-objects *themselves*, however, are nothing but "that which is immediately perceived" in essential consciousness. But to say that the *content* is public is to say nothing radical. It is to say only that what is immediately perceived by one perceiver has a causally determined resemblance with what is immediately perceived by another. Thus, if one should acquire the ability to share one's idea of a unicorn by simultaneously causing other spirits to passively perceive resembling content, one would have effectively acquired the capacity of telepathy (and to make one's ideas public). However, human spirits do *not* have the capacity to cause other human spirits to perceive their own imagined or kinesthetic ideas. Insofar as only God is capable of causing multiple minds to perceive the same idea, he is the foundation of the public world, just as he is the source of reality.

SECTION FIVE: THE PROBLEM OF TIME

One of the most powerful considerations in favor of a phenomenalist reading of Berkeley is his perplexing treatment of time. According to Berkeley, God's ideas are eternal archetypes, while our ideas are temporal (natural) copies. And for Berkeley, time is fundamentally subjective: It consists in the succession of ideas within the mind of a given finite spirit. Consequently, time may be relative to each individual finite perceiver (Berkeley recognizes the possibility time may flow faster for one spirit and slower for another). God, by contrast, is atemporal insofar as he does not experience a succession of ideas at all. Rather than perceiving successively, he perceives ideas "at once."

One of the first difficulties is this: If what God perceives is eternal, while what we perceive is temporal, how is it possible for divine ideas to resemble our own? One way to motivate this concern is to appeal to Berkeley's own *Dialogues* argument against indirect realism. There he argues: "How then is it possible, that things perpetually fleeting and variable as our ideas, should be copies or images of anything fixed and constant?" (*3D* I 205). Given that God's ideas must be eternally constant, it would seem that our own ideas cannot resemble God's.

Yet Berkeley's claim in this argument against indirect realism needs to be understood within context. He goes on to explain what he means: "Or in other words, since all sensible qualities . . . are continually changing upon every alteration in the distance . . . how can any determinate material objects be properly represented or painted forth by several distinct things, each of which is so different from the rest?" (*3D* I 205–6). The difficulty for the indirect realist is that there are a variety of qualitatively different ideas supposed to be referred to the same material thing (the ideas change depending upon circumstances). How can one and the same permanent thing resemble the many things which do not resemble each other?

This is not a problem which undermines the claim that God's ideas resemble our own. For even if our own ideas are qualitatively different, God can have as many ideas as there are perceivers. This potential variability does not undermine that God can perceive everything that we perceive. Remember that according to Berkeley, the only way to conceptualize what God perceives is to use our own ideas as a model. There is therefore an inevitable requirement that God's ideas be conceptualized as resembling our own.

The difference between our own experience of ideas and God's experience of ideas is that we experience them in succession. God, by contrast, is supposed to perceive them "all at once." Yet the fact God perceives all of his ideas at once, does not preclude those ideas being ordered for him (ordered with respect to their perceptual sequence for human spirits). Why should the fact that for God the ideas are perceived altogether, while for us they are perceive successively undermine the qualitative resemblance between our ideas and God's? It seems possible that even a human can recall a sequence of events at one and the same time, even though she had before experienced those events successively. Why should this undermine the resemblance?

One worry concerns the duration of ideas. Consider that the qualitatively same sound may have a longer or shorter duration. If God is infinite, then perhaps his own ideas have an infinite duration while our own ideas do not last nearly as long. Although God may perceive the sequence of ideas "all at once," all of his ideas in that order may have an infinite duration. This seems to undermine the view there is an *exact* qualitative resemblance between God's ideas and our own since the temporal duration is different. If this is so, it seems to follow that God's ideas are numerically distinct from our own, returning us to the difficulties discussed in the preceding section. Moreover, the problem arises how to conceptualize God's ideas. Is it possible for us to conceive of an idea of infinite duration using merely a finite idea as the basis? A more likely possibility is that his ideas have no duration at all (rather than an infinite one). But even so, there is a difference with respect to duration and all the difficulties discussed above still seem to follow.

Aside from these difficulties concerning resemblance, there are other problems with Berkeley's vexing account of time that may also press toward a phenomenalist reading. Like Descartes, Berkeley maintains that the soul always thinks. However, rather than maintaining the view (powerfully rejected by Locke) that the soul thinks even while we sleep, Berkeley deploys his subjective theory of time: When a soul is sleeping, no time passes for it; so there is no difficulty of its nonthinking existence during sound sleep. Berkeley explains in the *Principles*: "Time therefore being nothing, abstracted from the succession of ideas in our mind, it follows that the duration of any spirit must be estimated by the number of ideas or actions succeeding each other in that same spirit or mind. It is a plain consequence that the soul always thinks." (*PHK* I §98).

Yet this raises problems for an account of the existence of sensible things when one sleeps and before one was born. God's perception of the tree in the quad (while one sleeps) hardly seems to help if God's perception is *atemporal*. One wants to say that the tree continues to exist *in time* during one's sleep. Moreover, if time is relative to the perceiver, it would seem that nothing happens before the perceiver is born (at least, relative to the perceiver). Yet an appeal to the external existence of things in the mind of God hardly seems to help. Berkeley surely needs to allow that things continue to exist while one is asleep and before one was born if he wants to avoid flouting common sense. And he does. Philonous says:

> Now it is plain they [sensible things] have an existence exterior to my mind, since I find them by experience to be independent of it. There is therefore some other mind wherein they exist, during the intervals between the times of my perceiving them: as likewise they did before my birth, and would do after my supposed annihilation. (*3D* II 230–31 my insert)

All of these considerations make a phenomenalist account tempting. Aside from avoiding the problem of resemblance between God's ideas and our own, it also provides a uniform account of the existence of sensible things in case one does not perceive them: One provides counterfactual statements about what one would perceive (or would have perceived) under certain circumstances. For example, to say the tree exists in the quad (while one is sound asleep) is simply to say that had one been awake, standing in the quad, one would have perceived the tree. To say a tree came into existence during the Creation of the World, is to say that had one attended the Creation, one would have perceived the tree become perceivable. Indeed, Berkeley himself seems to provide just this analysis. Philonous says:

> Why, I imagine that if I had been present at the Creation, I should have seen things produce into being; that is become perceptible, in the order described by the sacred historian. (*3D* III 251)

More generally, in distinguishing between the eternal and tempo-ral existence of things, Philonous claims that with respect to the latter, things have a *relative* and *hypothetical* existence. Something comes into temporal existence when God decrees it should become perceptible (to humans) and ceases its temporal existence once it becomes imperceptible to us again (*3D* III 252).

Related to this passage is *another* concern which seems to press in favor of phenomenalism: Not all of God's ideas are real (or created) for us. Presumably, there are many ideas which God perceives which he does not decree that human spirits perceive. As a consequence, it is *not enough* for an idea to exist temporally that it be perceived by God. Something *more* is required. In particular, what seems to be required is an appeal to God's will and his causal efficacy.[12]

Yet there is also a difficulty lurking here which afflicts this phe-nomenalist account. Recall that the phenomenalist reading hinges on denying that God's ideas (and collections thereof) are to be identified with the things themselves. Instead, divine ideas are involved only insofar as God's will is concerned. However, the preceding objection suggests that it is possible that we *can* conceive of the things that God *might* have created (but didn't) such as a three-headed purple dog (to borrow and modify an example).[13] If God knows everything, then he knows this and so even possible objects (like three-headed purple dogs) exist in his mind. But how are we supposed to make sense of this in a phenomenalist reading?

The obvious answer is to simply use our own imagination of a three-headed purple dog to understand what exists in God's mind. In such a view, to say a three-headed purple dog exists in God's mind is just to say the idea of such a dog exists there. But, then, why not say that the things we *do* perceive (such as normal dogs) likewise exist in God's mind as ideas? In such a view, however, one has *identified* the everyday items with ideas in God's mind, and hence rejected phe-nomenalism. The only possibility is to account for the three-headed purple dog in God's mind *only* in terms of counterfactual statements about what human spirits would perceive, had God created such dogs by making them perceptible to us.

However, while items like three-headed purple dogs can exist in God's understanding, they are *not* determined by his will with respect to us (i.e., he does not cause them to be perceived by us under such and such circumstances). According to Berkeley, the sensible things that we perceive are made perceptible to *us by decree*. And the three-headed purple dog, by hypothesis, is not involved in such decrees. Consequently, it is hard to see how this possible object can be given an adequate counterfactual analysis. Given that it is not perceptible to us *at all*, there will be no counterfactual statements about what we would perceive were we to meet certain appropriate conditions.

A defender of the phenomenalist interpretation may attempt to extend the account by appealing to further counterfactual claims (about what would have been perceptible to us had God issued certain decrees), but now the account becomes a little bit too messy and its attraction starts to fade. It seems far simpler to say that we can conceive of the three-headed purple dog existing in God's mind. But if so, we have identified it with God's ideas (rather than appealing only to counterfactual claims about our own ideas).

The difference between fantastic ideas like this and the ideas that are perceptible to us in time is that while the former have not been made perceptible to us by decree, ideas of normal dogs (by contrast) have been made so perceptible. While phenomenalism is thereby officially rejected, the phenomenalist point has been well taken that more is required for an item's existence than God's sheer perception of it: Not only must it be perceived by God, it must be decreed by God to exist. In such a view, however, the things that exist independently of us are *nonetheless to be identified with God's own ideas* and so the phenomenalist reading has been rejected.

How, then, can we answer the concerns about time that press us toward a phenomenalist reading? Begin by contrasting two different accounts of Berkeley's claim that the speed of time can vary relative to the perceiver. In the first view, ideas are conceptualized like frames of a moving picture. Time moves faster when the frames move by faster (the wheel on the projector speeds up). Here, the speed of time is measured in terms of the number of ideas (frames) per minute. The problem, of course, is that such an account appears circular: One cannot appeal to time as a measure of the speed of time.

In the second view, the duration of any idea is measured in terms of the number of changes in other ideas that occur simultaneously with it. For example, suppose that two people witness an attempted murder where the victim screams. The duration of that scream may seem very long to one person and very short to the other. It will seem longer to the first, if there is a greater number of changes (i.e., a greater succession in ideas) which occur simultaneously with the

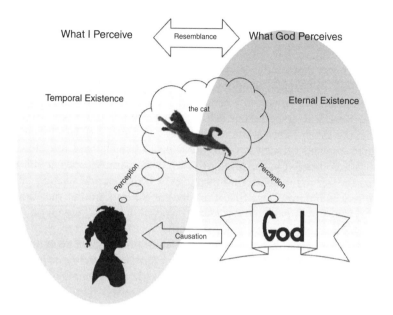

Berkelian Theory

scream. Imagine that the first notices the slow ticking of a clock. She perceives each second change in the spatial position of the hand. The other person does not notice as many changes. For her, the second hand is at 12 at one instant and at 11 the next. Rather than observing 55 changes, she has only observed 1. Since the succession of ideas is less for her, the duration of the scream seems shorter.

Aside from avoiding the problem of circularity, this second account solves the preceding difficulties. First, the duration of a given idea is not intrinsic. Instead, the duration of a given idea is relative to the changes in other ideas which attend it. As a consequence, it is possible for the same idea to have different durations for different perceivers. And the fact that ideas have no duration for God does not undermine the claim that God and human can perceive one and the same idea. There is, therefore, no difficulty conceiving of God's ideas, since they exactly resemble our own. What *is* difficult to conceive is a complete lack of succession in ideas. However, we do have an understanding of relative constancy (through a change in other ideas). While we do not have a complete understanding of absolute constancy, we can understand that is like relative constancy minus the succession.

Moreover, we have a better understanding of what Berkeley means in claiming that time is subjective. Given that we customarily measure time in terms of temporal events (such as the rising and setting of the sun, the movements of a clock hand), we can certainly allow that temporal objects exist before we were born and while we are sleeping. Such items, while ideas in the mind of God, can be measured in terms of such physical occurrences (which are also nothing but ideas ordered in the mind of God). For example, one can allow that the tree in the quad continued to exist while one was sleeping and moreover, acknowledge that it existed for 8 hours during that time. This is just to appeal to other ideas (involved in the movement on the clock, the rising and setting of the sun).

However, genuine time for Berkeley does not concern such objective measurements. How long an hour or day can seem to one person may be different for another. And the question of genuine temporal passage concerns the number of changes perceived. Thus, while one can acknowledge that certain events occurred before one was born and while one was sleeping, these events have no subjective duration (for one). The events that occur while one is sleeping are "instantaneous."

None of this undermines Berkeley's claim that things acquire a relative or hypothetical existence in time. While this does suggest a counterfactual analysis is involved, this does not yet lead to a phenomenalist reading. The phenomenalist more strongly denies that "unperceived things" are collections of ideas. But it is entirely acceptable to allow that what distinguishes God's idea of mere possible things from his idea of actual things is that the latter (unlike the former) are perceivable to us. And what makes those latter ideas perceivable to us is that they are governed by certain decreed conditionals such that when we act in certain ways, God causes those ideas to exist within us. For example, the tree in the quad is perceivable to me because if I walked into the quad with my eyes open, then I would perceive it.

Such a view allows us to understand how things come into being and pass away. The tree exists at the point in time when it becomes perceivable to humans, and it becomes perceivable once certain counterfactual claims are true. In particular, it exists, when it is true that upon performing certain actions, God will cause any human spirit to perceive it. And it ceases to exist when this is no longer true. For example, a tree comes to exist when it becomes true that upon moving its bodily limbs in certain ways, a human spirit will experience certain tangible ideas.

This means that what gives some of God's ideas a temporal (ectypal) existence for us is that they are governed by the Laws of Nature. Thus, what keeps a sensible thing in temporal existence, unperceived by me, is not merely the fact that God continues to perceive it, but moreover that it is part of a conditional or natural order pertaining to human behavior. More specifically, it exists in time because certain conditionals about human perception are currently in effect. It will cease to exist once those conditions are no longer in force. Thus, the temporal existence of a sensible thing is determined by the Laws of Nature, just as its publicity and reality are likewise determined. Consequently, it is finally not so surprising that Berkeley's Argument for Perception is ultimately grounded in an Argument from Causation. In affirming the premise that sensible things exist independently of my perception of it, I take it that much more is involved than meets the eye: One is effectively affirming the reality, publicity, and temporal existence of the thing. And this, as we have seen, requires grounding in the Laws of Nature.

CHAPTER NINE

THE RETRENCHMENT

Reading: *PHK* I §85–156

We have now considered Berkeley's account of reality and his arguments for this view. In this chapter, I want to examine Berkeley's Retrenchment of the Sciences, as well as returning to the question of philosophy and its (dis)agreement with common sense. Since this is such an important issue for Berkeley, it is imperative to consider in detail the degree to which Berkeley takes his own views to agree with the vulgar, and also to evaluate the degree to which Berkeley actually successfully stays true to common sense.

SECTION ONE: THE RETRENCHMENT

Arithmetic and Geometry

A difficulty that Berkeley must accommodate in rejecting abstract ideas is how universal (scientific) knowledge is possible in his view: It was generally recognized that the sciences concerned *universal* (not particular) truths. How can one know that *all* humans are mortal? What is the *object* of knowledge in this case, if not the universal nature of humanity? Is it necessary that one have knowledge of each and every human being individually?

Berkeley's overall solution is to admit the existence of *general ideas that are not abstract*. Such ideas are not formed by a process of abstraction; rather some particular idea is used as a *sign* to represent *all* other particular ideas of that sort (*PHK* I §16). For example, the idea of John, while particular in itself, can be made a general idea when it functions as a *sign* for all other ideas of particular humans. Insofar as the sciences concern universal truths, the objects of scientific knowledge are nothing but *signs.*

In Berkeley's view, both geometry and arithmetic take signs as their objects. For example, while the idea of some black line is itself particular, it becomes general when used as a sign for all lines. The object of geometrical knowledge is not that one idea of a black line, but rather that idea *qua* general idea (i.e. *qua* sign).

Yet how one can establish a universal truth once and for all? How can one show that Pythagorean Theorem holds of *all* right-angled triangles? Just because one shows that the theorem holds of a single right-angled triangle, it doesn't follow one has shown that the theorem holds for all of them. Berkeley's answer to these questions involves an appeal to discursive consideration. While one uses a particular idea of a triangle in the demonstration (as in a diagram), one only *mentions* those features which are relevant to the proof at hand. When demonstrating something about all triangles, one does not avail oneself of any of the particularities of the triangle used in the diagram. For example, one does not appeal to the fact that the triangle is right-angled in a demonstration about the triangle in general. Thus, Berkeley hopes to show how universal knowledge can be secured without any reliance on abstraction.

Signs fundamentally concern the guiding of action and are effectively *rules* governing human conduct. Knowledge, for Berkeley, then does not consist in a perception of abstract ideas, but involves rather an "apposite choice and skillful management of signs" (*ALC* VII §11). Thus, knowledge of geometry involves general knowledge of sensible extension (tangible extension in particular) taken as signs for each other (and as therefore behavior guiding). As such, mastery of these signs enables one to know how to act around any given tangible extension. In practice this means that the mastery of the signs is tantamount to the capacity to execute, for example, the same proof through the same discursive consideration on all represented extensions. As a consequence, for Berkeley, any departure from the utility of geometry in determining action yields nonsense.

Given Berkeley's views about abstraction and intelligibility, he is led to a very strict position about the divisibility of finite extension. As I mentioned at the beginning of this book, Berkeley is interested in rejecting the widely accepted view that finite quantities of matter are infinitely divisible. In rejecting matter entirely, of course, this problem is solved. However Berkeley more strongly rejects the notion of the infinite divisibility of finite extension as either void of meaning or else a contradiction in terms.

His argument is that extension is nothing but a sensible idea and one cannot perceive any given idea of extension to consist of an infinite number of parts (try it yourself!) (*PHK* I §124). Since there is nothing more to an idea than what is perceived, it cannot have an infinite number of parts. Nor is it possible to break down the idea infinitely through a process of division. Finally, one shall, at some finite point, reach *minimum* ideas which constitute the limits of perceptibility. As a consequence, Berkeley thinks that it is incoherent to suppose that extension is infinitely divisible. If extension is not taken as a sensible idea, then by the intelligibility constraint, it would seem that "extension" is void of meaning. One cannot abstract from the sensible qualities to create a pure notion of extension, Berkeley argues. Instead, one would invariably have to eliminate the sensible idea altogether (*PHK* I §125).

The "mistaken doctrine" of the infinite divisibility of finite extension arises for Berkeley precisely because one confuses the general sign with its particular nature. For example, one confuses a black line of one inch taken as a sign for all lines with the particular black line itself (*PHK* I §126–28). While the actual black line itself may not be divisible into a thousand parts, it stands for all lines—and as a consequence stands for much longer lines, which are themselves capable of division into a thousand parts. One then erroneously treats the black line of one inch (and, inevitably all lines regardless of size) as divisible into a thousand parts. The particular error that finite extensions can be divided infinitely arises, for Berkeley, because it is confused with its function as representing all lines—including lines of infinite length which are indeed divisible into an infinite number of parts.

As with geometry, the objects of arithmetic are signs. However, while natural science is concerned with the divine signs in nature and geometry is concerned with general tangible extension, arithmetic is concerned with signs that are purely of human construction. Thus, while there is an important sense in which both natural science and geometry are about the world, arithmetic as a science is about the signs of human systems of calculation. This is not to say that arithmetic truths do not, for Berkeley, hold of things in the world (such as money and marbles). The issue, rather, is that arithmetic as a pure science is not supposed to concern particular kinds of things (such as money and marbles). But, then, what does it concern?

In the view that Berkeley rejects, numbers are collections of units where our idea of a unit is abstract. For Berkeley, there is no abstract idea of unity. Indeed, number for Berkeley is, like the other primary qualities, entirely relative and mind-dependent: Number is "entirely the creature of the mind" (*PHK* I §12). His argument for this is that we can't count things unless we know what kind of things we are counting. Thus, counting presupposes determining in advance the kind involved; and kinds, for Berkeley, are arbitrarily determined by human terms. Berkeley writes: "We say one book, one page, one line; all these are equally units" (*PHK* I §12).

Instead, Berkeley argues, arithmetic is about the signs themselves used in systems of counting. He points to the development of different counting systems with increasing degrees of efficiency from strokes, to Roman numerals, to the Arabic. Methods were then developed to enable the conversion of signs used to stand for parts of collections into signs for the whole collection. These methods concern the conversion of signs specifically. And general arithmetic truths concern neither particular kinds of thing in the world nor abstract numbers, but rather the signs of the numbering system itself. Commentators have suggested that Berkeley endorses a version of mathematical *formalism* and that, indeed, Berkeley is the first to initiate such a view.[1] And because arithmetic only concerns the signs of a human system which is designed primarily for human practice, Berkeley argues, speculative arithmetic (the study of arithmetic for its own sake, divorced from practice) has no clear purpose. Indeed, insofar as speculative arithmetical claims are abstracted from "all signs, words, and things numbers" (*ALC* VII §5) they are going to be *meaningless*. Knowledge of arithmetical truths concerns not abstract ideas, but rather the "skillful use and management" of signs (*ALC* VII §12).

Natural Science

Berkeley's views on natural science involve the rejection of essences (or natures) as the object of scientific study. The rejected view says that the material substances in nature have essences which determine the properties a thing can gain and lose; the essence determines the powers that the thing has. In this view, essences are cited as the source of change, that by which substances secure their capacity to explain change in the world. In rejecting this view, coupled with his commitment to the view that spirits are the only causes, Berkeley offers a very different vision of natural science.

For Berkeley, the Lockean view (that we are ignorant of the real essences of substances in nature) yields a deplorable form of skepticism. Instead, Berkeley argues that everyday items in nature are nothing but collections of ideas. As a consequence, there is nothing beyond the phenomena (i.e., the regular occurrences of sensible ideas) that might outstrip our capacities to know. Despite this departure from the Lockean position, however, Berkeley is following Locke in pushing toward a new view of natural science; indeed he is radicalizing it.

In the older Aristotelian account that Locke attacks, scientific knowledge is supposed to be a universal understanding of the properties that flow necessarily from various essences. In Locke's view, we cannot attain this type of knowledge. Instead, we can only secure "experimental knowledge"—knowledge that involves observing the phenomena and making categorizations and predictions on the basis of this (*E.* 4.3.26, 556–57). Thus, while one cannot know the real essence of gold (which determines *why* it has all of the properties that it does), one can only, through experimentation, determine various properties the gold *has*. In this way, one can observe regularities among sensible things, but one is not going to be in a position to find necessary connections which allow one to infer from one phenomenon to the other, nor is one going to be able to claim that the observed regularity applies universally.

In Berkeley's view, the very hope for any knowledge of the first type is dispelled. Indeed, in both the *Principles* and the *Dialogues*, Berkeley observes that it is precisely this type of Lockean Ignorance which makes philosophers look ridiculous in the eyes of the world. In addition to rejecting this essence model of natural change, Berkeley identifies the modern mechanistic view that all change in nature is to be accommodated in terms of motion. In the brief *Dialogues* treatment of the Retrenchment of the Sciences, he points to the difficulty in explaining how motion can pass from one particle to another and in explaining how sheer motion can cause the rise of certain sensations in the mind (*3D* III 257–8). Here he is taking up Locke's pessimism about securing a basic understanding of body. According to Locke, we lack any knowledge of the real essence of body: As a consequence, we do not know how motion is transferred from one particle to another, or even how the particles themselves cohere together (*E.* 2.23.23, 308). Of course, the very problem is banished once matter itself has been jettisoned. Berkeley therefore leaves natural science with nothing but what Locke calls "experimental knowledge," which for Berkeley is all that is to be demanded.

In rejecting the Lockean appeal to unknown real essence, Berkeley also endorses the view that spirits are the only causes. However, by this he does not mean that one ought to appeal to spiritual essences in order to explain changes in nature in accordance with the essence model described above. One does not appeal to the essences of spirits in order to determine the properties that "flow" from them. Instead, natural science focuses only on the phenomena itself (leaving the study of spirits to the domain of metaphysics).

While the natural scientist is concerned with the regularity of the phenomena (and the Laws of Nature), metaphysics is concerned "with incorporeal things, with causes, truth, and the existence of things" (*DM* §71). In particular, metaphysics is concerned with the substances which support and cause the phenomena. However, spirits are not part of the Laws of Nature in the way that ideas are part of it. Spirits are not even related to time in the way that ideas are related to them. It is little wonder, then, that spirits are not the objects of scientific investigation. Indeed, in Berkeley's view there is an important sense in which they are not objects of knowledge at all. If they are known, it is by means of a different modality of knowledge—precisely the awareness of self as a knower of ideas. While one's self can function as the image (and general sign of) other spirits, and consequently one can acquire general knowledge of spirits, this knowledge had better not be confused with scientific knowledge of the world. In this way, not only does Berkeley retrench the sciences, he also draws a sharp line between the sciences and metaphysics where the latter concerns spiritual substances and the discursive intercourse among them and the former concern the signs used in that intercourse.

According to Berkeley the project of natural science is to ascertain the general rules which appear to govern such regularity on the basis of experience. This appeal to laws of nature, for Berkeley does not provide a causal explanation of *how* things happen; they only characterize the occurrence of phenomena at an increasingly high level of generalization. For example, Berkeley cites Newton's Principle of Attraction. While this characterizes the phenomena (the tides rise, bodies mutually draw to each other, particles of lead cohere), this—by itself—does not explain *how* this occurs. One does not know the *manner* by which particles cohere, or the *manner* by which bodies draw together (*PHK* I §103).

Instead of viewing the relations among phenomena as causal, Berkeley sees them as representational: What is *called* the cause may be nothing but the sign of the succeeding phenomena. Consequently, for Berkeley, the Laws of Nature are deeply semantic. This picture leads Berkeley to a very peculiar view of natural science. Recall that according to Berkeley, the phenomena studied by the natural scientist are general—and for Berkeley this means treating them as signs. Not only do ideas "stand for each other," but such semantic relations enable us to negotiate the world. It is precisely because we know that certain ideas attend other ideas (or will attend other ideas in case we move our bodies accordingly) that we can know how to behave under the various circumstances in which we find ourselves.

According to Berkeley, what science provides is a much broader knowledge of the regularities in nature through the formulation of general rules (which approximate the Laws of Nature). These general rules enable us to "make very probable conjectures, touching things that may have happened at very great distances of time and place, as well as to predict things to come; which sort of endeavour towards omniscience is much affected by the mind" (*PHK* I §105).

Yet while there are considerable advantages to the systematic study of the Laws of Nature, this doesn't mean that a person who hasn't studied science can't understand a sign in nature (*PHK* I §108). For example, without having understood the science, a man can certainly appreciate that a certain sound is the sign of an automobile or a bell. He needn't know, for example, the science of sound-waves. He needn't even know that no sound can be produced in a vacuum. And, since certainty in natural science is out of the question, it is also possible that this process of formulating general rules about the phenomena leads to mistakes about the signs themselves.

Since the point of this divine language is to direct human beings to act in particular ways, Berkeley thinks that scientists who study the Laws of Nature for their own sake (rather than with the divine purpose in mind) are like those who study the grammar of a book, rather than its meaning (they get lost in the fine print, if you will). And if the natural scientist is not ultimately eking out a deeper picture of reality (that outstrips the phenomena), then the scientific account has a value insofar as it gets the predictions right, and allows people to navigate the world more successfully. Consequently, Berkeley advises that it is undignified to dwell too much on the grammar of the divine language, without paying any attention to its very purpose. Instead, natural science should "enlarge out notions of the grandeur, wisdom, and beneficence of the Creator" by illustrating the "beauty, order, extent, and variety of natural things" (*PHK* I §109).

SECTION TWO: THE RESTORATION OF COMMON SENSE?

Preliminary Observations

Berkeley sees modern science as flying in the face of common sense by affirming that the world as it is in reality is very different from how it appears to us. In particular, it denies that there is anything like the colors and sounds that we immediately experience existing out there in the world. However, it also appears that common sense may have changed over the years. The appeal to sound-waves and light-waves is common enough now. Thus, Berkeley's explicit attack on this theory in the 21st century ought to be viewed as a *departure* from common sense. However, we do continue to act as if the phenomenal qualities of immediate sense-perception existed in the objects. In this way, Berkeley is indeed defending something we treat as true in our daily lives.

Moreover, the charge that Berkeley denies the existence of every-day items is simply false. For Berkeley, everyday items are collections of mind-dependent ideas. They are real insofar as the ideas which compose them are vivid, forceful, and orderly. More specifically, they are real insofar as they are part of the Course of Nature and governed by the Laws thereof. By contrast, the philosopher who identifies everyday items with material substance is led to deny their existence on the grounds that material substance is incoherent. Since Berkeley does not identify everyday items with material substance, he does not have to deny their existence. Instead, the issue turns on this crucial question: Is Berkeley's account of *what* everyday items *are* in accord with the vulgar?

Caution is required—Berkeley's relation to the vulgar differs in the *Principles* and in the *Dialogues*. In the latter, Berkeley attempts to reduce the philosopher's position to skepticism and opposition to common sense). As a consequence, he avoids criticizing the views of the vulgar and therefore gives the impression his own position is entirely friendly to them. By contrast, in the *Principles,* Berkeley aims to diagnose the underlying grounds for irreligious conduct, and he explicitly criticizes the vulgar as well as the philosophers.

The Vulgar on Mind-Independence and Causal Power

In the *Principles*, Berkeley represents the vulgar as believing that every-day items exist independently of any perception of them. Moreover, they attribute a causal power to everyday items as the source of our sense-perception. Certainly both beliefs (that tables and motorcycles can exist without somebody perceiving them, and that they are caus-ally efficacious) are commonsensical enough. And so it would seem that in rejecting these beliefs, Berkeley departs from common sense. Indeed, it would seem he *shreds* common sense, since for Berkeley, these beliefs are not only false, they are *contradictory*. Because the vulgar do not appreciate that sensible things are ideas, they incoher-ently believe that they can exist independently of perception. And owing to "cognitive closure" the term "cause" can only meaningfully apply to spiritual agents, so the view that ideas are causes is likewise incoherent.

Yet Berkeley also denies that, strictly speaking, it is *possible* to believe contradictions. On the face of it, this denial seems counter-intuitive. It is common enough to believe several propositions which turn out to be inconsistent with each other. So why does Berkeley think that it is impossible to believe a contradiction? The answer is that, for Berkeley, one cannot even conceive of a sensible thing exist-ing unperceived or as a cause. And if something can't be conceived, how can it be believed?

According to Berkeley, however, there is another sense in which one *can* believe in matter: "In one sense indeed, men may be said to believe that matter exists, that is, they act as if the immediate cause of their sensations, which affects them every moment and is so nearly present to them, were some senseless unthinking being" (*PHK* I §54). This does not concern one's capacity to conceive, but rather one's acting *as if* the cause of one's actions were unthinking. How should one characterize this behavior?

It's a little hard to imagine unless we contrast it with Berkeley's own view that God himself is the immediate cause of our sense per-ception. If people accepted Berkeley's view, they would behave more cautiously (and in conformity with what they took to be God's will). In particular, they would be ever responsive to the ubiquitous divine Governor. Thus, Berkeley speaks of a kind of "atheism" to which even Christians fall prey in their behavior. While avowing a belief in God, such Christians act only as if he were Creator (and not a Governor). So what is needed, according to Berkeley, is a recognition of God's close presence to us: "A clear view of which great truths cannot choose but fill our hearts with an awful circumspection and holy fear, which is the strongest incentive to *virtue*, and the best guard against *vice*" (*PHK* I §155).

This accommodates the vulgar view that unthinking things cause our sense-perception (and it accommodates therefore their belief in matter). However the distinction between a sensible thing's existence and its being perceived hasn't yet been discussed. While the issue is not addressed at all in the *Principles,* it is explicitly taken up in the Third Dialogue, where Hylas represents Philonous' view as violating the views of the vulgar: "But be your opinion never so true, yet surely you will not deny it is shocking, and contrary to the common sense of men. Ask the fellow, whether yonder tree hath an existence out of his mind: what answer think you he would make?" (*3D* III 235).

Philonous' answer is that the tree *does* have an existence out of his own mind. His claim is only that everyday items are dependent upon minds (some mind or other) not that they are dependent upon his *own*. The distinction is important, since the claim that everyday items are dependent upon *one's own mind* is outrageous. It would mean that these items cease to exist when unperceived by the specific person in question. Certainly, almost any person (regardless of how "vulgar") could understand this suggestion and reject it as ludicrous. Philonous' point, then, is that he does *not* affirm such an unacceptable position.

Instead, the issue is whether everyday items can exist unperceived at all by any mind. Note the *delicacy* of the issue. One needs to think about it. If you present this thesis to nonphilosophers, my suspicion is that while they will ultimately affirm that everyday items can exist unperceived, it will also require some reflection on their part. It isn't immediate and it isn't obvious. Notably, for Berkeley, the very distinction between perception and existence involves an *abstraction* made by the philosophers. So it doesn't seem like a distinction for the vulgar to draw. Why, then, does Berkeley claim in the *Principles* that the vulgar view sensible things as capable of existing unperceived, when it seems as if it is a view utterly unconsidered by the vulgar in the first place?

The answer can be found in Philonous' response to Hylas: The view that sensible things actually exist independently of all perception is *not* something that the Christian vulgar believe since they believe that God exists and perceives everything. Only *some* philosophers, atheists, and "heathen" believe that sensible things exist independently of perception (since they don't believe in an all-knowing God, but believe that sensible things exist even when they are not perceived by humans). In light of Berkeley's account in the *Principles*, then, we should expect that the difference between the Christian vulgar and the atheists is that the former act as if God existed while the former do not. The impossible belief (sensible things exist unperceived by any mind at all) ought to be accommodated likewise in terms of behavior; and this time, one expects the behavior will be "worse." While negligent Christians may act as if God is not the immediate source of sense-perception (and suppose they needn't be so dutiful), an atheist who doesn't even believe in God or the afterlife at all, would presumably feel greater freedom in behaving poorly. (Or at least that's no doubt what *Berkeley* thinks!)

Yet while Berkeley claims agreement with the Christian (and all monotheistic) vulgar that sensible things do not exist without being perceived, he does note a subtle difference with respect to the reasoning involved. Berkeley points out in the Second Dialogue that there is a difference between believing that all sensible things must be perceived because an omniscient God exists and believing that an omniscient God exists because sensible things must be perceived in order to exist (*3D* II 212). While the (Christian) vulgar subscribe to the former, they do not subscribe to the latter.

This difference can be understood in terms of the contrast in view with respect to causation: While the vulgar believe that their sense-perception is caused by the sensible things themselves, Berkeley believes sense-perception is immediately caused by God. Thus, the vulgar cannot conclude the existence of God from the fact that sensible things are independent of them (i.e., are caused from without). And in acting as if everyday items (collections of ideas) were the causes of sense-perception, they *ipso facto* treat the items as capable of existing unperceived, since no causal efficacy is observable in our ideas.

By contrast, Berkeley can conclude from the independence of sensible things (i.e., their being caused from without) that God exists, since it is absurd that ideas are causally efficacious. Thus, it turns out that Berkeley's position does not depart from the views of the (Christian) vulgar in ways that are often supposed. Indeed, the *only* difference actually concerns views about *causation*. Before I discuss this departure in greater depth, however, I want to stop to consider two other aspects that concern Berkeley's allegation that he is actually in agreement with the vulgar.

Sameness and Unity

Berkeley's happy accord with the vulgar that the tree exists independently of *one's own* sense-perception works only in the vulgar use of "same." As we saw in the last chapter, the question whether human spirits and God perceive numerically one and the same sensible thing when considered from a philosophical view has no factual (nonverbal) answer. It simply depends on how one describes the situation. The philosophers' expectation of numerical sameness (or numerical distinctness) among ideas perceived by different perceivers derives from overly refined (abstract) ontological views. Instead, the claim that multiple human spirits and God perceive the same sensible thing comes to nothing more than the more superficial claim that there is a (causally determined) resemblance that obtains among what we all perceive. We follow the vulgar in their use of the word "same" not because there is any deep underlying philosophical reality which secures genuine numerical identity, but only because this way of speaking is useful.

In assessing whether Berkeley's position ultimately squares with common sense, it is an important question whether he is in the right about the view of the vulgar in supposing that human spirits can sense-perceive "the same thing." When I perceive a loud sound, and you perceive a loud sound and in common usage we say we sense-perceive "the same" sound, is anything more being said then that there is a (causally determined) resemblance between what we sense-perceive? To be clear, the question is not whether we *mean* "causally determined resemblance" (which is fortunate for Berkeley, since we obviously *don't* mean that). The question is whether we are making any claims about strict numerical identity.

On Berkeley's behalf it is worth noting that the word "same" is certainly used in ways that are "loose" and which scarcely seem to require the strictness of a philosopher. Thus, a person may say: "Oh, look they're wearing exactly the same dress!" and mean that the two are wearing resembling instances of a dress rather than numerically one and the same dress. Indeed, it seems to me that in ordinary discourse, the word "same" is *usually* used in this way—cases of claiming strict numerical identity are rare.

The second issue worth considering is Berkeley's Collections Thesis according to which everyday items are nothing but collections of sensible qualities. In his view, this thesis is supposed to reflect the attitudes of the vulgar. However, on the face of it, this doesn't seem clear. For Berkeley, the vulgar believe that one immediately sense-perceives everyday items. And Berkeley concludes from the fact that one immediately sense-perceives only sensible qualities (color, sound, etc.) that everyday items are nothing but collections of sensible qualities. Yet, this leads to a view in which everyday items lack a unity that one might have wanted. A sheer collection of ideas with a word applied to it scarcely seems like the kind of unity possessed by a chair. The question, for our purposes, then, seems to be whether the vulgar are committed to a more serious unity. If they are, it seems Berkeley's account might depart from the vulgar in this respect.

This problem of unity comes especially to the fore when considering the question whether in seeing a motorcycle and touching a motorcycle, one sense-experiences the same thing. Nor can the problem be evaded by relegating vulgar sameness to mere similitude. For the issue here is precisely the fact that the visible ideas and the tangible ideas do *not* resemble each other: Visible ideas can only *look like* other ideas; tangible ideas can only *feel like* other ideas. There is no sameness in *any* sense of the word.

In Berkeley's view, these ideas are grouped together under the same word—any unity however is both artificial and superficial. The philosophers, for Berkeley, make the mistake of supposing that there is a real essence which binds these together and explains them. This, however, is a misconstrue of the actions of the vulgar:

> And indeed there is cause to suspect several erroneous conceits of the philosophers are owing to the same original: while they began to build their schemes, not so much on notions as words, which were framed by the vulgar, merely for conveniency and

dispatch in the common actions of life, without any regard to speculation (*3D* III 246).

As I discussed in Chapter Six, there are different views about how to interpret Berkeley on this issue. In one view, one *does* immediately see and touch the same motorcycle (i.e., the same collection of ideas). In another view, one only *mediately* sees and touches the same motorcycle (i.e., the same collection of ideas). Strictly speaking, in this last view, one immediately sees only colors (and light), while one immediately touches qualities such as size, shape, and solidity. The sense-perception of an everyday item, by contrast, requires *mediate* perception.

If the first view is right, then Berkeley seems in greater accord with the vulgar (who believe we immediately perceive everyday items), while in the second view he seems to depart from it at least somewhat (in claiming that we don't immediately perceive them). I considered another interpretation, however, in which Berkeley distinguishes between the visible everyday item and the tangible one. This view has the advantage of allowing the vulgar to immediately perceive everyday item(s). However, it also attributes the error to the vulgar of supposing that they immediately see and touch the same thing.

It is worth noting that in the *Essay Towards a New Theory of Vision*, Berkeley recognizes what he sees as a common error of supposing that we immediately see and touch the same thing: Most everybody falsely treats objects of sight only mediately perceived as immediately perceived (*NTV* §45), so this error results from confusing the signifier with the signified. For example, in communicating through the use of words, we rarely pay attention to the words themselves, but rather the ideas suggested by them: "in the very same instant the sound and the meaning enter the understanding: so closely are they united that it is not in our power to keep out the one, except we exclude the other also. We even act in all respects as if we heard the very thoughts themselves" (*NTV* §51). So it comes to pass that visible ideas and tangible ideas are "most closely twisted, blended, and incorporated together. And the prejudice is confirmed and riveted in our thoughts by a long tract of time, by the use of language, and want of reflection" (*NTV* §51): In this account, words which are used for tangible items come to be applied to visible ones as well, just as the same word is used to refer to both itself and the signification ("rock" can be used to refer to the word rock and the hard rock).

What is important for our purposes here is that in the *Essay* (unlike the *Dialogues*) Berkeley explicitly outlines an error that would seem to apply even to the vulgar—namely of blending tangible and visible ideas together, and in thereby supposing that we immediately see what we immediately touch. This suggests, however, that the vulgar suppose a greater unity of the everyday item than is indicated in the *Dialogues*. For it now turns out that the vulgar are *wrong* in supposing one and the same thing is both the immediate object of sight and touch. Instead, the relation between the immediate objects of sight and touch is arbitrary, and the fact the same word is applied to both is likewise arbitrary.

Causation Revisited

It turns out that Berkeley's major break from the vulgar is actually his denial that everyday items are causally efficacious. What does he have to say for himself on this point? Berkeley *knows* this is a departure. Indeed, this departure is tantamount to his disapproval of the common behavior of folk which is indicative of a failure to believe in God as a Divine Governor (i.e., as the immediate cause of our sense-perception). Yet in the *Dialogues*, because his agenda is to reduce the philosophers to skepticism and a departure from common sense, he deemphasizes this. Instead, he cites the Christian scripture, claiming that this doctrine is explicitly endorsed therein (*3D* III 236).

However, in the *Principles,* Berkeley says that one ought to "*think with the learned, and speak with the vulgar*" (*PHK* I §51). Thus, one can continue to say that fire heats, water cools, and so forth (rather than saying that spirits heat, etc.) just as one says the sun rises and sets despite the fact that the earth, not the sun, is in motion. The important point for Berkeley is not the turn of phrase, but rather the behavior that ensues: "In the ordinary affairs of life, any phrases may be retained so long as they excite in us proper sentiments, or dispositions to act in such a manner as is necessary for our well-being, how falsesoever they may be, if taken in a strict and speculative sense" (*PHK* I §52).

What is especially curious, however, is that while Berkeley says that one can speak with the vulgar in saying that fire heats and water cools in the *Principles*, he spends most of the First Dialogue, having Philonous embarrass Hylas for admitting that sugar is not sweet and fire is not hot. Why should one be any more embarrassing than the other? And if Berkeley can speak with the vulgar in saying fire heats, why can Hylas not simply speak with the vulgar and say that fire is hot? The answer I think is that Hylas *can* do this. Or at least, he tries to speak with the vulgar at the beginning of the Third Dialogue: "the vulgar retain their mistakes, and for all that, make a shift to bustle through the affairs of life" (*3D* III 228).

However, Berkeley also has two responses to this move. First, Hylas' position (unlike Berkeley's) in addition to leading to the preceding, yields a version of Lockean Ignorance about everyday items. Thus, it leads to a far worse departure from common sense by opening the door for an unacceptable skepticism. Second, the arguments provided in the First Dialogue go much further, and in fact show that the very notion of material substance is incoherent. Because Hylas identifies everyday items with matter, he is thereby led to deny the existence of everyday items themselves, which is absurd. In effect, this complaint about parity is in some sense fair. And it is only because philosophical materialism leads to an even deeper skepticism (and, indeed, its own eventual annihilation) that Berkeley's position on immediate causation can come out ahead in this respect.

Why do the vulgar fall into the error of supposing that our sense-perception is caused by the sensible things themselves? And why do the philosophers suppose it caused by things resembling our ideas? In the *Principles*, Berkeley explains that neither recognize the contradiction involved in supposing ideas (or things like ideas) are causally efficacious. Moreover, unlike human spirits (which are marked out by an identifiable visible body), the Governing Spirit does not have such an easily identifiable "badge." The very regularity by which God operates is taken as mitigating against there being a spirit, since "inconstancy and immutability" is characteristic of the human spirit, and therefore recognized as a mark of freedom.

And while in *Alciphron*, Berkeley is not concerned with immediate causation, he again points out how regular occurrences become common, and are then overlooked:

> Hence, a common man, who is not used to think and make reflexions, would probably be more convinced of the being of a God by one single sentence heard once in his life from the sky than by all the experience he has had of this visual language. (*ALC* IV §15)

The very regularity of the Divine Language is why it is over-looked, and miracles are required by God to get the attention of human spirits. Indeed, it is precisely this regularity which leads to the vulgar error of confounding signifier with signified, and supposing that we immediately see tangible objects. In the *Essay*, Berkeley further explains that because the Divine Language transcends all cultural (and linguistic) variation, and because it is learned immediately upon entering the world and pervades our daily lives, it does not stand out with the same hallmarks as a human language which is limited to cultures and which one can recall learning (*NTV* §144).

Yet this does not detract from the "miraculous" nature of the Divine Language, which when one reflects upon it, ought to strike one with amazement. Imagine, Berkeley argues, a sighted newcomer to a land inhabited by people born blind. She would be capable of informing and directing the inhabitants about what they would touch when they moved in certain ways. Her knowledge would appear incredible and inexplicable. Such is the sense of wonder, argues Berkeley, which has become lost on us as a consequence of the ubiquity and regularity of God's communication with us. It is a sense of wonder, argues Berkeley, which needs to be recovered.

CONCLUSION

I conclude this book by offering a brief assessment of Berkeley's philosophy. As we have proceeded, I have drawn attention to difficulties and controversial assumptions when I have felt it especially necessary. However, it is worth taking a step back to assess Berkeley's argumentative strategies within a bigger picture. In order to do so, I turn to the views of David Hume, the apparent empiricist successor to Berkeley's idealism.

BERKELEY AND HUME ON CAUSATION

It is somewhat ironic that Berkeley's most serious (and explicit) departure from common sense concerns his views about causation. Yet the "guts" of David Hume's philosophy involve an attempt to provide a theory of causation and our natural inclinations to engage in causal reasoning. Indeed, Hume's account of causation seems to have been very seriously inspired by Berkeley's own account of suggestion. In Berkeley's view, frequent experiences of the co-occurrence of two ideas generate a habit or tendency, such that upon experiencing the one, the other will be suggested to the imagination. Hume's account explains the fact that we draw causal inferences (despite the fact they are, for him, unjustified).[1] This constant conjunction of cause and effect generates a habit which causes a vivid idea of the effect to be produced when an impression of the cause is received.[2] Moreover (and this is the unique part of Hume's theory), while no necessary connection between cause and effect can ever be perceived, the habit itself generates an impression of necessitation (i.e., the feeling of psychological compulsion in moving from one perception to the next), which is then erroneously projected onto the objects themselves.[3]

Both philosophers use an appeal to the generation of a habit to produce certain ideas in the imagination, which arises upon the experience of constant correlations. One important difference, however, is that for Berkeley "suggestion" is used to explain how we come to understand *signs*. It is a notion which helps Berkeley elucidate his theory of *meaning*. In his view, the vulgar wrongly suppose that sensible things (ideas) are causally efficacious. They are confusing a causal relation with a semantic relation. And this prevents them from following the instructions of the Divine Governor.

By contrast, Hume uses this habit to explain why humans *naturally* engage in causal reasoning. In his own view, humans draw causal inferences and treat perceptions as causally efficacious precisely because of the general principles which govern the psychological operation of the mind. He endorses an error theory about necessitation in supposing that we falsely project the necessary connection into the objects themselves which itself involves nothing more that the internal experience of the compelling habit itself.

BERKELEY AS SKEPTIC

Why does Hume overturn Berkeley's position? Hume perversely brands *Berkeley* a skeptic:

> [M]ost of the writings of that very ingenious author [Berkeley] form the best lessons of scepticism, which are to be found either among the ancient or modern philosophers . . . He professes . . . to have composed his book against the sceptics . . . But that all his arguments, though otherwise intended, are, in reality, merely sceptical, appears from this, *that they admit of no answer and produce no conviction*. Their only effect is to cause that momentary amazement and irresolution and confusion, which is the result of scepticism. (*Enquiry*, p. 155)

Obviously this charge would have been *anathema* to Berkeley. And clearly Hume is using the term "skepticism" in the loose way that Berkeley had used in the *Dialogues* (which is the work to which Hume is here referring). He charges Berkeley with skepticism not because Berkeley professes to know nothing of the world, nor because he denies the existence of matter. Rather, he brands him a skeptic because Berkeley's *own arguments* engender a kind of *perplexity*:

Arguments "which admit of no answer" yield a conclusion that is nonetheless unbelievable. While the thesis may seem interesting, it is never fully *accepted as true.*

Hume appears to endorse the legendary view of Berkeley as "irrefutable" but nonetheless "unbelievable." And indeed, there is something to Hume's criticism. If it is true that Berkeley's conclusions are never accepted by vulgar and philosophers alike (and indeed, we somehow, simply *cannot* believe them), then Berkeley's project fails in its own terms. Berkeley's entire purpose is to return men of speculation to practice by demonstrating their abstractions vacuous and inciting them to virtuous conduct. In so doing, Berkeley wants to help change the behavior of the vulgar which demonstrates a belief in the causal power of everyday items (and a disregard for the Divine Governor as the immediate cause of our sensations). If his conclusions will never be accepted by the philosophers and the vulgar alike, then Berkeley's project is a "bust."

Unsurprisingly, Hume's own account of causation provides a psychological account of why people draw causal inferences. In such a view, people are simply going to treat the world causally. Rather than constituting a reply to Berkeley's argument, it effectively affords a psychological explanation of why nobody believes Berkeley. On this issue of God as a universal, immediate cause, Hume is very clear that it is simply *unbelievable*: "it seems to me that this theory of the universal energy and operation of the Supreme Being is too bold ever to carry conviction with it to a man, sufficiently apprized of the weakness of human reason . . . We are got into fairy land ere we have reached the last steps of our theory" (*Enquiry*, p. 72).

SPIRITUAL CAUSATION

In rejecting Berkeley's position, however, Hume has more work to do. Berkeley claims that the term "cause" can be given content by one's own awareness of oneself as a causally efficacious agent: One can self-consciously cause ideas of the imagination (and internal kinesthetic ideas) at will. If so, Berkeley has a genuine way of accommodating causation that does not require Hume's relegation of necessitation to the sheer experience of psychological compulsion and the projection of it upon the objects perceived. Instead, one is immediately aware of oneself as a cause.

Hume considers such an account. However, he also raises several concerns about this position. The core concern is that while one might be aware of one's volitions (and the ideas which ensue), one is not aware of any necessary connection between the two. Nor is one aware of volition itself as having any kind of causal power within it. Just as one is aware of two successive perceptions in the case of external objects (one perceives the water being heated, then one perceives the water boiling), likewise one is aware only of a volition followed by an effect. And the appearance of any necessity between the two simply arises from our projecting the feeling of psychological compulsion onto the volition and attendant effect.

It is an interesting question how Berkeley might respond to this. If this is the model he accepts—namely, the view that in the causation of one's own ideas one is aware of individual volitions followed by individual effects—then the same reasons which lead him to reject causation in the external world should likewise lead him to reject causation in the case of the mental as well. Such a view was endorsed by Malebranche (whom Berkeley in part aimed to address on this score); and it would appear to threaten Berkeley's philosophy in a very fundamental way: If spirits cannot be legitimately viewed as causes, then surely his entire philosophical system collapses.

This concern is important in Berkeley scholarship. However, I would like to suggest that Berkeley may have an answer to this Humean argument. It isn't clear to me that Berkeley actually endorses this model which involves the observance of particular volitions followed by particular effects. Such a view has other problems besides the Humean one mentioned above. First, if a volition is an intention, then it seems to require some content (*what* is being intended). Thus, if one intends to cause the idea of a unicorn, the volition should include ideational content involving the image of a unicorn. But insofar as the idea is already included within the volition, it would seem that any subsequent attempt to produce the idea would be redundant. Second, if one needs to appeal to a volition in order to explain the creation of an idea, then doesn't one need to posit a new volition to explain the creation of the volition? If so, there will be an infinite regress. If not, then why do we need to appeal to a particular volition in the first place?

It is interesting that Berkeley does not provide an analysis of what it would mean to say that volitions exist. Recall that for Berkeley the existence of an idea consists in being perceived, while the existence of a spirit consists in perceiving and willing. But in what does the existence of a volition *itself* consist? Berkeley nowhere says. And in my proposed interpretation, Berkeley's account of essential consciousness includes only two elements—subjective-objects and one's own existence. There is no room for volitions as additional entities over and above spirits and ideas.

My suspicion is that Berkeley may not *need* individual volitions (taken for entities over and above spirits and ideas) in order to explain mental causation. If the existence of an idea consists in being perceived, then it seems to me the way to cause it to exist would be precisely *to perceive it*. Consider the case of active imagination: One can conjure up the idea of a unicorn, imaginary sounds, and so forth. But how are these objects created? Berkeley can say that it is *by* perceiving them that they come into existence. In other words, it is through one's essential consciousness of oneself and one's subjective-object that one brings about the existence of that object.[4] Presumably, in that awareness of oneself, one would be aware of oneself as an active thing—an agent or source of causal responsibility for the idea. Thus, Berkeley could distinguish between this form of active perception (willing, volition) and the passive perception involved in sensory-experience where subjective-objects do *not* exist because one perceives them. The phenomenology of pain and pleasure involved in such passions would make one aware that one was *not* the causal source in such cases.

Of course, even if this account is defensible, Hume has other concerns to press. He observes that the production of ideas appears quite remarkable—indeed, it seems like a case of producing something out of nothing. But in such a case, one is *not* aware of *the means* by which one produces them. One is not aware of the *modus operandi* by which ideas are produced (*Enquiry*, p. 68). But if so, one is not truly aware of the necessity by which they are produced.

This issue is especially interesting since Berkeley himself does not seem to allow that one is aware of any such *modus operandi* either. At least Berkeley is clear that *mysterious* spiritual activities such as divine grace and inspiration are definable only in terms of their causes and effects. No distinct conception of the *modus operandi* is available. However, Berkeley might also respond by saying that the existence of a *modus operandi* or a relation of necessity with the effect would precisely *undermine* the very notion of creation of something out of nothing to begin with. Instead, the search for such a mysterious connection between oneself and one's ideas is not to be found anywhere. Indeed this connection is not a *thing* at all. Rather, one must quite simply act (by producing ideas) through one's perception of them. To expect a perceivable *modus operandi* by which one spontaneously creates ideas from nothing is to confuse perceivable ideas with the taking of action in the creation of one's ideas spontaneously.

Hume has other concerns, however. It isn't clear why one can produce some ideas and not others. One can produce the idea of a unicorn, but not the idea of one million unicorns. Why not? The latter is too complex—it outstrips the capacity of one's imagination. But why? Surely there is an underlying explanation (of which one is unaware). But if so, one does not have a handle on the causal connection between will and idea. Again, one's capacity to produce ideas is affected by how much sleep and food one has had. When one gets tired, one thinks less well. But this again suggests that there is much that is not understood about the causal relation between will and idea.

Berkeley does not have much to say about these issues, and it isn't clear whether he has the theoretical resources to accommodate them. While I think that he can, in the end, explain the existence of various limitations on the capacity of human spirits to produce ideas (by appeal to the human body), it is far from obvious.[5] And, in any event, it is clear enough that his own account of the mind is exceptionally thin (largely, because there is not much to the mind at all, other than the fact that it is a willing, perceiving agent). Indeed, Berkeley explicitly denies that spirits are objects of knowledge (i.e. a subjective-object) at all, thereby separating it from the domain of the sciences, leaving any analogous study of the mind out of the question.

By contrast, Hume's major agenda is to provide a scientific account of the human mind. He thinks that it is plain that one engages in causal reasoning about the mind just as one does with regard to items such as billiard balls. One concludes that passions (such as desire, anger, and the like) will yield certain kinds of action (*Enquiry*, p. 83). Based upon experience, one learns about a person's character and makes inferences about future behavior (*Enquiry*, p. 91). For example, one expects a certain person to arrive late based upon knowledge of character. Indeed, in Hume's theory of causation, human beings can be expected to naturally draw these types of causal inferences about each other given the constant correlations which inevitably lead to relevant habit to draw the inferences.

Yet Hume still has more work to do. In particular, he needs to eliminate Berkeley's own account of the mind (i.e., spirit) and show how it is at least possible for perceptions to exist unperceived by the mind. Hume argues for the coherence of the view that perceptions can exist unperceived by appeal to the vulgar view that everyday items can exist unperceived. Since the beliefs of the vulgar ultimately concern perceptions, argues Hume, their belief that everyday items can exist unperceived, requires at least the coherence of the view that perceptions themselves can exist unperceived. Hume argues:

> When I view this table and that chimney, nothing is present to me but particular perceptions, which are of a like nature with all the other perceptions. This is the doctrine of philosophers. But this table, which is present to me, and that chimney, may and do exist separately. This is the doctrine of the vulgar, and implies no contradiction. There is no contradiction, therefore, in extending the same doctrine to all the perceptions. (*Treatise,* Appendix, p. 634)

Recall that according to Berkeley, the vulgar are guilty of a contradiction in supposing that sensible things (ideas) can exist independently of being perceived. Hume appears to be simply *denying* Berkeley's radical thesis without any argument. He may be taking it as his starting point that Berkeley's position is simply unbelievable and hence false. Hume concludes from this that it must likewise be non-contradictory to suppose that perceptions (or ideas) themselves exist unperceived. In effect, he concludes that thoughts (perceptions, ideas) can exist without being objects of consciousness awareness. He is thereby led to deny the reflexivity of thought.

How does Hume accomplish this? He proposes that the mind is nothing but a heap of connections and that immediate awareness of an object (or perception) can be explained strictly in terms of the causal impact that a perception makes upon the heap (*Treatise,* p. 207). In such a view, it is entirely possible for such perceptions to exist without making a causal impact upon a heap of perceptions. Consequently, it is possible for them to exist unperceived.

This is a great departure from Berkeley's insight (in the Master Argument) that all ideas must be accompanied by an "I." In Hume's view, if we are aware of ourselves, we are aware of nothing but a bundle of perceptions (*Treatise*, p. 252). His view, it seems, is that certainly one can conceive of how a perception could exist without there being this additional consciousness of self (which turns out to be nothing more than an awareness of the bundle that one is). Thus, in his approach, the reflexivity of thought is effectively denied by showing how it is possible to pull the self and its objects apart from each other. And this requires an alternative analysis of the self (or, if you will, consciousness that one exists).

As I noted much earlier, however, there is actually a difficulty with this account, which may have motivated Hume's notorious criticism on his own account of personal identity in the Appendix to the *Treatise*. Consciousness of a plurality of perceptions does not seem to have the necessary unity to constitute consciousness of one's own existence. But if so, Hume's analysis would fail as an account of self-consciousness, and his elimination of Berkeley would also fail.

KEY ASSUMPTIONS

Does Berkeley win? Does he beat back Hume? Is he actually irrefutable? I don't see why. Much of Berkeley's arguments hinge on two key sets of assumptions which are very controversial. (Hume accepts the first, and tries to reject the other). First, Berkeley assumes that the significance of terms must generally be fixed by (prelinguistic) mental content. This requires that we can even identify a kind of phenomenal "given" prior to the workings of culture and language. Moreover, it ultimately grounds intelligibility in this prior mental content. However, one might (for example) argue that the meaning of terms is often determined simply by their usage and their role within a larger context of discursive behavior. In such a view, intelligibility would not require prior mental content.

Indeed, Berkeley himself has sometimes been taken as defending such a view. The reason for this concerns his thesis that terms such as "force" and "grace" can be meaningful even though distinct ideas can be annexed to them, and their meaningfulness is connected to their capacity to guide and incite to action and provoke passion. Yet, as I have argued, even in these cases Berkeley requires that these terms be defined, and the terms used in the definitions themselves are given semantic content by prior mental content. Certainly his claims that extensionless color and unperceived sensible things are oxymorons, requires this strict view about intelligibility.

At any rate, if this assumption is rejected, then it is clear that Berkeley cannot defend his immaterialism. Even his argumentative strategy in the *Dialogues* (which depends so much upon appeals to common sense and ordinary linguistic usage) also depends upon his antiabstractionism and therefore his appeal to this model of intelligibility. Indeed, it is needed precisely at the juncture at which Berkeley argues that extension itself is mind-dependent and hence cannot exist in an unthinking substance (thereby demonstrating the very notion of material substance to be incoherent). The rejection of material substance as unintelligible is the lynchpin, however, of his reduction of the philosophers' position to skepticism.

The second crucial set of assumptions concerns Berkeley's views about consciousness. For example, Berkeley assumes that thought is essentially reflexive. This, coupled with his particular model of essential consciousness, is required for his understanding of the very notions of ideas and spirits and the dependence of the former upon the latter. If occurrent thoughts, for example, can exist even if one is not conscious of them, as Hume tries to show, then the very principle of substantiality which binds spirits and ideas is broken. And the fact that Hume's analysis fails (or at least *seems* to fail), does not mean that the question whether all thought is inherently reflexive has been answered. After all, Hume attempts to show this by following Berkeley's model of consciousness in which the variable elements are subjective-objects. But it isn't clear that this is the best or correct analysis. Certainly, the question whether phenomenal thoughts can be separated from essential consciousness is a fundamental question even today. And it is crucial in assessing Berkeley's success.

I conclude, then, by observing that while it is highly doubtful that Berkeley is irrefutable, it is also clear that he was an exceptionally subtle and profound thinker. Too often Berkeley is underrated and dismissed because the views that he defends initially strike one as outrageous and plainly false. What seems to be ignored is the bigger picture—Berkeley's project and the complex argumentative strategies he executes to secure his project. Certainly, the deepest assumptions which shape his views remain salient to this day. And he still has something to tell us about what are now commonsensical views about secondary qualities such as sound and color. While the philosophy of Berkeley may inevitably perplex, this is ultimately a testament to the peculiar genius that is Berkeley.

NOTES

PREFACE

[1] William Butler Yeats, "Blood and the Moon," The Variorum Edition of the Poems (Macmillan: New York, 1957).

[2] From a *Letter to Des Bosses*, March 5, 1715, (trans. and eds.) Richard Ariew and Daniel Garber *Philosophical Essays* (Hackett Publishing: Indianapolis, 1989).

[3] James Boswell, *The Life of Dr. Johnson*, August 6, 1763, George Birbeck Hill (ed.) and L. F. Powell (revised) (Clarendon: Oxford, 1934).

[4] Robert C. Solomon, *Introducing Philosophy: A Text with Integrated Readings*, 6th ed. (Harcourt Brace & Company: New York, 1997).

CHAPTER 1

[1] My account of Berkeley's life borrows heavily from A. A. Luce's *Life of Berkeley* (Thomas Nelson and Sons: London, 1949) and David Berman's *George Berkeley: Idealism and the Man* (Clarendon: Oxford, 1994).

[2] Luce, p. 2.

[3] Luce, p. 3.

[4] Berman, 1994, p. 17–20.

[5] Bertil Belfrage, *George Berkeley's Manuscript Introduction* (Doxa: Oxford, 1987), pp. 27–45.

[6] Margaret Atherton, *Berkeley's Revolution in Vision* (Cornell University Press: Ithaca, 1990), pp. 3–4.

[7] Benjamin Rand, *Berkeley and Percival: The Correspondence of George Berkeley and Sir John Percival* (Cambridge University Press: Cambridge, 1914), p. 89.

[8] A loyalist to the exiled Stuart King James II and his descendants after the "Glorious Revolution" of 1688–89 led to the ascension of Mary II and William III.

[9] Rand, p. 62.

[10] Berman, 1994, p. 94–97.

[11] E. J. Furlong and D. Berman, "George Berkeley and *The Ladies Library*," *Berkeley Newsletter* 4 (December 1980), pp. 4–13.

[12] Published in the *Miscellany* (1752) as *Verses on the Prospect of Planting Arts and Learning in America* (*Works* VII, p. 369).

[13] Berman argues that the reason for this increase in recognition was Berkeley's high profile from his Bermuda Project, p. 120.

[14] James Wallace, *A New History of Philosophy: Volume Two: From Descartes to Searle*, 2nd ed. (Harcourt Publishers: New York, 2000), p. 410.

[15] David Hume, *A Treatise of Human Nature*, 2nd ed., L.A. Selby-Bigge (ed.) with revisions and notes by P. H. Nidditch (Clarendon Press: Oxford, 1978), p. 17.

[16] Boswell, *The Life of Dr. Johnson,* sub 1763; Thomas Reid, *An Inquiry into the Human Mind on the Principles of Common Sense,* (ed. w/introduction) Timothy Duggan (University of Chicago Press: Chicago, 1970), Introduction, Section V, p. 14.

CHAPTER 2

[1] Second Meditation. René Descartes, *Meditations on First Philosophy*, *The Philosophical Writings of Descartes*, 2 volumes, John Cottingham, Robert Stroothoff, and Dugald Murdoch (trans.) (Cambridge University Press: Cambridge, 1984).

[2] First Meditation.

[3] Second Meditation.

[4] Third Meditation and Sixth Meditation.

[5] Immanuel Kant, *Foundations of the Metaphysics of Morals*, First Section, 2nd ed., Trans. with intro by Lewis White Beck (Macmillan: New York, 1988).

[6] David Berman, *A History of Atheism in Britain: From Hobbes to Russell*, pp. 64–67 (Croom Helm: New York, 1988).

[7] Some of the major deists include: Lord Herbert of Cherbury (1583–1648), Charles Blount (1654–93), John Toland (1670–1722), Anthony Collins (1676–1729), Thomas Woolston (1670–1733), and Matthew Tindal (1657–1733).

[8] Berman, *A History of Atheism in Britain*, pp.70–92.

CHAPTER 3

[1] This name ("The Master Argument") was coined by André Gallois in his article, "Berkeley's Master Argument," *Philosophical Review* 83 (1974), pp. 55–69.

[2] Kenneth P. Winkler, *Berkeley: An Interpretation* (Oxford University Press: Oxford, 1989), pp. 183–87.

[3] Winkler, p. 186.

[4] I borrow this expression from Henry Allison, *Kant's Transcendental Idealism: An Interpretation and Defense* (Yale University Press: New Haven, 1983), pp. 261–62. However, I use it specifically to refer to elements of essential consciousness (such as thoughts) which are *not* viewed as mental states.

[5] For further discussion see Roderick Chisholm, "On the Observability of the Self," *Philosophy and Phenomenological Research* 30 (1969), pp. 7–21; and Sidney Shoemaker, "Introspection and the Self" in Peter A. French, Theodore E. Vehlin, and Howard K. Wettstein (eds.) *Studies in the Philosophy of Mind*, Midwest Studies in Philosophy 10, (University of Minnesota Press: Minneapolis, 1986), pp. 101–20.

[6] See Chisholm.

[7] Hume, *Treatise of Human Nature*, p. 252.

[8] For this example, see Chisholm.

[9] In the Appendix to the *Treatise*, pp. 633–36.

[10] The expression was coined by Colin McGinn. See his *Problems in Philosophy: The Limits of Inquiry* (Blackwell Publishing: Oxford, 1993).

CHAPTER 4

[1] I am indebted to John Carriero for my understanding of the First Dialogue. While our respective readings are different, I have been greatly influenced by his own reading and by the particular issues of concern to him.

[2] For example, see John Yolton, *Perceptual Acquaintance from Descartes to Reid* (Basil Blackwell: Oxford, 1984).

[3] For some considerations which tend to suggest such a view, see John Carriero, "Berkeley, Resemblance, and Sensible Things," *Philosophical Topics* (2003) 31: 1, 2, 21–46. See p. 29.

[4] Galileo, *The Assayer* (1623).

[5] For this objection, and a related discussion see I. C. Tipton, *Berkeley: The Philosophy of Immaterialism* (Methuen: London, 1974), pp. 226–36.

CHAPTER 5

[1] I suspect Malebranche may offer a view of this type in *The Search after Truth,* Thomas M. Lennon and Paul J. Olscamp (trans. and eds.), (Cambridge University Press: Cambridge, 1997), p 441.

[2] Lisa Downing makes this point and shows how it can be used to undermine even direct realism. Lisa Downing, "George Berkeley," *The Stanford Encyclopedia of Philosophy (Winter 2007 Edition)*, Edward N. Zalta (ed.), http://plato.stanford.edu/archives/win2007/entries/berkeley/.

[3] Robert Boyle, "Excellency and Grounds of the Mechanical or Corpuscular Hypothesis," (1674).

[4] What has been called the Likeness Principle, will be examined in greater depth in the following chapter.

CHAPTER 6

[1] For example, see Wilfred Sellars' "Empiricism and the Philosophy of Mind" in *The Foundations of Science and the Concepts of Psychoanalysis,*

Minnesota Studies in the Philosophy of Science, Vol. I, H. Feigl and M. Scriven (eds.), (University of Minnesota Press: Minneapolis, 1956).
[2] For example, see Berman, 1994, pp. 148–55.
[3] For a defense of this view, see Pitcher, *Berkeley* (Routledge: London, 1977), pp. 62–90.
[4] Sixth Meditation, *CSM* II, pp. 50–51.
[5] Winkler, p. 40. See J. L. Mackie, *Problems from Locke* (Oxford University Press: Oxford, 1976).
[6] For example, Mackie and Winkler.
[7] Phillip D. Cummins in "Berkeley's Likeness Principle" in C. B. Martin and D. M. Armstrong (eds.), *Locke and Berkeley* (Doubleday: New York, 1968), pp. 353–63.
[8] Winkler, pp. 141–49.

CHAPTER 7

[1] Phillip D. Cummins, "Berkeley's Manifest Qualities Thesis," in Robert Muehlmann (ed.), *Berkeley's Metaphysics: Structural, Interpretive, and Critical Essays* (Pennsylvania State University Press: University Park, 1995), pp. 107–26.
[2] Malebranche, p. 450; Hume, *Treatise of Human Nature*, p.165.
[3] *Discourse on the Method*, Part VI, *CSM* I, p. 140. In pointing to this connection, I am drawing from David Kline's "Berkeley's Divine Language Argument" from Ernest Sosa (ed.) *Essays on the Philosophy of George Berkeley* (D. Reidel Publishing: Dordrecht, 1987).
[4] On this point, see Kline.
[5] See Atherton, pp. 172–94.
[6] George Pitcher, "Berkeley and the Perception of Objects," *Journal of the History of Philosophy* 24 (1986), pp. 99–105.
[7] For a compelling defense of this reading, see Margaret Atherton, "The Objects of Immediate Perception," in Stephen Daniel (ed.) *New Interpretations of Berkeley's Thought* (Humanity Books: New York, 2007), pp. 107–19.
[8] George Pappas, *Berkeley's Thought* (Cornell University Press: Ithaca, 2000), pp.181.
[9] Pappas, pp. 172–82.

CHAPTER 8

[1] I follow Kenneth Winkler (1989, p. 193) in drawing this distinction.
[2] Winkler, pp. 207–16.
[3] See Charles McCracken, "What *Does* Berkeley's God see in the Quad," *Archiv für Geschichte der Philosphie* 61 (1979), pp. 280–92; and "Berkeley's Realism" in Stephen Daniel (ed.) *New Interpretations of Berkeley's Thought* (Humanity Press: Amherst, New York, 2007), pp. 23–44.
[4] Other commentators have written of "the continuity argument." Since this way of characterizing the argument is misleading, I have avoided this label.

[5] Jonathan Bennett argues that Berkeley falls prey to an ambiguity in 'depends' in providing what is a fallacious argument. *Locke, Berkeley, and Hume: Central Themes* (Clarendon Press: Oxford, 1971), p. 212.

[6] Winkler (1989) defends this view, pp. 212–16.

[7] McCracken (2008) uses this as an argument, p. 31.

[8] See Bettcher, *Berkeley's Philosophy of Spirit: Consciousness, Ontology, and the Elusive Subject* (Continuum: London, 2007), pp. 74–79.

[9] For this view, see A. C. Grayling, *Berkeley: The Central Arguments* (Open Court: La Salle, 1986).

[10] J. D. Mabbott, "The Place of God in Berkeley's Philosophy," reprinted in C. B. Martin and David M. Armstrong (eds.) *Locke and Berkeley* (Cambridge University Press: Notre Dame, 1968), pp. 364–79.

[11] Bettcher, 2007, pp. 88–95.

[12] Pitcher, 1977, pp. 171–72.

[13] Pitcher, p. 171.

CHAPTER 9

[1] See Douglas Jesseph, pp. 88–122, esp. 118–20.

CONCLUSION

[1] David Hume, *Enquiry Concerning Human Understanding*, pp. 24–39.

[2] Hume, *Enquiry*, pp.40–55.

[3] Hume, *Enquiry*, pp. 60–79.

[4] One of the benefits of this reading is that the question how Berkeley's Argument from Perception can succeed without collapsing into the Causal Argument is answered. For Berkeley, the view that an idea is not caused by me is equivalent to the view that it can exist unperceived by me. This is because one can only cause an idea by (actively) perceiving it.

[5] See Bettcher, 2007, pp. 86–87

FURTHER READING

[1] For a more comprehensive list, see *Works* IX pp. 147–50.

[2] For a more comprehensive list, see *Works* IX pp. 147–50.

FURTHER READING

WORKS PUBLISHED BY BERKELEY[1]

1707 *Arithmetica* and *Miscellanea Mathematica* (London)

1709 *An Essay Towards a New Theory of Vision* (Dublin)

1710 *A Treatise Concerning the Principles of Human Knowledge* (Dublin)
1734 2nd edition (London)

1712 *Passive Obedience* (Dublin)

1713 *Three Dialogues between Hylas and Philonous* (London) 1725 2nd edition
(London), 1734 3rd edition with *Principles* (London)

1715 *Advice to the Tories Who Have Taken the Oaths* (London)

1721 *De Motu* (London)

1721 *An Essay Towards Preventing the Ruine of Great Britain* (London)

1732 *Alciphron: or, the Minute Philosopher* (Dublin) 1732 2nd edition
(London), 1752 3rd edition (London)

1733 *The Theory of Vision, or Visual Language, Shewing the Immediate
Presence and Providence of a Deity, vindicated and explained* (London)

1734 *The Analyst; or, a Discourse Addressed to an Infidel Mathematician*
(Dublin)

1735 *A Defence of Free-thinking in Mathematics* (Dublin)

1735 *Reasons for Not Replying to Mr. Walton's "Full Answer" in a Letter to
P.T.P* (Dublin)

1735–37 *The Querist* (Dublin)

1738 *A Discourse Addressed to Magistrates* (Dublin)

1744 *Siris: A Chain of Philosophical Reflexions and Inquiries Concerning the
Virtues of Tar-Water, and Divers Other Subjects* (Dublin)

1749 *A Word to the Wise: or, an Exhortation to the Roman Catholic Clergy of
Ireland* (Dublin)

1740 *Maxims Concerning Patriotism* (Dublin)

1752 *A Miscellany* (Dublin)

PUBLISHED POSTHUMOUSLY[2]

Philosophical Commentaries (Berkeley's notebooks 1707–08).

Draft of the Introduction to the *Principles* (1708).

Berkeley's correspondence with Samuel Johnson (1729–30).

RECOMMENDED COLLECTIONS AND ANTHOLOGIES OF BERKELEY'S WORK

M. R. Ayers (ed.) *Philosophical Works Including The Works On Vision* (Dent: London, 1993).
This useful anthology includes *NTV, PHK, 3D, DM, TVV, PC*, and the philosophical correspondence between Johnson and Berkeley.

A. A. Luce and T. E. Jessop (eds.) *The Works of George Berkeley, Bishop of Cloyne*, 9 volumes (Thomas Nelson and Sons: Edinburgh, 1948–57).
This remains the definitive collection of Berkeley's work.

BIOGRAPHICAL INFORMATION AND PHILOSOPHICAL BACKGROUND

D. Berman *George Berkeley: Idealism and the Man* (Clarendon Press: Oxford, 1994).

A. A. Luce *The Life of George Berkeley, Bishop of Cloyne* (Thomas Nelson: London, 1949).

C. J. McCracken and I. C. Tipton (eds.) *Berkeley's Principles and Dialogues: Background Source Materials* (Cambridge University Press: Cambridge, 2000).

OTHER INTRODUCTORY SOURCES

J. Dancy *Berkeley: An Introduction* (Blackwell: Oxford, 1987).

R. Fogelin *Berkeley and the Principles of Human Knowledge* (Routledge: London, 2001).

T. Stoneham *Berkeley's World: An Examination of the Three Dialogues* (Oxford University Press: Oxford, 2002).

B. Umbaugh *On Berkeley* (Wadsworth/Thompson: Belmont, CA, 2000).

K. P. Winkler (ed.) *The Cambridge Companion to Berkeley* (Cambridge University Press: Cambridge, 2005).

ONLINE RESOURCES

The Berkeley Newsletter http://people.hsc.edu/berkeleystudies/
The International Berkeley Society http://georgeberkeley.tamu.edu/
The Stanford Encyclopedia of Philosophy http://plato.stanford.edu/

RECENT BOOKS ABOUT BERKELEY (GENERAL STUDIES)

D. Berman *George Berkeley: Idealism and the Man* (Clarendon Press: Oxford, 1994).

H. M. Bracken *Berkeley* (Macmillan: London, 1974).

A. C. Grayling *Berkeley: The Central Arguments* (Open Court: La Salle, 1986).
R. G. Muehlmann *Berkeley's Ontology* (Hackett: Indianapolis, 1992).
G. Pappas *Berkeley's Thought* (Cornell University Press: Ithaca, 2000).
G. Pitcher *Berkeley* (Routledge & Kegan Paul: London, 1977).
J. R. Roberts *A Metaphysics for the Mob: The Philosophy of George Berkeley* (Oxford University Press: Oxford, 2007).
I. C. Tipton *Berkeley: The Philosophy of Immaterialism* (Methuen: London, 1974).
K. P. Winkler *Berkeley: An Interpretation* (Oxford University Press: Oxford, 1989).

RECENT COLLECTIONS OF ESSAYS (GENERAL STUDIES)

S. H. Daniel *New Interpretations of Berkeley's Thought* (Humanity Books: New York, 2008).
S. H. Daniel *Reexamining Berkeley's Philosophy* (University of Toronto: Toronto, 2007).
K. P. Winkler (ed.) *The Cambridge Companion to Berkeley* (Cambridge University Press: Cambridge, 2005).
R. G. Muehlmann (ed.) *Berkeley's Metaphysics: Structural, Interpretive, and Critical Essays* (Pennsylvania State University Press: University Park, P.A., 1995).
E. Sosa (ed.) *Essays on the Philosophy of George Berkeley* (D. Reidel Publishing: Dordrecht, 1987).
D. Berman (ed.) *George Berkeley: Essays and Replies* (Irish Academy Press: Dublin, 1985).
W. E. Creery (ed.) *George Berkeley: Critical Assessments*, 3 vols. (Routledge: London, 1991).
C. M. Turbayne (ed.) *Berkeley: Critical and Interpretive Essays* (University of Minnesota Press: Minneapolis, 1982).

RECENT BOOKS ABOUT BERKELEY (SPECIAL TOPICS)

B. Arsić *The Passive Eye: Gaze and Subjectivity in Berkeley (via Beckett)* (Stanford University Press: Stanford, 2003).
M. Atherton *Berkeley's Revolution in Vision* (Cornell University Press: Ithaca, 1990).
T. M. Bettcher *Berkeley's Philosophy of Spirit: Consciousness, Ontology, and the Elusive Subject* (Continuum Press: London, 2007).
C. Bradatan *The Other Berkeley: An Exercise in Reenchantment* (Fordham University Press: New York, 2006).
R. J. Brook *Berkeley's Philosophy of Science* (Martinus Nijhoff: The Hague, 1973).
C. G. Caffentzis *Exciting the Industry of Mankind: George Berkeley's Philosophy of Money* (Kluwer Academic Press: Dordrecht, 2000).

D. E. Flage *Berkeley's Doctrine of Notions: A Reconstruction Based on His Theory of Meaning* (Croon Helm: London, 1987).

D. M. Jesseph *Berkeley's Philosophy of Mathematics* (Chicago University Press: Chicago, 1993).

P. S. Olscamp *The Moral Philosophy of George Berkeley* (Martinus Nijhoff: The Hague, 1970).

P. Walmsley *The Rhetoric of Berkeley's Philosophy* (Cambridge University Press: Cambridge, 1990).

INDEX